1993

THE INTERNATIONAL POLITICS OF SOUTH ASIA

THE
INTERNATIONAL
POLITICS OF
SOUTH ASIA

Vernon Marston Hewitt

Manchester
University Press

Manchester and New York

distributed exclusively in the USA
and Canada by St. Martin's Press

Published by Manchester University Press
Oxford Road, Manchester M13 9PL, UK
and Room 400, 175 Fifth Avenue, New York, NY 10010, USA

Distributed exclusively in the USA and Canada
by St. Martin's Press, Inc., 175 Fifth Avenue,
New York, NY 10010, USA

A catalogue record for this book is available from the British Library

Library of Congress cataloging in publication data
Hewitt, Vernon Marston.
The international politics of South Asia/Vernon Marston Hewitt.
    p.   cm.
Includes index.
ISBN 0-7190-3392-6 (hardback). – ISBN 0-7190-3393-4 (pbk.)
    1. South Asia–Foreign relations.   2. South Asia–Politics and government.   I.
Title.
    DS341.H49   1992
    327.54–dc20
                                                                      91-33522

ISBN 0 7190 3392-6 *hardback*
0 7190 3393-4 *paperback*

Printed in Great Britain
by Bell & Bain Limited, Glasgow

Contents

List of figures and maps *page* vii

Preface ix

An introduction to the international politics of South Asia 1

1 The states of South Asia (I): bi-lateral relations 15

2 The states of South Asia (II): the international setting 63

3 The domestic politics of South Asia: state–society relations and regional stability 103

4 South Asia and the world economy: transition and the imperatives of reform 154

5 Future prospects for regional stability and disarmament in South Asia 195

Epilogue 224

Bibliography 230

Index 239

Figures and maps

Figures

1 South Asia: population by state *page* 4

2 Basic indicators   5

3 Economic indicators   155

4 Total external debt   158

Maps

1 North-East India   42

2 China, India, Aksai Chin   42

3 Sri Lanka   43

4 Pakistan   112

5 India   135

For Michael Peter Askham
Bosworth College, Desford
1975–1977

'If we shadows have offended, think but this –'

Preface

Many people have assisted me in this project, and several colleagues from the Politics Department, University of Bristol, have read through various drafts of chapters and made comments and criticisms. I would like to thank Nick Rengger and Mark Wickham-Jones for their valuable support and encouragement: Nick for ensuring that I was in touch with events throughout the complex world of International Relations, and Mark for ensuring that what was written up made sense. I would also like to thank Terrell Carver for tearing himself away from his vast administrative duties to read through the completed draft.

Subrata Mitra at Hull was invaluable for his collaboration on ideas over ethnicity and secularism within India, and Sumit Ganguly of Hunter College, New York, must be thanked for giving me an opportunity to work on Indian nuclear weapons policy throughout 1990. Simon Lawson *et al.* of the Indian Institute Library, Oxford were extremely helpful throughout the latter part of 1990 and early 1991. In times of cuts and shortages I would also like to thank Bristol Library's inter-library loan scheme without which I would have had to criss-cross the country chasing up references.

Finally I would like to thank the Warden and Fellows of Nuffield College, Oxford for providing me with visitor's facilities during Hilary Term 1991, and for ensuring a conducive atmosphere for a period of intensive work on the manuscript. I am particularly in debt to Andrew Adonis and David Butler, and to the many students who befriended me during my stay. I am also indebted to the many Bristol students who have shown an interest in South Asia. The final results of the work remain, of course, my responsibility alone.

In carrying out the research for this book I have been made aware of the sheer scarcity of single-authored, comparative studies written on

South Asia. While such books exist for other regions, South Asia has tended to remain divided both by country and by academic discipline. Works comparable to Naomi Chazan, D. K. Fieldhouse or Richard Hodder-Williams on Africa,[1] or Charles Anderson and Gary Wynia on Latin America[2] are almost totally absent. By contrast, each year sees the addition of a series of edited books on South Asia. Notable works include Harriss and Alavi,[3] Wilson and Dalton,[4] and most recently Craig Baxter et al.[5]

Given the complexities of South Asia it is little wonder that the temptation has been to farm out areas of expertise and bring them together under the loose rubric of a general theme or relatively tight editorial control. The lone author, attempting to paint out a broad canvas that is both conceptually and empirically accurate, would appear to be at a distinct disadvantage. Someone who has been brought up on the sophistication of party politics in India will not necessarily be able to discuss the consequences of income distribution on political stability in Pakistan. Indian (or Pakistani) specialists with a background in colonial politics or the immediate post-colonial period cannot be assumed to be competent to write about foreign policy or security aspects of the states of South Asia in the late 1980s.

There are nonetheless distinct problems with edited works that mitigate against their obvious clarity. Apart from problems in style and continuity, the drawbacks are often epistemological; this affects the way in which the various problems and issues of a country's or a region's development are conceptualised. Increasingly issues such as economic development, party-based political participation, and national security are perceived as being separate and unrelated. Rather than relating them collectively to aid our comprehension of specific regions of the world, such separated 'categories of the understanding' – narrowly drawn and jealously guarded by a host of specialists – dissipate our efforts and divide our results.

Part of the problem here is the current crisis within the humanities and the attitude towards comparative methodology. In head-long reaction to past excesses, unfulfilled promises, and prospects for funding, western universities (and in particular British ones) have encouraged extreme specialisation of research based upon 'recognisable' areas of study. The cumulative effect of this is that scholars have undergone a sort of intellectual involution which contributes both to the fragmentation of the social sciences and to the proliferation of separate but often identical cells of inquiry. Comparative politics is either actively discouraged on the grounds that it lacks a 'true disciplinary' home, or becomes a mere rhetorical exercise in listing what things are different, similar or merely interesting.

For studies in South Asia, this trend in academic specialism has been made worse by the old orientalist emphasis upon the uniqueness and diversity of the 'sub-continent' (still to the British as good a euphemism for India as the 'Raj'). This stress has down-played the similarities of, and the connections between, the differing states of South Asia and has constructed a series of almost unbridgable gulfs between the pre- and the post-independence periods, and between the countries themselves.

The reverse side of this dilemma is that narrowly-defined 'area studies' are excluded from the wider areas of academic enquiry going on within the broad church of the humanities on 'professional' grounds, and the belief exists that somehow such wide interests are suspect, even unscholarly. It may come as a surprise that issues that are central to western political theory, western theories of international justice, and matters of economic and political integration are also central to the future of the South Asian states as they attempt to construct enduring national identities, develop their economies, and construct durable and defensible state boundaries.

While studies on European integration need not necessarily discuss the continental dimensions of the Indian federal system, much would be gained if they did, particularly on the issue of fiscal policy. Discussions on affirmative action and radical pluralism would also do well to look at the various reservation policies within India aimed to assist in the economic development of 'backward' sections, and the problems they have faced in weighing the demands of one backward section against another, especially when definitions of economic hardship become inexplicably bound up with ascriptive notions of caste.

The result of all these prejudicial habits of mind has been not only the creation of serious gaps in the literature on South Asia as a region, and as a sub-region of the wider international arena but, much more seriously, a lack of interest in comparative studies *per se*. It is high time that someone restated the advantages of this approach. In the classic work *Social Origins of Dictatorship and Democracy*, Barrington Moore noted that: 'In the effort to understand the history of a specific country a comparative perspective can lead to asking very useful and sometimes new questions. Comparisons can serve as a rough negative check on accepted . . . explanations.' Yet more significantly Moore concluded that the acts of comparison, and the appreciation of similarities and differences 'constitute a *single intellectual process*, and make such a study more than a disparate collection of interesting cases ... That comparative analysis is no substitute for detailed investigation of specific cases is obvious.'[6] No degree of diligent editing or direction can constitute such a process, and although the amount of material that needs to be examined may well make the job of writing comparative texts unrealistic, there are profound reasons why they should be attempted. It is odd that, twenty-five years after Moore's brilliant (even if flawed) book, we should have so forcefully to remind ourselves of the value of such an approach.

Vernon Hewitt,
Bristol, 30 April 1991

Notes

1 Naomi Chazan, *Politics of Contemporary Africa*, London, 1986. D. K. Fieldhouse, *The Economic Development of Black Africa 1945–1980*, London, 1986. Richard Hodder-Williams, *Introduction to the Politics of Tropical Africa*, London, 1984. There is the laudable exception of B. H. Farmer's *An Introduction to South Asia*, London, 1983.

2 Charles Anderson, *Politics and Economic Change in Latin America*, Princeton, 1967. See also Gary Wynia, *The Politics of Latin American Development*, Cambridge, 1984.

3 J. Harriss and H. Alavi, *The Sociology of Development Series: South Asia*, London, 1987.

4 A. J. Wilson and D. Dalton, *The States of South Asia*, London, 1982.

5 C. Baxter, *Government and Politics in South Asia*, Boulder, 1987.

6 B. Moore, *The Social Origins of Dictatorship and Democracy*. London, 1967, pp. x–xi

An introduction to the international politics of South Asia

The expression 'international politics' has a rather dated feel about it. It appears to lack, for example, both the analytical rigour of the term 'international political economy', as well as the fashionability and *immediacy* of the words 'international relations'. Yet in spite of these potential drawbacks I have good reasons to use it. For the purpose of this book 'international relations' is too narrow to yield significant domestic and regional insights because of its association with realism, and its overtly systemic approach that concentrates on states as the component parts of an anarchic international environment. This global perspective, with its emphasis upon power and coercion, is inherently western in its bias. Even if packaged as a specialist area study (or worst still, a subject for the so-called 'strategic' analyst) such views have an odd effect upon the size and importance of South Asia, similar to that caused by looking at a large object through the wrong end of a telescope. What is by itself impressive becomes small and marginal, uninteresting and slightly out of focus.[1] A systemic approach to regional politics exaggerates the importance of superpower involvement, and fails to realise that the prime dynamic behind a great deal of foreign policy arises within a domestic context of pressing economic and political instability, and even one of increasing environmental degradation.[2]

On the other hand the term international political economy is also too narrow for the task in hand, even though it draws much-needed attention to the links between political elites, resource allocation, and the types of economic regimes. In his book *The Political Economy of International Relations*, Robert Gilpin concentrates on the dynamics between international market forces (that in principle have no bounds and seek continuously to increase their domain), and the nation-state, which is inclusive and territorial. For Gilpin the key questions raised by an international political economy perspective are how the state and its associate political processes affect the production and distribution of wealth and, in particular, how political decisions and interests influence the location of economic activity.[3] There have been many significant works on particular countries within the South Asia region, but none have moved to incorporate – through linking up issues of economic growth with foreign policy – an approach that deals with both regional and international linkages.[4] Moreover, like the systemic literature of the realists, most of the writings on political economy are biased – for obvious reasons – towards the 'core' economies of the United States and the Pacific, and not necessarily the more peripheral areas of the world.

We end then, through default, with the somewhat archaic expression of 'international politics'. In many crucial respects the term is related to what the late Hedley Bull referred to as the 'world politics' paradigm, a paradigm that transcends the distinction between the study of international relations and the study of domestic politics by focusing upon the global political system of which the states system and the national political systems are both part.[5] As such, this approach stresses the connections between the national, regional and international arenas as mediated through the institutions of state and government, particular cultural and ideological values, and particular desires and aspirations. At the most general level, the international system is dominated by an integrated capitalist world economy, and until very recently, security alliances based upon global bipolarity. Regionally, the states of South Asia share a common history and a common constitutional legacy. Domestically, the politics of South Asia are dominated by either the decay of established political institutions (as in India and Sri Lanka) or the difficulties that arise when trying to create new ones (as in Bangladesh and Pakistan). All the states are beset by a growing assertion of regionalism and ethnicity, problems of political legitimacy, and the stresses caused by volatile political participation, or the demands for political participation.

Defining the region

As with all regional concepts, the territorial dimensions of South Asia is rather fluid and open to criticism. In its annual reports the World Bank classifies Pakistan as part of Europe, Middle East and North Africa, a notion that ignores cultural and linguistic ties that make Pakistan a fundamental part of the South Asian region, but one which stresses the religious affinities between Pakistan and the Arab world. One of the reasons why India has never appreciated Pakistan's suggestions for a South Asian nuclear free zone is that Pakistan's definition of South Asia excludes China, while India's does not. Since China is already a nuclear power (and has no stated intention of renouncing the use of nuclear weapons) this distinction is a rather crucial one to make. Furthermore, for a regional study centred upon India and Pakistan, China presents something of problem. In order to simplify matters I have treated China as both a regional and an extra-regional power, because although she clearly lies outside of South Asia, she impinges directly on India's perception of her wider Asian interests, and since the mid-1960s has been in cosy alliance with Pakistan. China is neither a superpower in an economic sense (despite an important and increasing aid profile in the Third World since late 1960s) nor in a military 'power projection' sense, although recent changes in military doctrine, especially with reference to sea power, imply that this may be changing.[6]

For the main purposes of this study however, the region of South Asia contains the states of India, Pakistan, Bangladesh, Sri Lanka, Nepal, Bhutan and the Maldives. Sikkim will be dealt with as an integral part of India (to which it ceded in 1975). Tibet will be referred to briefly, although since the 1950s it has, for good or ill, fallen into the domain of the sinologist. I will discuss the Indian ocean with reference to the Indian Union Territories of the Andaman and Nicobar Islands, Daman and Diu and the Lakshadweep archipelago.

My definition largely ignores the relations between Pakistan and the Islamic world of the Middle East, and perhaps more seriously excludes Afghanistan with its ethnic and cultural links across the Pakistan border into Baluchistan and North West Frontier Province. It also ignores India's associations with the states of East and Central Asia, especially Burma (which was administered as part of British India until the mid-1930s). Yet the historical, political and economic legacies of a shared colonial past give the region, so defined, an obvious co-hesiveness. The area also has a distinct geographical identity.

The sovereign states of India, Pakistan, Bangladesh, Nepal and Bhutan constitute an area situated between the Himalayan mountain range and the Indian Ocean littoral, bordered to the west by the mountains of the Hindu Kush and the Kandahar plains, and to the east by the Chittagong, Mizo, Chin, Naga and Patkai hills on the Bangladesh–Burmese border. The Republic of the Maldives is situated just over 500 km to the south-west of Sri Lanka,[7] and the Indian island

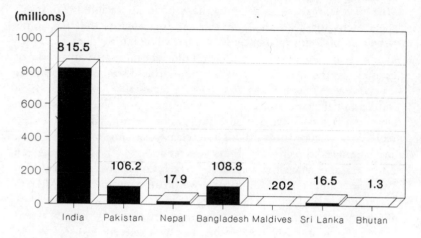

Figure 1 South Asia: population by state
Source: World Bank Report, 1990

dependencies of Lakshadweep, Daman, Diu and the Andaman and Nicobar Islands. For much of the century, the entire area was either under British colonial administration, or as in the case of Nepal and Bhutan were sovereign states under varying degrees of British paramountcy. All of the states with the exception of Bhutan and Nepal, are currently members of the British Commonwealth of Nations.

A brief profile of the states of South Asia

The size and population of these states differ enormously: from the micro-state of Bhutan with a population of just over 1.4 million living within an area of 47,000 square kilometres, to the Republic of India with a population in excess of 800 million and a territorial area of 3,288,000 square kilometres.In the late 1980s the population of South Asia accounted for one-fifth of the total global population. Each month, the regional population increases by about one million individuals, a demographic trend that maintains continual pressure upon the resources and productive capacities of the respective states. Moreover, the population is extraordinarily young – in the mid 1980s 40 per cent was below the age of 15.

The qualities of life vary between states and most significantly

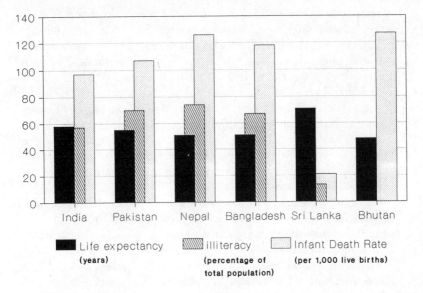

Figure 2 Basic indicators
Source: World Bank Report, 1990

within states. The average life expectancy in India is 57 years, although landless labourers in the states of Bihar and Orissa are much less likely to achieve this. In Sri Lanka, life expectancy is 71 years, a figure that compares favourably with Britain's figure of 75, and Japan's 78. Levels of literacy vary between the states and within the states. Bhutan is worse than India, while Sri Lanka boasts the highest mean average of adult literacy. Within India, the southern state of Kerala has an adult literacy rate of over 70 per cent, while the east state of Orissa has a rate under 30 per cent.

As would be expected, the economic powers of these states reflects their size. In 1988/9 India's Gross Domestic Product (GDP) was approximately US $270.64 billion, making it approximately the tenth largest economy in the world. For the same period, Pakistan's GDP was calculated at US $39.07 billion. By contrast Nepal's productive capacity was just over US $3 billion. Close by, the state of Bangladesh – the erstwhile 'East Wing' of Old Pakistan – has a GDP of US $19.01 billion. Most of the economies of the South Asia region are mixed economies, containing various mixes of public and private enterprises and various styles of economic planning aimed at achieving industrialisation.

Each state of South Asia has followed a slightly different set of development strategies since independence. India has been the most inward orientated of the regional economies and has until very recently operated one of the most inflexible planning systems. The most significant consequence of this is that India's share of world trade is remarkably low given the size of her economy, similar to that associated with the old non-market economies of Eastern Europe. Nepal and Bhutan rely heavily upon Indian trade, while the Maldives is associated economically more with the states of East Asia. The Bangladesh economy remains hostage to rapid population growth and extreme variations in the climate which inhibit much-needed improvements in agricultural output.

The most obvious links between the region and the wider international community are those of trade and aid. All the South Asian states, regardless of their respective strengths, rely upon concessional borrowing and grants from multilateral institutions such as the World Bank and the International Monetary Fund (IMF), the Colombo Plan, European-based aid consortia, and bilateral assistance with the US, Europe, and increasingly Japan.

Somewhat paradoxically, while India remains a net receiver of aid, she is herself a source of financial contributions to the states of Nepal and Bhutan, and has since the mid 1980s extended credits to Sri Lanka. This is in addition to various aid schemes aimed at Africa and the Far East in the fields of financial and technical assistance, and in addition to contributions to the Colombo Plan and the Asian Development Bank.[8]

The region contains a huge and complex mix of sociocultural identities, dominated by the primacy of language and religion. Within India herself, the social diversities are notorious: fifteen national languages, eighty primary dialects, and six major religions. Despite its smaller size, Pakistan boasts as many differences, with tribal and Pushto speakers in the North, Sindi and Punjabi speakers to the southwest, and with a minority of Urdu speakers closest to the institutions of national power. India is a secular republic, despite the fact that over 80 per cent of the population are Hindus. Pakistan, Bangladesh and the Maldives are all Islamic republics of the Sunni sect. Pakistan has a small but articulate minority of Shi'ites, and various tribal and animist societies are situated in Baluchistan and North West Frontier Province.

Sri Lanka's second republican constitution, promulgated in 1978, underlines the supremacy of Buddhism as the official religion, while recognising the rights of its Christian, Muslim and Hindu minorities to practise their own religions unmolested. Nepal is a monarchical Hindu state, while the Bhutanese monarchy – the *Shabdrung* – is heavily influenced by Tibetan Lamaist Buddhism, despite the large presence of Nepalese immigrants speaking Nepali and Hindi dialects.

The kingdom of Sikkim – formally a part of the Indian federal system since 1975 – is inhabited by the large tribal group known as the Lepcha, although as with Bhutan, the area is dominated by a growing number of Nepalese Hindu immigrants. The monarchical tradition of the *Chogyal* drew from both the Buddhist and Hindu traditions of royalty before being formally abolished by indigenous political parties calling for greater democracy and closer association with India.

While many of these societies are very old – India can (and does) boast one of the oldest cultures in the world dating back to *c.* 2500 BC – the present territorial boundaries are new. None of the states of South Asia are nation-states in the classic sense of the term; they are, rather, juridical and territorial. Although supported by the precedents and requirements of international law, they lack, to varying degrees, established national identities and even in some cases legitimate governments.[9] The sovereign state of Pakistan only came into existence in 1947 when it was carved out of the north-western (West Pakistan) and the north-eastern (the erstwhile East Pakistan) wings of British India on the basis of a homeland for the Muslims of South Asia.

The problems of irredentism

No writing on the bilateral relations within the region would make any sense without an understanding of the legacies of Partition and on the subsequent forms of Indian and Pakistani nationalism. The boundaries drawn up in the closing weeks of British rule crossed areas of ethnic and cultural affinity and divided them between the successor states. Because of this, one of the most enduring legacies of the colonial period for South Asia remains that of unresolved boundaries and unspecified borders. This legacy has been a cause of considerable regional friction and stress, and dominates the regional policies of all the states.

Tamils in the southern Indian province of Tamil Nadu, for example, have a long-standing historical association with the Sri Lankan Tamils long settled in the north-east of the island and the Sinhalese – the majority on this small island – fear India's affinity with the Sri Lankan

Tamils. Despite the creation of a Muslim state of Pakistan, there are almost 100 million Muslims living within India.

In spite of the secession of East Pakistan in 1971 on the basis of Bengali nationalism, there are still over 250,000 Urdu-speaking non-Bengalis living in what is now Bangladesh. Ironically, these people emigrated from India on the eve of Partition to live in an Urdu-speaking state! Since the mid 1970s they have been seeking to return to Pakistan – a state that none of them have ever seen. Tribal movements across the sensitive Chittagong Hill tracks, which form part of the Indian–Bangladesh border, continue to complicate relations between New Delhi and Dhaka. Tribal identities also cross-cut the Afghan and Pakistani border (the so-called Durand Line), where linguistic and religious ties have given rise to the calls for a separate 'Pashtustan'.

This high degree of ethnic and cultural diversity, irrespective of concepts such as a composite Indian, Pakistani or Sri Lankan identity, not only raises domestic issues such as the problems of nation-building, 'national' languages, or federal government, but is also an issue that directly influences the political, economic and military relations between the states themselves. Put simply, the problem is one of irredentism – the presence of cultural affinities across borders that threaten the integrity of a specific territorial unit by claiming allegiance to apparently older and more potent symbols than the flag or the national anthem.[10] The presence of such allegiances invites governments to interfere within the 'internal politics' of a neighbouring state and to make claims for territorial expansion.

The classic example in South Asia is the province of Jammu-Kashmir, which is claimed by Pakistan on the grounds that it is Muslim, but which is currently part of the Indian federation. Irredentist problems have also added a particular dimension to Indo–Sri Lankan relations, with Sinhalese fears that a separate Tamil state (or even an autonomous Tamil state within a federal Sri Lanka) will fall under the control of Indian Tamils in the nearby state of Tamil Nadu.

The extraordinarily high degree of ethnic, cultural and linguistic overlap in South Asia both within and between states gives rise to the fear of 'balkanisation': a process wherein parts of the territorially-defined state attempt to cede on the grounds of ethno-linguistic self-determination, or opt to join another South Asian state. This paranoia is in part a legacy of the Partition of British India itself, since the Indian National Congress Party were bitterly opposed to Pakistan and attempted to argue that, far from requiring their own state, the

Muslims of South Asia would have nothing to fear from a united India. From the Indian position at least, Pakistan had seceded from the Union of India in 1947, an interpretation heavy with legal implications since it implied 'that if it [Pakistan] failed to survive the traumas of its creation, the Muslim areas would have to return to the Union of India'.

These experiences of territorial disintegration were seriously reinforced in 1971 when Pakistan collapsed following a short but bloody civil war, which ended in the third Indo-Pakistan war. Since the mid 1980s India has faced several sustained campaigns from areas determined to form their own sovereign states on the basis of apparent national identities: in the Punjab, throughout the troubled north-eastern states (particularly in Assam), and in Jammu and Kashmir. Because of the central importance of Kashmir, domestic violence in the 'valley' is particularly crucial to Indo-Pakistan relations.

Secessionist demands are not confined to the larger states of the region, however. The most tragic example of secession based upon a subnationalist movement comes from Sri Lanka, where since 1983 the Sri Lankan Tamil minority have been at war with the Sinhalese majority. Bangladesh too – perhaps the most homogeneous state of the region – has had difficulties with a Hindu minority, with tribal groups crossing the Burmese border, and with some rebel activity in the north-east.

It is because of the problems associated with irredentism and subnationalism that South Asia is one of the most violent regions in the world. India has recently witnessed instances of Hindu–Muslim violence on a scale not seen since Partition. In the first seven months of 1990, 1,159 people were killed in Jammu-Kashmir, while 2,420 died in the Punjab. In Pakistan, serious ethnic violence in and around the city of Karachi continued to claim innocent lives and became part of the general domestic crisis that led to the dismissal of the Benazir Bhutto government in August 1990. Towards the end of the year, the Ershad regime of Bangladesh was swept out of power by a student-based movement that seemed to be quite independent of the (many) established political parties.

Following the withdrawal of Indian troops from Sri Lanka in March 1990, the Sri Lankan government resorted to large-scale military operations against the Tamil bases in and around the Jaffna peninsular. In response, the Tamil Tigers – the main Tamil rebel group – began a campaign of murder and assassination. In November 1990, a European Parliamentary Report stated that since 1987, over 60,000 people have been killed in ethnic violence throughout the island. Even in the Himalayan kingdom of Nepal, a pro-democracy movement – influenced by events in Eastern Europe – led to the scrapping of a party-less political system after a ban that had been in force since 1962. Pro-Nepalese agitations to establish a Gurkha state also affected the kingdom of Bhutan, Nepal and parts of the Indian state of West Bengal.

While such degrees of domestic instability cannot be ignored in either the regional or the international context, to concentrate solely on political violence would nonetheless distort the regional picture. Amid various political crises, almost all of the states in question took part in some form of 'normal' political process such as elections and referenda.

Since the restoration of a democratic government in 1988, Pakistan has been to the polls twice. Following the resignation of V. P. Singh in November 1990, India has witnessed the caretaker government of Chandra Senkhar. His resignation in March 1991 opened the way for a mid-term election in mid May 1991 that was delayed in the wake of Rajiv Gandhi's assassination in the Southern Indian state of Tamil Nadu. Perhaps the most dramatic – and unlooked for – event in the region has been the electoral victory of the Bangladesh National Party following the collapse of the Ershad military regime. As part of her return to democratic politics, Bangladesh is preparing for presidential elections sometime in the near future.

Issues, themes and arguments

Irredentism, and the associated fear of internal disintegration, are very much at the top of the regional agenda, and are powerful forces shaping the wider international policies of the South Asian states. Another central component of state policy throughout the region concerns the imperatives of economic growth and development. The states of South Asia – even India – remain part of what is still referred to as the Third World, and as such, they confront all the problems of poverty, slow growth, and poor trade performance.

The key relationship that emerges in this study is that between the need to maintain the dynamic of economic development and social integration, and the need to maintain territorial integrity and a growing, legitimate sense of nationalism. At the heart of the South Asian region is the historical legacy of Partition and the relationships between secular India, Islamic Pakistan and the future of Kashmir: an issue that has proved to be far more enduring than the Bengal crisis of 1971 or the Soviet invasion of Afghanistan in 1979.

The book concentrates on the interconnectedness of economic, social and foreign policy. Chapter 1 begins by looking at the current interests and concerns of the South Asia region, and concentrates on bilateral relations since 1947. The chapter stresses the centrality of Indo-Pakistan relations, and touches upon India's wider concerns with China and China's links with Pakistan. The Non-Aligned Movement (NAM) and the Commonwealth are discussed with reference to the evolution of Indo-Pakistan relations.

Chapter 2 looks at how the states of South Asia have related historically to the superpowers and to the wider international institutions such as the United Nations, the US-sponsored defence packs of CENTO and SEATO, to the British Commonwealth of Nations, and to the international institutions of the Islamic world. Chapter 3 lies very much at the centre of this study. It examines the problems caused by rapid social change and political instability, both in terms of irredentism and the fear of disintegration. The importance of Chapter 3 reflects my conviction that domestic politics, and the perceptions and priorities of political elites, are the vital starting point to understanding of regional insecurity, and foreign policy in general.

Chapter 4 examines the links between South Asia and the international economy in a period of economic uncertainty, and amid domestic concerns over the future of economic liberalisation within India. The chapter also examines the economic links between the South Asian states themselves, focusing on the recently-formed South Asian Association of Regional Co-operation (SAARC). Although the region has so far managed to escape the worst excesses of debt, the next decade may well be crucial to deciding whether the earlier momentum of the 1980s is maintained. The domestic consequences of India and Pakistan coming under further (and stricter) IMF conditionality are also taken into consideration. Finally, Chapter 5 looks at India's future in South Asia in an era of growing multipolarity, and the future of the region within the current thinking on the so-called New World Order. The chapter examines the likelihood of either India or Pakistan deploying nuclear weapons, and assesses the consequences such deployment would have within the region and throughout the world with reference to the Nuclear Non-Proliferation Treaty (NPT), international sanctions, and collective security arrangements. Could both states afford to run the risk of international condemnation, and would nuclear weapons increase or decrease regional stability? One central question that has had to be posed since 1989 is, with the ending of the cold war, whether the way is open for further regional co-operation within South Asia, or whether further mistrust and hostility is to be expected.

No contemporary study of international politics, whatever its regional bias, can ignore the collapse of what used to be called – with a certain degree of Anglo-Saxon malice – the Soviet Empire. Current discussions about the New World Order (NWO) are dominated by five issues: the importance of stability within the Middle East; the inexorable disintegration/redefinition of the Soviet Union; the socio-economic problems of the 'new' East European states; the crisis of the post-war global economy, and the environmental crises of global warming and ozone depletion. All of these issues are of critical importance to the states of South Asia, bringing about opportunities for new beginnings in their domestic, regional and international policies, as well as highlighting the risks of further failures.

While India has never been a radical power, she has always professed to uphold a particular vision of the world within which the interests of the newer, post-colonial states are paramount. While India accepts the concept of an ordered international society based upon the rule of law, she has consistently (and successfully) rejected an international order based upon American hegemony. Part of her success in resisting Washington's overtures (that have been at once seductive and callous) involved a careful use of Soviet aid and assistance from the mid-1960s onwards. Throughout the 1970s and 1980s India was willing to trade off western technological sophistication against Soviet cheapness, and use Soviet support to defend India in the higher councils of global diplomacy without becoming a mere satellite of the Russian 'Great Game'. The success of Indo-Soviet relations has been the candid appreciation of their mutual interest. It was Nehru himself – the first Prime Minister of India, who noted that India and the Soviet Union shared a geopolitical perspective on the world: 'We are their second front, and they are ours.'[11] While Soviet aid has been small relative to western bilateral and multilateral assistance, it has been concentrated in key sectors, especially arms procurement and energy projects. Without Soviet help, the price of India's defence modernisation would have been vastly inflated. The possible demise of the USSR – or a least a Soviet Union that is economically and strategically exhausted – leaves India potentially exposed in a capitalist world economy with which she has surprisingly few links. One of the most interesting paradoxes that emerge in this study is how an area of the world containing over 800 million people, the world's fourth largest military machine, and one of the world's oldest cultures should be – *by itself* – so marginal to the economics of South Asia and the world system generally.[12]

It is not incumbent upon an general study to offer any firm or fast conclusions, yet what emerges at the end of the book is an overwhelming emphasis upon the need for economic restructuring in order to maintain the momentum of development policies, and to ensure a conducive security environment which lessens the fear generated by irredentism. Economic and social development should be the prime concern of the states of South Asia with regard to both their regional and their international agenda. The generation of economic wealth will assist the creation of strong national identities and help in the integration of backward regions and provinces, which will in turn help in matters of security. As Barry Buzan has recently noted, 'for the third world states themselves, the idea of national security borders on nonsense unless strong states can be created'.[13] Strong state here means wealthy. In turn, secure, integrated and dynamic economies will command a higher profile within the world economy in terms of trade and investment. These are the challenges for the South Asia region in the 1990s.

Notes

1 This is not the case with the book by B. Buzan and G. Rizvi, *South Asian Insecurity and the Great Powers*, Basingstoke, 1985 which although focusing upon the ways in which superpower rivalry has reinforced the security complex, nonetheless drew useful attention towards some of the vagaries of domestic politics and coined the very useful analytical term 'security complex', a term that has been further developed in the second edition of Buzan's book *States, People, Fear*, London, 1991. Many writers have made contributions to works on the foreign policy of India generally, or a specific bilateral relationship. R. W. Bradnock's *Indian Foreign Policy Since 1971*, London, 1990 is timely but brief. P. Duncan's book, *The Soviet Union and India*, London, 1989 is a good example of just how useful the case-study approach can be.
2 See the introduction to the second edition of B. Buzan's book, *People, States, Fear*, London, 1991.
3 R. Gilpin, *The Political Economy of International Relations*, Princeton, 1987, p. 9.
4 There has been a tendency to extend the concept of security to deal with issues of economic stability and development. See C. Thomas, *In Search of Security*, Brighton, 1987 and also P. Saravanamuttu and C. Thomas, *Conflict and Crisis in South-North Security*, London, 1989.
5 Hedley Bull, *The Anarchical Society*, London, 1977, p. 297.
6 See G. Segal, 'China', in E. Karp, *Security With Nuclear Weapons? Differing Perspectives on National Security*, Oxford, 1991.

7 The island of Ceylon was renamed Sri Lanka in 1972, following the promulgation of the island's First Republican Constitution. For reasons of clarity I shall use the term Sri Lanka.

8 The 1989–90 Ministry of External Affairs *Report* listed twenty-four countries as in receipt of Indian aid (p. 4).

9 See R. H. Jackson, *Quasi-States: Sovereignty, International Relations, and the Third World*, Cambridge, 1990, especially Ch. 4.

10 For an interesting introduction to the subject of irredentism, see Naomi Chazan (ed.), *Irredentism and International Politics*, London, 1991.

11 Cited in Ramesh Thakur, 'Normalising Sino-Indian Relations', *The Pacific Review*, 4, 1991, pp. 5–18.

12 Interestingly enough, Bradnock makes this point with reference to India's economic relations with the South Asian region itself. *India's Foreign Policy*, p. 58.

13 B. Buzan, 'People, States and Fear' in E. Azar and Chung In-Moon, *National Security in the Third World*, London, 1988, pp. 14–43.

1

The states of South Asia (I): bi-lateral relations

A cursory view of South Asia reveals the extent of India's centrality. She is the only state that shares borders and cultural affinities with all the other states. India has 72 per cent of the territorial area, 77 per cent of its population and approximately 78 per cent of the region's natural resources. It has recently been noted, by observers within India and especially within the region, that it is her long-term goal to translate this physical domination into a political one: this is certainly the perception of India's neighbours, especially Pakistan, who from the moment of her birth feared apparent Indian designs against her. One Bangladeshi analyst noted recently that 'the international role of a state is essentially a function of its power capabilities and an elite's perception of their role . . . India has all the nascent tendencies for great power ability.'[1]

This chapter reviews the regional aspirations of each state in terms of both military and economic ability, and will concentrate on Indo-Pakistan rivalry as it emerged after independence. Despite her size, Pakistan has refused to concede to India the role of regional hegemon, and has made it clear that she must be judged as India's equal by the smaller states of South Asia and by the wider international community.

The interactions of regional and international state systems can be most clearly conceived with reference to what Buzan and Rizvi called a 'security complex'.[2] This refers to a subsystem of the international community of states that for reasons of geography, history and culture are directly related to each other. This concept allows an understanding of the states of South Asia from a genuinely regional perspective and not as a mere extension of the international security environment as perceived by the superpowers. As we shall see, present international realignments are a cause for concern for the simple reason that they do not correspond with changes of perspective within the region itself.

India: the emerging military giant?

In general terms India's foreign policy has been shaped around the enduring principles of non-alignment, both with reference to the international system as a whole, and initially with reference to China and Pakistan.[3] In 1957 Nehru had noted that 'the cold war is based not only upon hatred and violence, but also upon a continuous denunciation, on picking out the faults of others. I tried [in a recent visit to the Far East] to reverse this process, even when I differed radically from those that I addressed.[4] Internationally, non-alignment meant keeping out of cold war 'denunciation', and forgoing western offers to join in defensive alliances against the Soviet Union and viceversa. It was India's express hope that her immediate neighbours would also deny foreign countries the use of military bases and facilities, and construct their policies along lines similiar to New Delhi. For India, the main issues confronting the newly independent states were surely those of socioeconomic development and growth, which required regional stability and global peace.

Yet the colonial legacies of poor border demarcation and the bitter division of Pakistan from India proved difficult to resolve though consultation alone. Immediately after 14 August 1947 a war broke out between India and Pakistan over the state of Kashmir. Other conflicts between India and Pakistan took place in 1965 and 1971, and between China and India in 1962. Since then, India's foreign policy has been somewhat Janus-faced; within the region it has attempted to provided the state with a coherent defence doctrine committed to the use of force, while internationally it has stressed non-interference and dialogue, a stance that has allowed a relatively poor country room to manoeuvre within the emerging post-colonial world.

Increasingly these two foreign policy postures have clashed. In recent years the association between non-alignment and pacifism (always specious) has given way to the belief that India, like any other state, is concerned with developing and projecting national power. After 1962 an involution of preoccupations took place. India became less concerned about having a high international profile in various fora, and more concerned about strengthening the components of its military power. Non-alignment became, more or less, a loose synonym for a traditional *realpolitik* approach.[5] In the early 1980s the clearest indication of an Indian 'Monroe' doctrine for the region was given by Sen Gupta: 'No South Asian government must ask for extensive military assistance with an anti-Indian bias. If a South Asian country genuinely needs to deal with a serious internal conflict it should ask for help from neighbouring countries, including India.'[6]

The expansion of India's military potential initially relied upon US and British help. From the mid-1960s onwards, India increasingly turned towards the Soviet Union for both weapons imports and technological assistance to create an indigenous arms industry aimed primarily at China, and then increasingly at Pakistan.

In 1953 Indian army personnel numbered between 325 and 355,000 men. In 1989 India had the fourth largest army in the world. In 1990 the army numbered over one million men. While the army continues to take the lion's share of the Indian defence budget, both the air force and the navy have been considerably expanded since the mid-1970s.[7] In 1989–90, the Indian air force consisted of 836 combat aircraft, twelve armed helicopters and five transporters. Throughout the 1980s India has pressed ahead with an ambitious naval modernisation programme. By 1989, the Indian navy numbered 47,000 men (excluding 5,000 in the manned air force wing and 1,000 marines). The fleet consisted of twenty-eight principal surface vessels, including two aircraft carriers, five destroyers and twenty-one frigates. She also has seventeen operational submarines including one Soviet-made nuclear *Foxtrot* under loan. In 1989 it was announced that India plans to construct her own nuclear submarine, following on from the success of her indigenously produced frigates.

Soviet assistance in the 1980s had given the Indians access to the MiG-29s (Flogger) which are produced in India under a turn-key arrangement, and access to the latest Soviet-designed battle tanks.[8] By 1986 however, India was attempting to gain access to western technology through various licensing agreements with French, German and American companies, and had already purchased a squadron of Mirage 2000 jet fighters. An attempt to negotiate for the licensed production of the Mirage jet in India had fallen through because of escalating costs and balance of payments difficulties. The Soviets continue to provide between 60 and 70 per cent of Indian arms imports, while India is now self-sufficient in a a whole range of ordnance productions.

In 1989 it was announced that the Indian government would be setting up a special trading committee to encourage the export of arms to raise much-needed foreign capital to be ploughed back into weapons modernisation. Unlike the states of Brazil (or China), India has not actively sought to export arms in the past, one reason being her domestic commitment to principles of non-violence and her sensitivity to the arms industry.[9]

Following the establishment of the Integrated Missile Programme in 1983, India has also been able to research and develop an Inter-Continental Ballistic Missile and an Intermediate Range Missile, tested in 1988 and 1989 respectively.[10] Since the early 1970s India has also undertaken independent satellite production which has involved extensive collaboration with the Soviet Union, the European Space Agency and indeed NASA.

India draws upon the third largest pool of qualified technicians and engineers throughout the world, and these have been deployed not just within space and ballistics research, but also in her civilian nuclear power programme. India is self-reliant throughout the nuclear fuel cycle, using natural uranium for her CADMUS-type reactors and for her generation of R–5 reactors. Supplies of enriched uranium for the Tarapur station came firstly from the U.S. and then from France. India is committed to an ambitious extension of her civilian power programme, and supplies many Third World states with nuclear expertise. All of these technological achievements, a satellite and missile programme, and a general consensus on the need for civilian nuclear power have implied to many observers that India has also been working on a nuclear weapons programme. Indeed in the mid 1970s the evidence seemed overwhelming, following India's detonation of a so-called 'peaceful' nuclear device in 1974.

The test alarmed Pakistan and led to sustained attempts by Pakistani scientists to develop their own device. As in so many other things, Indian accusations against Pakistan duplicated Pakistani allegations against India. Talk of the infamous Islamic bomb was started in Pakistan in the mid 1960s, and appeared to gain momentum during the 1970s – mainly through the enthusiasm of Pakistan's civilian President, Zulfikar Bhutto, who had earlier been the cabinet minister for energy. In the early 1990s Pakistan was convinced that India was working on a highly sophisticated process of inertial confinement fusion to produce a hydrogen bomb without risk of international detection. In turn Pakistan has accused the Indians of secretly developing or even stockpiling nuclear weapons.

Commenting on the scope and nature of India's military developments since the mid-1970s, a Pakistani observer stated that 'it requires no great insight to divine what India envisions for herself – the status of the 3rd or 4th great world power by the end of the century'.[11] That this status involves a known nuclear capability apparently goes without saying. Since the 1974 test, India and Pakistan have stood on the brink of escalating a conventional arms race into a nuclear one, being both 'threshold states' and non-signatories of the Nuclear Non-Proliferation Treaty.

Such technical developments give contemporary India an oxy-moronic image of a Third World superpower. This long list of Indian achievements clash with well-held concepts and images of mass poverty, political corruption and the vagaries of a caste-based society. Both these images are subject to exaggeration. There has been a tendency to overstate India's indigenous technological capability, both in the field of weapons production, and in the wider field of industrial research and development. This exaggeration is particularly prevalent in the Pakistani literature on India and Indian intentions. Yet it also follows that the classic 'Third World' stereotypical image of poverty and squalor – held still by many Westerners – is also highly misleading.

The limitations to Indian military power?

Even in those areas where India has adapted foreign technological designs to suit her particular needs in both the military and industrial spheres, the finished products have often been unsatisfactory and have ended up containing a large proportion of imported components. Even when licensing agreements have explicitly handed over patents to Indian developers from foreign companies there have been difficulties in continuing production once all foreign collaboration has ended. Current examples of such difficulties can be found in the development of an indigenous Light Combat Aircraft (LCA).

The design for the LCA now incorporates the General Electric's F–404 engine produced in America, since the Indian-produced engines could not meet the Indian Air Force specifications. The plane also includes imported radar and missile guidance systems. Although not typical of all joint ventures, the apparent fate of the LCA is nonetheless illustrative of wider drawbacks. Production costs for the LCA have escalated because of a reduction in the number ordered by the air force, especially following the MiG-29 deal, and it has been calculated that by the time the LCA is deployed with the Indian Air Force, it will already contain redundant technology.

In a recent article, Raju Thomas has remarked that when the project is completed 'the only thing Indian on the LCA will be the coconut which, in accordance with Indian traditions is broken over the prototype'.[12] There are similar problems with the Indian-produced battle tank, whose home-produced engine has so far proved inadequate for the army.

These weaknesses are also found through India's wider industrial and corporate sector as well. The electronic and computer software industries, areas of strength within the Indian economy and encouraged to export in the mid 1980s, were unable to compete abroad since their designs were quickly superseded by western or Japanese patents. Again joint ventures – often successful in opening up new areas for software production and marketing production – often fail to innovate on acquired information. Moreover, the traditionally lucrative markets such as the Soviet Union and Eastern Europe are turning increasingly to the West and East Asia.

While such weaknesses do not detract from the sheer size of India's military machine, it raises questions about its credibility and its effectiveness in any future conflict. It is by far the largest within the South Asia region. In 1988–9 India spent US $9.8 billion on her armed forces, compared to Pakistan's expenditure of US $2.63 billion and China's expenditure of US $5.64 billion.[13] Despite budget cuts in 1989 by the Gandhi government, the defence estimates were increased by 8.9% by the V. P. Singh government in 1990 because of increased tension along the Kashmir border with Pakistan. Outside the region her military modernisation programme has caused some anxiety in Australia and Indonesia, where it is believed that the extent of her rearmament is unnecessary for any 'legitimate' defence. Mohammad Ayoob noted recently that 'Indonesian concerns about Indian intentions have been recently heightened by India's attempts to augment her naval power and acquire a power projection capability in the vicinity of the sub-continent'.[14] Anxiety has been especially caused by Indian naval developments in and around the Port Blair base on the Andaman and Nicobar islands. Within the region, Pakistan has consistently denounced India's rearmament as part of a plan to destroy Pakistan's sovereignty and 'undo Partition'. These denunciations have continued despite US support, and the supply of advanced US weapons, and despite Indian claims that she is merely trying to match the developments of Pakistan, and more distantly, China.

Pakistan and the search for parity

The great difficulty for Indo-Pakistan relations is that India's perceptions of the Pakistani conspiracy is mirrored almost exactly by the Pakistani view of the 'Indian grand design', a design within which Pakistan has at best a secondary, decorative role, or at worst, no role at all. From the Indian position, Pakistan was (until very recently) a military-led, authoritarian government – the 'Sparta of Asia' – whose regional policy was aggressive and dishonest, and premised upon the eventual collapse of India.

After the Radcliffe Boundary Commission of 1947 created a 'moth-eaten Pakistan state', Jinnah was determined to maintain parity with India, and turned first to the British, then to the Americans and then to the Chinese. The success of this extra-regional search for support is plain to see within contemporary Pakistan: by the late 1980s Pakistan had assembled a powerful and well-integrated army of 480,000 personnel (excluding reserves), and an air force made up of at least 451 combat aircraft. In contrast to India, most of these are western (American, British and French) and have been imported into Pakistan under various international security arrangements aimed at the Soviets. The Pakistan navy, partially to offset Indian developments, has increased quite dramatically in the last two years, although at seventeen principal surface combatants and six submarines it has remained much smaller than India's. The fleet is made up of seven destroyers and ten frigates. Over the last year purchases and leaseback arrangements with the United States and Britain have doubled the tonnage of the Pakistan fleet. There is some speculation that the Pakistanis are about to purchase a nuclear submarine from China.

Until very recently the security environment of Pakistan was comparable to that of Israel. To the north and east lay the mass of India with its apparently implacable hatreds, while to the west lay Afghanistan and Iran. After 1979 and the Soviet invasion of Afghanistan, over 3 million Muslim refugees crossed into the North West Frontier Province and the Baluchistani province of Pakistan. Such circumstances – coupled with the apparent threat of further Soviet attacks against Pakistan herself – appeared to justify a dramatic increase in weapons procurement and a demand for sophisticated weapon technologies from the United States.

These weapons were eventually provided by the Reagan administration in the face of vigorous Indian protests that, far from being deployed against the Soviets (or the Soviet-backed Afghan government), they would end up being deployed against India. The settlement of the Afghanistan situation at Geneva in 1988 has eased the refugee situation somewhat, although the internal stability of Afghanistan and

B

the fate of the Mujahadeen resistance is still a matter of concern for Islamabad. Current disagreements between the United States and Pakistan over Islamabad's nuclear capabilities and nuclear research programme have led to a cut-back in both military and economic aid. Cut off from extra-regional support, Pakistan has entered the 1990s acutely aware of India's indigenous military power. In 1989 one Indian analyst noted (somewhat too emphatically, perhaps) that 'India's military power greatly exceeds that of Pakistan's . . . and the weight that Bangladesh and Sri Lanka are able to bring to bear is minimal. The problems for Pakistan are accentuated by the relative decline in Pakistan's defensive capability.'[15]

Pakistan's size relative to India raises acute problems of defence. Flat open borders in the Punjab and Sind area favour armoured infantry and tank warfare. What is referred to as 'in-depth defence' – the ability of a state to absorb an initial attack and over-extend an enemy's supply lines – is made particularly difficult for Pakistan because of her geographical 'narrowness' *vis-à-vis* India, and the proximity of her main communication centres to the Indian border. Most of her rail and road networks travel on south-west/north-east axis and would quickly fall to an advancing Indian army if the forward defences fell or pulled back, and would remain vulnerable to Indian air strikes. Indeed, in 1965 the Indian army crossed the international border in the Punjab/ Sind areas and directly threatened Lahore and Rawalpindi.[16] It is not surprising therefore that Indian demands in the 1980s for 'deep strike' fighter capability – leading to the purchase of Jaguar and Mirage – caused particular concern in Islamabad, even if India argued that her purchases of deep strike fighters was itself in response to the Pakistan purchasing of F-16s from the USA.

Because of India's industrial and economic size relative to Pakistan, it is likely that the longer hostilities continue, the more likely that India will win in any potential conflict. Given the physical inability of Pakistan to resist a determined Indian land attack, several western analysts have suggested that Pakistan's official defence doctrine has become overtly *offensive*. In times of regional tension and crisis the Pakistan military are inclined to pre-empt any Indian moves and launch attacks against India's forward positions before they could cross the international boundary.

As will be discussed, both the 1965 and the 1971 conflicts show some aspects of this strategy, since in both conflicts Pakistan calculated that her best option was to strike against India first. In 1991, Sumit Ganguly cited Stephen Cohen's remarks that since the mid 1980s, both India and

Pakistan have moved to 'offensive defence' strategies. If Cohen's observations are correct, in such circumstances incidents of misperception, misinformation or error could well precipitate a war.[17]

Whether or not Pakistan can maintain (or retain?) military parity with India is a difficult question to access. Pakistan has attempted to match India not through sheer numbers (an impossible task given her relative size) but through more sophisticated technologies such as the F-16s fighter bomber. A sheer listing of numbers of planes, ships and men does not give much insight to how successful they will be in wartime. Different weapon systems and types of planes have different strengths and weaknesses, as do the command structures and strategic flexibility of the respective armies. Various defence analysts have noted that Indian defence doctrines – especially with regard to her navy and the ideas of 'floating sea control' and carrier-battle groups[18] – are antediluvian, expensive to maintain and vulnerable to air and submarine attack. Moreover, since the Gulf crisis over Kuwait, analysts have noted the poor performance of much Soviet hardware against so-called western 'smart' weapons.

Pakistan has followed a different course to India in terms of economic and military development. Her reliance upon foreign weapons imports is much greater than India's since no real attempt has been made to develop an indigenous arms industry. Her technological sophistication is nonetheless impressive, although she lacks India's economic and industrial depth. In 1989 Pakistan tested her own surface-to-surface missile. Yet this reliance means that Pakistan has been far more vulnerable to arms embargoes than India, a fact that merely acts to increase her insecurity more. Pakistan's military strength is clearly a force to be reckoned with, even if Indian critics imply that it has been bought at the price of national dependence upon the US. They are especially impressive when it is recalled how the origins of the state were so shaky. In 1947 few believed that Pakistan would survive at all.

If Indo-Pakistan relations have been characterised by wars and profound mistrust, what are the chances for a peaceful settlement and a normalisation of relations in the immediate future? Throughout 1990 both states were on the brink of a war, while earlier in 1987 both states panicked each other while holding large-scale military manoeuvres close to the border areas. A considerable part of the problem behind Indo-Pakistan relations is that what India considers to be her legitimate defence requirements appear to deny the legitimate defence requirements of others, especially Pakistan: India's insistence that

Pakistan should not go to the US for arms, or that New Delhi should vet what arms Pakistan can buy, remains unacceptable to Pakistan. Yet Pakistan's continual refusal to acknowledge the 'realities of regional power' (a euphemism for Indian predominance) is a source of continued irritation to New Delhi.

The evolution of Indo-Pak relations

Since 1962 successive Indian governments have justified their military modernisation programmes on the basis of actual border violations. India's threat perceptions of Pakistan remain despite the disintegration of the Eastern Wing in 1971, as do her concerns about a nuclear China and her unresolved territorial ambitions on India. These perceptions have been historically and politically constructed. Indo-Pakistan relations can in fact be traced to the nature of Hindu–Muslim politics within British India. A great deal of writing has discussed the crisis that followed the bifurcation of the British Raj along so-called communal lines, and it is only necessary here to reiterate the essential points.[19]

Pakistan was created as a consequence of the 'two national theory' advanced by the Muslim League, a nationalist political party, which stated that the Hindu and Muslim communities within the Raj constituted two separate nations. It followed from their arguments that when the British granted India independence, they must do so to two states, not one.[20] This argument was resisted by the Indian National Congress Party, the main source of opposition to the British. Under the leadership of a westernised, secular middle class, the Congress claimed to represent all Indians regardless of their religion, language or race.

Despite initial resistance, the British conceded to the idea of Partition just a few weeks before leaving the sub-continent. The geographical randomness of the subsequent boundary award, the speed with which the international borders were demarcated, and the peculiarity of creating a state of Pakistan made up of two wings separated by over 1,000 miles of Indian territory, are the direct consequence of British disengagement from the sub-continent.

Despite various and complex ideas of confederacy and loose federal arrangements, Jinnah was able to use the cry of 'Islam in danger' to create the fear that, *within the Muslim minority provinces* of British India, the Congress talk of secularism would not be enough to protect Muslim rights after 1947. Yet – and this is the most astounding irony of Partition – the territorial domain of the Pakistani state would be situated in Muslim majority areas in which the Muslim League was not well represented or, in some cases, not even present at all. Nor is it clear what views Jinnah had over the Muslims of Bengal, since many of his references to 'Pakistan' refer exclusively to the North West.[21] Once Partition had been agreed upon (and the idea is, as so many ideas appear to be, the brainchild of Earl Mountbatten, the last Viceroy), the process of creating a two-wing state took priority.

The first and foremost problem that the British and the League faced was how to create a sovereign state in two separate parts of the Raj that had no real previous interrelationships, very few natural resources, very little urbanisation, no significant industrial development and virtually no infrastructure. All they had in common was the fact they were populated by Muslims. Following the breakdown of the interim Indian government set up in early 1946 before the British had accepted the 'inevitability' of Pakistan, the Viceroy divided the executive council into two sub-committees, one for the eventual state of Pakistan and one for the Indian dominion. The problem was however that until the actual formation of Pakistan, the government of India remained intact so that 'the Leaguers were in effect ministers without portfolios in the existing secretariats of British India' and, more significantly, the sub-committee on Pakistan was 'a cabinet claiming to be a government, but as yet without any ground under its feet or a roof over its head. Mountbatten showed his contempt when he let slip that the government of Pakistan would have to make do with a tent in the initial years of independence'.[22]

While it is not necessary to go into the details of the process of state formation in Pakistan, the legacy of Partition is vital. Partition left a serious psychological scar on Indo-Pakistan relations. Over 2 million people are said to have died following independence, as Muslims left for Pakistan, and Hindus left for India. The spectre of social and territorial disintegration has remained within both India and Pakistan to this day, despite the change in generation.[23]

The demarcation of the international border left many serious anomalies in and around the Chittagong Hill tracks of East Bengal, the Kutch of Rann area in the West, parts of the Punjab and, most seriously, the then princely state of Kashmir. Partition created a state with a 1,400-mile border with India to the west, and a 13,000-mile border with Afghanistan. In 1947 the Afghan government argued that, with the ending of British India, the Afghan-Indian border (the so-called Durand Line) was invalid and that significant parts of the new state ought by right to be within Afghanistan.[24] The situation of East

147,834

Pakistan created a logistical nightmare for Pakistan's defence requirements especially in the face of potential Indian hostility and irredentist claims from Afghanistan. The Radcliffe award had also failed to clarify the border between East Pakistan and Burma in the area of the Naaf river.[25]

Once the territorial dimensions of Partition had been accepted, controversy continued as to how the assets of the Raj were to be divided between the two dominions. As Jalal notes: 'The Partition machinery set up to determine Pakistan's share of the assets of undivided India had seventy-two days in which to dismantle a government structure it had taken the British over a hundred years to construct . . . Settling who was to get what . . . took place against a backdrop of unprecedented communal carnage.'[26] Every financial asset was fought over – postal services, civil servants, sterling balances and most significantly of all, the armed forces. After Partition, for example, all of the ordnance factories were situated within India and there were serious disagreements over the allocation of surplus stores. After protracted negotiations, Pakistan was given 17.5 per cent of the financial assets of the Raj, most of which was held up within India until 1948/49. Pakistan's share of the undivided British Indian army came to just over 30 per cent (140,000 out of 410,000), 40 per cent of the navy and 20 per cent of the airforce, although much of the air force remained on Indian territory. Yet because of the immediacy of hostilities, Pakistan was never to receive the full settlement. Rs750 million should have been repaid to Karachi, yet India was to suspend payments after Rs200 million.

In such circumstances, it was appreciated that from the onset of her existence, and for some time to come, Pakistan's 'defence potential' would be poor: of sixty-seven battalions with British India, only thirty-five went to Pakistan and even these were stripped of their Hindu and Sikh companies. Once the prospects of war appeared over Kashmir, India refused to allow any military stores or hardware into the hands of the Pakistani army. Jinnah accused the Indian National Congress of attempting to 'strangle Pakistan at birth'.

The security environment within South Asia was thus deeply hostile to Pakistan's existence.[27] The first priority – even above that of setting up district and provincial governments – was to defend herself against India's perceived determination to undermine her and reintegrate her into a reunified India. The first part of Pakistan's strategy was to construct a highly centralised state with a powerful military establishment that would prevent India utilising internal instability in the first turbulent years to show up Pakistan's existence as somehow illegitimate. The only way this military establishment could be built was to turn to foreign, extra-regional help.

The open invitation by Pakistan to 'foreign powers' in the early 1950s led to an Indian condemnation that has never really stopped. Yet Pakistan has argued that India's subsequent policy of non-alignment, and the need for cold war rivalry to be kept out of the South Asia region, was a rather purple Indian version of simple power politics, a cunning disguise of Indian expansionist interests dressed up in the language of moral virtues. This belief is still held to this day. A recent Pakistani commentator has pointed out that: 'It is significant that many Indians, when they speak of the *Indian* land mass cannot refrain from making it clear that what they are really talking about is the entire South Asian region.'[28] For reasons of size and weakness Pakistan still has no option but to seek multilateral agreements to regional problems, either through the United States, the Middle East or China to checkmate India's obvious advantage. Such a policy is diametrically opposed to India's stress upon bilateralism and her regional primacy.

There is little danger in exaggerating Pakistani paranoia over India: India remains the prime focus of Pakistan's foreign policy, and the degree of this obsession distorts much of her thinking on India and Indian politics. Waseem has noted that: 'Ever since the emergence of Pakistan, India has been our greatest preoccupation in the context of international relations, . . . and yet what is most often dished up to us as so-called scholarly analysis on India's internal and external policies are all highly subjective . . . even inaccurate.'[29]. The importance of Hinduism is often stressed and India's claims to secularism dismissed as mere propaganda. Yet for all the strengths of Indian scholarship on Pakistan, much can be said of India's preoccupations with the 'Muslim mind' in which prejudice is dressed up as scholarship. In the preface to a book entitled (tellingly) *Understanding the Muslim Mind*, Rajmohan Gandhi – the grandson of Mahatma Gandhi, noted stoically: 'Any nuclear clash between India and Pakistan (may God forbid it) would, in part, be due to history. Though living side by side for centuries, Hindus and Muslims have never adequately understood or trusted one another.'[30]

The Kashmir issue

As the domestic situation within the Indian state of Jammu and

Kashmir deteriorated from 1987 onwards, it looked to many that India and Pakistan stood on the brink of a fourth war. Pakistan revived old hopes that the province might well one day wrest itself from the Indian Union. In 1987 there was a serious escalation of tension in the Kashmir area, with both sides exchanging heavy artillery fire over the so-called Line of Control (LOC). The situation was diffused when President Zia and Prime Minister Rajiv Gandhi met at Jaipur, ostensibly to watch a cricket match. In August 1990 further fighting took place in the Siachen glacier area, where a large number of casualities were caused by frostbite.[31]

The 1990 crisis – the worst for some time – followed in the wake of a serious breakdown in Kashmir during which India had deployed a large number of troops to deal with anti-Indian riots, and to root out a separatist organisation – the Jammu and Kashmir Liberation Front (JKLF) who were agitating for an independent state. Despite Indian accusations of Pakistan's complicity, Pakistan seems as unwilling as India to entertain the idea of an *independent* Kashmiri state, although this idea is being suggested by such organisations as the JKLF.

If Partition itself has been the subject of much anguished and rhetorical writings, so too has been the drama of the Kashmiri Maharaja's indecision about whether to join the Dominion of India, become an independent Kashmiri state, or become part of Muslim Pakistan. Having a Hindu leader over a Muslim majority state, Pakistan's claims to the kingdom seemed to be justified on the basis of the two-nation theory. Moreover Kashmir's proximity to Pakistan also favoured the Radcliffe principle of grouping together contiguous Muslim majority areas.[32] Following implicit Pakistani support for a tribal invasion into the valley to help their fellow Muslims, the Maharaja signed up to secede to India and received immediate military help. This led to outrage in Karachi and an immediate conflict between the two dominions.

While timely Indian moves prevented the 'tribals' from taking the capital Srinagar, the Indians did not succeed in totally removing the Pakistani army, leaving Pakistan in control of an area of approximately 30,503 square kilometres referred to as 'Azad' (free) Kashmir. Both states continue to claim the state in its entirety. One commentator noted that India's 'arguments for holding on to Kashmir are hollow, fallacious, shifting and confused'.[33]. Indian academics often reiterate the same accusation in reverse. Both states have pressed on with the integration of their respective portions of Kashmir into their wider political frameworks, and both states remain committed to 'restoring' Kashmir to their respective political federations.

Nehru referred the matter to the United Nations Security Council in 1947, allegedly following the suggestion of the Viceroy. In a letter sent in November 1947 to his Pakistani counterpart, Liquat Ali Khan, Nehru also held out the prospect of settling the issue through a plebiscite, a matter that had already been discussed earlier between Jinnah and Mountbatten. The subsequent role of the UN in the Kashmir problem profoundly shocked Nehru, since Pakistan was not only able to canvas international support, she was also able to elicit sympathy on a whole series of issues that were, from the Indian point of view, matters for bilateral negotiation only. Initially supportive of the presence of the United Nations Observers Group for India and Pakistan (UNOGIP) and a UN-regulated ceasefire line, India gradually came to see the observation group as unwarranted interference. In 1948 Nehru noted bitterly: 'I must confess that the attitude of the great powers [on the question of Kashmir] has been astonishing. Our experience of international politics and the ways things are done in the higher regions of the UN has been disappointing to the extreme – no doubt all this will affect our conduct of international relations in the future.'[34]

The handling of the Kashmir issue by the international community goes a long way to explaining India's antipathy to the role of 'external' mediation in regional affairs. This aversion would, over time, become directed not just against third-power mediation, but also against most forms of multilateral negotiation within the region itself. Following the United Nations fiasco, India was determined to solve the Kashmir crisis on the basis of bilateral relations with Pakistan. She was, however, to accept brief Soviet mediation after the 1965 war with Pakistan.

The 1947–8 conflict was halted through a combination of Indian diplomatic naivety, the weakness of the respective armies, and the curious fact that a British Commander-in-Chief (Field Marshal Sir Claude Auchinleck) was in command of both Indian and Pakistani forces and a large percentage of the office corps on both sides were also British.[35]

Yet India's perceptions of a pernicious, calculating Pakistan were set firmly in their mould. Matters were made worse when in 1958 the civilian government in Pakistan was removed by a military coup. The dispute between Indian and Pakistani nationalism was now heightened through the conflict of a democracy against a military oligarchy. Extreme and mutual threat perceptions stalled attempted political dialogue, with India turning down a Pakistani offer of a mutual defence pact in the late 1950s. Ayub Khan in his autobiography *Friends, Not Masters* believed that the future for Indo-Pakistan relations was bleak because of Indian arrogance.

Indian mistrust was further reinforced after the 1965 conflict. India's military humiliation over the 1962 border clash with China (discussed below) had revealed serious weaknesses in India's military capability. In early April 1965 the Pakistan army carried out a careful probe of India's defences in the Rann of Kutch area. Satisfied that Indian moral was low, Ayub Khan launched the infamous *Operation Gibraltar* to take Kashmir by force. The result of the conflict was another draw that failed to alter the already existing UN ceasefire line. To Pakistan's surprise, India had launched an attack across the international Punjabi border, and the key Pakistani assumption – that Muslim Kashmiris would welcome the Pakistanis as liberators – badly misfired. The stalemate was made official through the Tashkent Declaration of January 1966 signed in Soviet Central Asia, which reinstated the *status quo anti*.

The period between 1965 and 1971 saw little improvement between the two states over Kashmir. The restoration of democracy in Pakistan in 1971 (a fact welcomed by India as a precondition for the normalisation of Indo-Pakistan relations), and the current civilian regime of Naswar Sharif (who is himself a Kashmiri) have not provided the kind of political breakthrough desired. Since 1972, Indo-Pakistan relations have oscillated between open hostility and suggested reconciliation. In December 1985, Prime Minister Rajiv Gandhi and President Zia-ul-Haq signed an agreement not to attack each other's nuclear installations, an agreement that was reiterated in 1988 by the then Pakistan Prime Minister Benazir Bhutto. Pakistan has offered various solutions to the standoff between them, from a joint non-nuclear agreement, to a 'no first strike' agreement, but the Indian response has always been mistrustful of Pakistan's real intentions, and guarded about her own. Mutual mistrust also characterises The Kashmir issue. Hence the prospects for an opening in Indo-Pakistan relations, even after the restoration of democracy in Pakistan, remain remote.

The Pakistan civil war 1970–1971

Pakistan's fear of Indian plans aimed at her destruction have been part of the domestic political agenda since 1947 and was dramatically substantiated with the loss of East Pakistan, during a civil war, in which the predominantly West Pakistani government refused to concede Bengali demands for greater autonomy. What made matters so critical is that Bengal's success in breaking away rested on *Indian* involvement. Very few colonial states have disintegrated since independence, and although the geographical separation of East from West made Pakistan's case rather unusual, the fact that 1971 happened at all (with the loss of 56 per cent of Pakistan's population and 32 per cent of its territory) terrified future Pakistani governments that, with future Indian help, Pakistan would disintegrate further. Sajjad Hyder, who was Pakistan's High Commissioner in New Delhi in the run-up to the Bangladesh crisis, noted in a recent book: 'Our perceptions of India are that, beneath a thin veneer, the Indian leadership and a sizeable segment of Indian opinion continue to regard the formation of Pakistan as an historical error and that given the opportunity they would wish in some way to redress the situation.'[36] The degree and extent of Indian involvement in the civil war has been well documented, and the war has produced several studies from both the Indian and the Pakistani side's.[37] While India acted to make the most out of Pakistani difficulties, she was also provoked into action by the fear of general instability in her own troubled north-eastern area caused by a massive influx of Bengali refugees – up to 10 million by August 1971. Unsure of the ideological views of many of the refugees, India feared that they would add to her problems with left-wing groups in the state of West Bengal.

During the late 1960s West Bengal was the scene of intra-communist violence and fighting between the Left and the Congress Party in power at the centre. The prospect of the 'two Bengals' falling to the left raised the spectre of a united Bengali nation under its own state, and a Marxist one to boot, giving rise to concern within India over the prospect of her territorial disintegration. India watched throughout the summer of 1971 as the Pakistani military abandoned any real search for a political solution with Mujib Rehman, the leader of the Bengal nationalist party, the Awami League. His arrest and incarceration in West Pakistan marked the beginning of a 'military solution'. By early September, it was clear that India was in favour of intervening directly, having stepped up her covert support for the Bengali rebels. In December 1971, with Indian military forces grouped in the eastern sector ready to 'liberate' East Pakistan, the Pakistan leadership in the west wing launched a pre-emptive air strike in the western sector against Indian airfields.

The resurrection of the Kashmir issue by the Pakistani leadership failed to distract the Indians from their primary objective of liberating Bengal or of rallying round the Bengalis to an issue that had never really concerned them in the first place. Fighting in the western sector was not as dramatic as that in the eastern sector. India's declaration of a unilateral ceasefire in the West on 17 December followed the fall of Dhaka (now the capital of Bangladesh) and some Indian gains over the Kashmir ceasefire line and in Sind and Pakistan Punjab.

Unlike the previous wars, the 1971 conflict fundamentally altered the balance of power within the region. The eastern wing was now an independent state, and erstwhile West Pakistan was in turmoil. The breakup of Pakistan confirmed India's long-held prejudice that religion could not provide the basis for enduring nationalism (and her public position that the 'two nation' theory was incorrect). 1971 confirmed India, in her own eyes at least, as the dominant regional power. The Simla Accord of 1972 (signed in the old summer capital of the British *Raj*) was the first significant bilateral agreement between India and Pakistan in which New Delhi attempted to get Pakistan to accept the 'realities of power within the sub-continent'. At first it seemed that Pakistan could do little to prevent the Indians from renegotiating events, especially with reference to Kashmir, in their favour.

India was able to bargain territorial gains made in Punjab and Sind for a readjustment of the old UN ceasefire line towards a new line of control (LOC) in Kashmir which improved India's forward positions. The Simla Accord also opened the way for the eventual recognition of Bangladesh by Pakistan (extended in 1974) and the return of PoWs held in the East. The 1973 repatriation agreement between India and Pakistan was complicated by Pakistan's initial reluctance to deal with Bangladesh, and Bangladeshi determination to place several prominent prisoners of war on trial in Dhaka. On 9 April 1974 India held a trilateral conference with Pakistan and Bangladesh, which further underscored her new-found influence within the sub-continent.

A great many myths have grown up around the so-called 'spirit of Simla' over the degree of its durability, and the degree of its success for India. Various studies on Indian foreign policy still hail the declaration as India's 'Congress of Vienna', the onset of India's key role as regional manager and regime builder, and the end of Pakistani hopes to be treated as an equal.[38] While there can be no doubt that India's intention was to try and use the 1971 victory to set the regional agenda in her favour, and to provide the framework within which Indo-Pakistan relations would evolve, it is questionable whether such an approach succeeded.

Pakistan's new civilian leader, Zulfiker Ali Bhutto, was anxious to settle with India on terms that would not discredit him domestically. Initially the mood was one of realism. After the war *The Pakistan Times* noted bleakly: 'we on our part have to rid ourselves of the fiction of equality of status with India. If India plays fair by us, if she does not seek to weaken or isolate us, we should advance rather than checkmate her legitimate regional interests.'[39] But this view did not last, if only for the simple reason that India did not appear to play 'fair' with Pakistan's security interests. The Simla negotiations were only concluded after protracted wrangling (and were settled late into the night, since neither side could afford to draw a political blank). The Indian Prime Minister faced accusations of a 'sell out' since it seemed to the right-wing parties that Pakistan had not been taught the lesson she deserved. Rizvi has noted that 'Pakistan has refused to acknowledge [her] inferior status . . . despite being truncated in 1971 . . . Pakistan remains determined to hold the balance of power in South Asia.'[40]

Although Pakistan's pursuit of military parity against India was severely weakened, she was able to turn for more external help to · China, and to the U.S after 1975. China was particularly useful to Pakistan during the period of isolation experienced under the Bhutto government, especially between Islamabad and Washington, and could well remain an important source of support during the current disagreements between the US and her most 'allied ally'.

On an official visit to Beijing in 1976 Bhutto cast further doubts on Pakistan's commitment to the spirit of Simla and to regional bilateralism. In the joint communiqué there appeared the telling lines that, while all was well in South Asia, 'only the Jammu and Kashmir dispute remains to be resolved peacefully in accordance with the right of self-determination recognised in the United Nations Resolutions and *accepted by both India and Pakistan*'.[41]

Bangladesh and the reaction against Indian dominance

A few weeks before his removal from power in December 1990, President Ershad of Bangladesh accused India of engineering popular unrest and assisting, as he put it, 'the octopus of destructive politics'. Since the early 1970s Dhaka has been in the habit of accusing India of 'anti-national designs' over either her suggestion to construct a link canal between the Brahmaputra and the Ganges river systems, or her general misuse of the now infamous Farraka barrage just fifteen kilometres from the Bangladesh border. For two states united by war against Pakistan, the cause of such hostility seems hard to find: did not Mujib Rehman fly back to a liberated Bengal, cheered on by a mass crowd of Indians during his stopover at New Delhi?

Having grasped the bull by the horns in 1971, India was determined to shape the political future of the new state both in keeping with her wider security interests in the north-east and as an insurance policy against China. This twin approach – a new departure for Indian foreign policy in the region – continued until the basis of secular Bengali nationalism collapsed, and the language of gratitude turned into charges of political domination.

Between 1971 and 1975 Bangladesh was tied to India through a whole series of bilateral treaties and agreements, and had become by 1975 the largest recipient of Indian aid. Having acted as the 'midwife' of the newest independent state in South Asia, it seemed a natural continuation of a close and intimate relationship. In 1975 Indian aid was in the region of Rs299.88 crore. India's *total* aid since the early 1950s to the Himalayan kingdoms of Nepal and Bhutan came to only Rs305.32 crore. Even after the sundering of the New Delhi–Dhaka axis, aid programmes continued. By 1979 India's commitment to Bangladesh was Rs335.27 crore.[42]

Immediately after the 1971 ceasefire had been declared, India granted Bangladesh Rs25 crore for immediate relief, as well as over £5 million sterling in foreign exchange to help stimulate reconstruction and trade. A majority of the aid programmes between 1971 and 1973 involved food grains and edible oils, although by 1974 Indian assistance had broadened out to deal with joint economic ventures in which Indian capital imports would help Bangladesh reconstruct her roads and railways. A 1974 agreement also covered co-operation in the fields of nuclear power and nuclear research.

By 1974 India had also concluded various border demarcations that had been outstanding at the time of East Pakistan's demise in and around the Indian territories of Assam and Tripura. Other agreements involved the incorporation of various Muslim Bengali enclaves into Bangladesh without compensation, although it was only in 1982 that India finally agreed to lease 'in perpetuity' the so-called Tin Bigha corridors that connected Bangladesh with four Muslim enclaves in the Indian state of West Bengal, and even to this day the agreement has not been fully implemented.

The keystone of Indian policy towards Bangladesh – and a vital input into the Bangladeshi perception of Indian intent – was the Twenty-Five Years of Friendship and Co-operation treaty signed in Dhaka on 19 May 1972. The co-operation referred to was as much strategic as it was economic. The treaty spelled out at some length that:

> neither country would participate in any military alliance directed against the other, both would refrain from aggression against each other, neither would give any assistance to a third party involved in an armed conflict against the other, and, in the event of an attack against either, the parties would immediately enter into consultations in order to take measures to eliminate the threat.[43]

In retrospect, given Bangladesh's size relative to India, such a candid assertion of bilateralism could only give rise to mistrust and suspicion. Bangladesh is surrounded by India on all sides, except for a poorly demarcated border with Burma. The cultural affinities between the two – refracted by fourteen years within a united Pakistan – could be both supportive and suffocating. To make matters worse, India was quick to send in constitutional advisers, the result being that the 1972 prime ministerial constitution of Bangladesh was a virtual replica of the Indian constitution of 1950, ignoring the presidential forms experienced under Pakistan.

By early 1975, when the domestic support for the Mujib regime was melting away in the face of anti-Indian propaganda and accusations of domestic corruption, the left wing of Bangladeshi politics argued that a glorious free Bengal had been reduced to a mere satellite, 'another Himalayan kingdom' within an extended Indian economic zone run by Indian traders and smugglers. To the political right – and inspite of previous charges of collaboration with Pakistan during the civil war – the Muslim fundamentalists charged that Bangladesh had escaped from the Punjabi embrace of West Pakistan only to fall under the Hindu juggernaut.

The events of August 1975 – the killing of a large part of the Rehman family and the rise of the military – ended India's hopes of a lasting friendship with Bangladesh and her hope that Bangladesh would remain democratic. When news reached New Delhi about the murder of Mujib, Indira Gandhi noted in response that 'we feel that there is an effort to disturb stability in the region . . . we cannot help expressing our deep concern over these events'. Pakistan, afraid that such a statement was the first tentative moves for another 'liberation war' (to remove the military and restore a democracy, a move that could have been legally bolstered by the 1972 Friendship treaty), warned of the serious consequences that would follow from any further Indian intervention.[44]

Bangladeshi–Indian relations deteriorated rapidly after August 1975. Most of the Awami League fled to India, while several former guerrillas took to the Myminsingh area of north-eastern Bangladesh to fight against an Islamic restoration under the title of the *Shanti Bahini*. Although it has been denied on numerous occasions, it is frequently asserted by the Bangladeshi authorities that India is supporting the rebels. Over the years successive Indian governments have accused Bangladesh of supporting her own rebellious tribes in the troubled north-eastern states, who are attempting to gain independence from New Delhi.

In 1981 the Indian navy laid claim to the Purbasha island that had been emerging in the mouth of the Hariya Bhanga river – one of the numerous rivers of the Ganges delta – since the 1970s. Indian attempts in 1984 to position fencing along the West Bengal/Bangladesh border led to incidents between India's Border Security Force (BSF) and the Bangladeshi Rifles.

Pakistani attempts to normalise relations with Bangladesh were complicated by India's role in the liberation of Bangladesh and her relationship with the Mujib Rehman regime. Prime Minister Mujib Rehman, the leader of the Bengali Awami League, was determined that before any negotiations could be made to release PoWs, Pakistan must acknowledge Bangladesh as a sovereign nation. This was a bitter pill to swallow, since Pakistan perceived it as a demand conveyed on the back of the Indian Army. By 1972 Bhutto had already come to see the Mujib regime as a set of Indian stooges imposed and maintained by New Delhi, and it was this prejudice, along with the problems of domestic reaction to the Simla Agreement, that delayed Pakistani recognition of Bangladesh until 1974. Moreover, Bhutto argued that since a Pakistani army had surrendered to an Indian army, there was no need to bring in the Bengalis at all. Relying upon Chinese support, Pakistan also blocked various attempts by India and the Non-Aligned Movement to introduce Bangladesh to the United Nations.

There were limits to how long the 'new' Pakistan could afford to sulk over the issue of Bangladesh however. The longer she ignored the proclaimed secular state for the Bengali, the more deeply entrenched Indian vested interests would become. Yet even after recognition was extended, Pakistan remained aloof from serious involvement until after 1975, and the demise of the pro-Indian government of Mujib

Rehman through a military coup. Ironically, it was only when President Bhutto himself had been removed in Pakistan by the army that Pakistan–Bangladesh relations improved dramatically. China did not recognise Bangladesh until the establishment of the Ziaul-Reham military regime in November 1975.

Throughout the 1980s both Pakistan and Bangladesh were committed to creating Islamic republics under the auspices of the military, a common task that created obvious affinities between their foreign policies with respect to secular India and to the Middle East. By 1988 and the death of President Zia, Pakistan returned to a quasi-form of civilian government and in late 1990 Bangladesh had momentarily rid itself of the army and was preparing itself for party-based, parliamentary elections. In what is perhaps a rather curious testimony to the 'two nation' theory after all, events within Pakistan and Bangladesh have remained closely associated long after the two wings had appeared to go their separate ways.

Developing close relations with Pakistan were vital for the Bangladeshi policy of escaping Indian dominance, and in generally pressurising the Indians into making some concessions on the issue of shared water resources.

The construction of the Farakka barrage started in India in 1962. The aim of the project was to divert water occasionally from the Ganges into the Hooghly to prevent the Calcutta-Howrah Port from silting up, especially during the pre-monsoon period when the flow of the north Indian river systems is dramatically reduced. The barrage would also provide irrigation facilities for India. The then province of East Pakistan objected that the resulting theft of water seriously affected her own irrigation projects, and threatened fresh water supplies further down in the delta by lowering the water table and increasing risks of salination.

Extensive consultations between India and Pakistan proved incapable of resolving the issue along the lines of the Indus River Treaty, and the matter was inherited by the Awami League government in 1971. Part of the problem – and a serious one with reference to international law – was India's insistence that the Farakka barrage was a barrage and Pakistan's insistence that it was in fact a dam. Pakistan referred the matter to the World Bank and to the United Nations.[45]

In 1972 India and Bangladesh decided to create a permanent Joint Rivers Commission (JRC) to attempt to agree on guidelines for shared usage of the Ganges. Yet by 1975 the talks were stalling amid Bangladeshi accusations of unilateral Indian action just before the onset of the July monsoons. In 1975 Bangladesh accused India of so reducing the water level in the Ganges that the Bangladesh Water Board pumping station at Hardinge Bridge was in danger of stopping, thus jeopardising extensive irrigation works. By 1980 a decision was taken to wind up the JRC and move to a series of interim settlements to share the water on a yearly basis – none of which have been to the lasting satisfaction of Dhaka.

Furthermore, India believes that the problems of shared water resources can be solved by joining the two major river systems in the north east – the Brahmaputra and the Ganges – by a link canal. This would enable greater control over the flow of the rivers and would help share scarce water resources by transferring water across the water-sheds and drainage basins of the two systems if and when it was required. Such a scheme, India believes, would also help trade and commerce. The canal would start and end in Indian territory but would be almost entirely located within Bangladesh, cross-cutting the Barind Upland and separating the extreme north of the country from the delta area. Bangladeshi objections are on ecological, technical as well as strategic grounds.[46]

Bangladesh has suggested an alternative scheme, which involves the construction of storage reservoirs and canal complexes in Nepal and India away to the north-east of the sub-continent. Such a scheme has the apparent advantages of providing Nepal a riverian outlet through Bangladesh (made possible by canal links across five rivers), as well as giving Nepal and north-west India access to hydroelectric power stations. Despite Nepalese agreement, India objects on the grounds that this scheme is too expensive, that it would involve too many other states, and it would flood valuable (and scarce) land in the Hindi-speaking provinces of northern India. In turn various Bangladeshi governments have pointed out that even the Brahmaputra – Ganges canal could not be a solely bilateral affair, since it would have to involve China as a 'watershed' state. This in turn would raise a hornet's nest of legal claims and counterclaims in a part of the world already thick with territorial disputes.

Since 1975 Bangladesh has returned to the former Pakistan practice of internationalising the Farraka barrage by referring it to The United Nations at the opening of the thirty-first session of the General Assembly (where both India and the Soviet Union protested), the Islamic Conference of Foreign Ministers and, to India's particular irritation, the summit of the Non-Aligned Movement in Colombo 1976. India has consistently refused to have any outside mediation in the affair, despite several precedents set in both the developed and developing world, and despite the involvement of the International Bank for Reconstruction and Development (BIRD) in the Indus Water Treaty.

In recent years, based upon the creation of the South Asian Association of Regional Co-operation (SAARC) in 1985, Bangladesh has tried further to involve the other regional states, especially Nepal, in a comprehensive settlement. Yet India's mistrust of multilateralism remains. On 2 June 1985, Rajiv Gandhi and President Ershad signed a moratorium of understanding (MOU) and decided to reconvene a Joint Committee of Experts which, like the JRC before it, has so far failed to come to any acceptable agreements. It is not known what policies Begum Zia's government will adopt. Her husband, Zial-Reham, was the architect of a Bangladeshi foreign policy that sought to distance the state from Indian dominance. The opposition to the canal scheme remains.

Finally, and unlike any other state in South Asia with the possible exception of Nepal, Bangladesh's regional policy is totally determined by her general poverty, and the degree to which her sovereignty can be compromised through environmental disasters. Bangladesh is not a powerful state in military terms. In 1989–90 its army numbered some 90,000 personnel, her navy was made up of three ex-British frigates, and her air force consisted of sixty-four combat aircraft.[47] In the late 1980s most of these units were busy dealing with domestic security matters as President Ershad attempted to address his country's economic ills and shore up his own political future. In 1990, with an estimated GDP of US $19.01 billion, the World Bank listed Bangladesh as the fifth poorest country in the world. The explanations for this continuing poverty are complex.

In part they are linked with political incompetence and war, in part with the misfortune of Partition and the consequences of the 1971 civil war. In a short but precise lecture to the British Royal Asian Society in 1988, Hugh Evans noted simply that 'Bangladesh is just over 16 years old . . . For a people to have to build a new state from scratch is unfortunate. To have to do so twice in 25 years seems almost extravagant.'[48] Bangladeshi priorities are first and foremost the need for economic and industrial development, but since 1971 these goals have proven elusive.

Between 1980 and 1988 Bangladesh witnessed two devastating monsoons, two droughts, one typhoon and one earthquake. The floods of 1988 alone resulted in over US $2 billion dollars of damage. There now exists overwhelming evidence that increased runoff in the northern Himalayas, caused by deforestation in Nepal and north-west India, has contributed to the ferocity of the floods and to the high degree of sedimentation. In 1988 a Bangladeshi English-language paper noted that 'the dimensions of this year's floods should make it clear to all that the complete destruction of Bangladesh is now a distinct possibility'.[49]

In April 1991, coastal Bangladesh was hit by a typhoon which claimed over 200,000 lives. Bangladesh's recognition that only regional co-operation can bring any lasting relief explains why Bangladesh took the initiative to create the South Asian Association Regional Co-operation (SAARC) in the early 1980s, but it has been difficult to prove to India that a forum for regional co-operation is anything other than an attempt by the other states to gang up against her. Yet any analysis of Bangladesh's foreign policy must stress the importance of environmental degradation. Policy formulation must be premised on the fact that 'the whole notion of security as traditionally understood in terms of political and military threats must be expanded to include the growing impact of environmental disaster'.[50]

Sino-Indian relations

What makes Pakistan's intransigence so irritating to enthusiastic students of India's strategic interests is that it detracts attention away from what some analysts believe is her 'real' rival, the People's Republic of China.[51] Much has been made about the asymmetry of Sino-Indian relations, with China's cultural and political heartlands far off on the Pacific coast, while in contrast, the remote Tibetan plateau looks down on to the Hindi heartlands of the Gangetic plains. Far from facing each other (as with India and Pakistan), India and China sit back to back, 'like two Asian giants in a perpetual sulk'. This asymmetry is given particular relevance since, as a nuclear power, China can potentially strike at India's main population centres while India cannot yet hit at China's, although recent missile tests have underlined India's clear potential. India remains concerned about China's nuclear capabilities and her nuclear modernisation programme. Because of technical bilateral agreements with Pakistan, the Chinese bomb is part of the general Indian anxiety over the 'Islamic bomb'. Ashok Kapor has noted that 'the Indian perception of her role in Asia needs to be viewed in conjunction with the Chinese world view' because India has long recognised that, unlike Pakistan, China is both an ideological and a cultural force to compete with throughout the Third World and throughout international politics generally.[52]

While formally outside the region, China is linked to India's immediate security environment because of unresolved border disputes with India to the north-east (including claims on Bhutan and Sikkim, and the present Indian states of Arunchal Pradesh and Assam) and to the north-west area of Aksai Chin, adjacent to Ladakh.

Although India has never claimed Tibet, it has implicitly supported Tibetan claims for greater autonomy from China both in the late 1950s and during subsequent periods of political instability. India provides the exiled Dalai Lama (the spiritual leader of the Tibetan Buddhists) a home in Dharamsala, in the Indian state of Himachal Pradesh. Interestingly enough, India has not allowed the Dalai Lama to form a government in exile, and the Indian government remained silent in 1987 over China's suppression of Tibetan-Buddhist agitation in and around Lhasa.

Even during the heyday of Sino-Indian co-operation, from 1949 until 1959, China did not drop her claims to substantially large areas of Indian territory. In 1950 and 1959, the communists moved to substantiate claims to Tibet despite Indian protests. The 1954 Agreement on Tibet (that recognised Tibet as an 'autonomous' region of China) established the importance of the 'five principles' of Panscheel which were: mutual respect for each other's territorial integrity; mutual non-aggression; mutual non-interference; equality and mutual benefit, and peaceful co-existence. Praised as 'bold, wholesome principles', they did not survive the border crisis of 1962 (although, as shall be discussed, they remain as the basis of the Non-Aligned Movement).

Since 1962 the implied Chinese negotiating position has been a trade-off between disputed territories over the MacMahon Line in the North-east for recognised Chinese sovereignty over Aksai Chin in the North-west. Zhou En Lai's 1960 statement referred to 'reciprocal abandonment of conflicting aims in the eastern and the western sectors', but India has refused to budge from what it considers its rightful inheritance.[53]

The Sino-Indian borders remained unresolved throughout the British period and were not, like the Kashmir crisis, a product of British disengagement. Settlements between *Raj* and Manchu China at Simla in 1914 made vague references to watersheds and 'natural boundaries' without verification, and with reference to remote areas that had been poorly mapped. Anxious to avoid great-power rivalry with the Russian

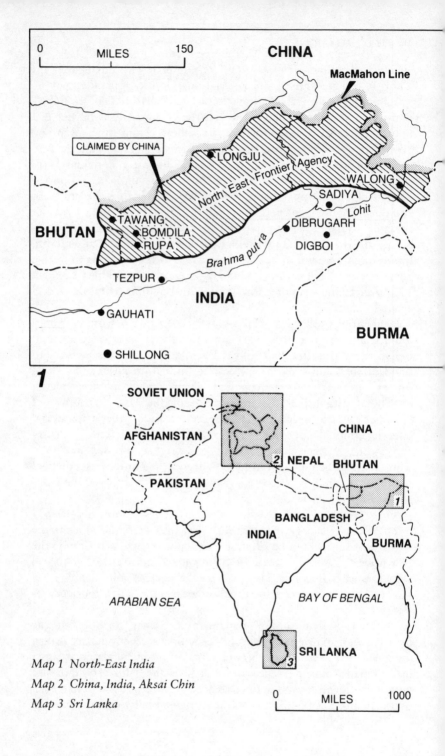

Map 1 North-East India
Map 2 China, India, Aksai Chin
Map 3 Sri Lanka

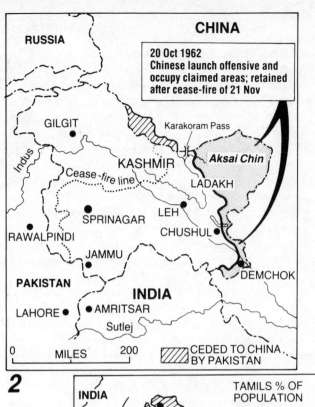

CHINA

20 Oct 1962
Chinese launch offensive and
occupy claimed areas; retained
after cease-fire of 21 Nov

RUSSIA

GILGIT

Karakoram Pass

Indus

KASHMIR

Aksai Chin

Cease-fire line

LADAKH

SPRINAGAR

LEH

RAWALPINDI

CHUSHUL

JAMMU

DEMCHOK

PAKISTAN

INDIA

LAHORE ● ● AMRITSAR

Sutlej

0 MILES 200

CEDED TO CHINA
BY PAKISTAN

2

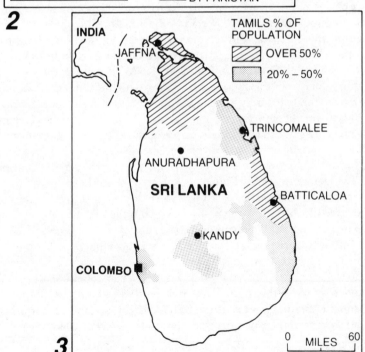

INDIA

TAMILS % OF
POPULATION

JAFFNA

OVER 50%

20% – 50%

TRINCOMALEE

ANURADHAPURA

SRI LANKA

BATTICALOA

KANDY

COLOMBO

0 MILES 60

3

Empire, the British – masters of practicality – had prefered the notion of 'buffers' and 'spheres of influence' to demarcated borders. To the players of the Great Game, China had not been a serious concern at all.

This particular Simla agreement was subsequently denounced by Mao Tse Tung in 1949 as one of a whole series of unequal treaties forced on China by the imperial powers, and one that would be renegotiated. India's inflexibility and her refusal to depart from a previous British discourse of demarcation frustrated China and finally precipitated an act of Chinese aggression. While Indian intransigence does not excuse the use of force, it illustrates that Sino-Indian negotiators approach the matter from quite different premises. In 1987 Raju Thomas noted that 'the border issue is not a difficult one *provided that the Chinese accept* the Himalayan Crest and the Indus river watershed as the legitimate and logical borders between the [two] countries'.[54] The problem arises from the Chinese refusal to recognise the 'legitimate' and 'logical' borders provided by geographical concepts such as 'crests' and watersheds. More recently Ramesh Thakur has stated that 'the Indian position on the border dispute appears to be inflexible even to sympathetic observers because it is based upon a legalistic framework of questionable authenticity with no scope for political manoeuvring'.[55] In turn India denounces Chinese assumptions of pre-1949 borders as arrogant and unrealistic. It is within this impasse, and in spite of several political initiatives from both sides, that the border issue has come to rest. India reinstated ambassadorial links with Beijing in 1976, despite earlier Chinese complaints over the merger of Sikkim with India in 1975, Chinese support for tribal rebels situated in the North-East, and rhetorical support for the various Marxist (so-called Naxalite) violence against New Delhi since the mid 1960s. In 1978, the Indian foreign minister A. B. Vaypayee went on a goodwill tour, and in 1981 the Chinese Foreign Minister Huang Hua visited New Delhi. During the ASIAD Games in New Delhi, in 1982, China complained over the presence of an Arunchal Pradesh dancing troupe in the opening festival. The Rajiv Gandhi visit of 1988 – the first visit of an Indian Prime Minister since Nehru's – did not visibly improve the pace of border negotiations.

In 1988–89, the Indian Defence Ministry's annual report still played the 'China card' as part of the justification to maintain Indian defence expenditure. Yet, since the 1962 war, and apart from the odd border panics such as those that occurred in 1987 along the Bhutanese/ Arunchal Pradesh sector of the MacMahon Line (and earlier around the Sumdurong Chu district) Sino-Indian relations have been significantly less tense than Indo-Pakistan relations. The two sets of equations cannot be separated because of the degree of Sino-Pakistan co-operation that began in the mid 1960s.

If historical and cultural misperceptions lie at the root of the Sino-Indian stand-off, they are further complicated by the fact that China's claims in the north-western sector impinged upon parts of Azad Kashmir and Indian controlled Ladakh. Parts of Azad Kashmir, having been under effective Pakistani administration since 1948, were given to China through the Sino-Pakistan border agreement of 1964 despite the fact that the area was in effect claimed by India.[56] Indian protests were ignored. Thus shared perceptions of India provided the cement between Pakistan and China, in spite of Ayub Khan's keenly-felt anti-communism, and the antipathy of the Americans to China prior to the 1972 breakthrough. After the 1965 war (when the Americans had temporarily withdrawn military assistance from Pakistan) China stepped into the breach as a major arms supplier to Pakistan and as a significant giver of aid. Throughout the 1970s, China provided Pakistan with about US $2.6 billion of weapons, and various soft loans and grants.

Because of this *entente cordiale*, India sees Pakistan and China as part of the same security dilemma. In the middle of the August war in 1965, China demanded that India should withdraw various observation posts from Sikkim that were apparently violating the border, thus raising the possibility of a two-front war. The fear that China would come to Pakistan's aid during a war with India has had a profound influence upon India's perception of her own legitimate defence requirements. The construction of the strategically significant Karakoram Pass Highway (that opened in 1978) further raised the possibility of Chinese forces being deployed to reinforce Pakistan in any future Kashmiri conflict. Yet China's failure to come to Pakistan's help in 1971 following India's invasion of East Pakistan was seen as a telling failure. Another important obstacle to Sino-Indian relations has been the degree of co-operation between the Soviet Union and India after the onset of the Sino-Soviet split.

The Himalayan kingdoms of Nepal and Bhutan

In 1989, P. N. Haksar, the guru of India's intellectual approach to questions of foreign policy, noted that 'India should not be concerned about Nepal. If they want to play their China card let them, it is of no consequence'.[57] Since 1988 various Nepali communiqués stated that in retaliation for an independent foreign policy (allegedly involving an arms deal with China signed in 1988) India had closed down all but two of the fifteen trade crossings into India which were vital for her survival. In 1989 India refused to renew the separate Trade and Transfer Agreements, arguing that it was her wish for them to be negotiated separately. By late 1989 the economic effects of the alleged 'embargo' were serious enough for the IMF to announce approved Special Drawing Rights (SDRs) of up to US $9,500,000 for immediate economic relief. World Bank estimates in late 1990 calculated that India's unilateral action had seriously reduced Nepal's economic prospects and were responsible for a virtual zero growth rate in FY 1989/1990.[58] India initially denied that her unilateral action was in retaliation for the purchase of Chinese arms, and cited the Nepalese refusal in 1988 to grant work permits to Indian residents, or deal with the problems of smuggling and re-exporting Indian produce.

India's policy towards Nepal gave rise to strong anti-Indian sentiments within the Nepalese court because it coincided with renewed Indian support for a widespread popular movement to reinstate a multi-party democracy after a long period of partyless, *panchayat* government. In a recent article, Leo Rose has speculated that the possible explanations for India's attitude towards Nepal are linked to several factors. One factor concerns the Nepali government awarding a building contract to a Chinese construction company, despite the closeness of the Indian border and the risks of spying.

Another factor certainly seems to involve the selling of arms, but most critically, the recent argument seems to have been started by 'a secret agreement between China and Nepal, apparently concluded in the late fall of 1988, providing for the exchange of intelligence'.[59] Even if such claims can be substantiated, can India's actions be justified, or are actions towards Nepal merely paranoic?

Nepal's perception of India is a stereotypical case of the 'small state' complex, in which she has attempted to play off Indian dominance by making diplomatic overtures towards China. This is also true of Bhutan, since both states exist in the cultural–political 'grey area' where Indian and Chinese cultural traditions mix. In 1768 Prith-vinarayan Shah, the Raja of Gurkha, announced to his court that Nepal was like a 'yam between two boulders' and that their policies to British India and Manchu China should, while playing them off for mutual benefit, provoke neither. Such a sound recommendation is still valid, although the logical consequences of such an understanding significantly constrain Nepal's (and Bhutan's) independence. Ramesh

Thapur has noted generally that: 'India views China as an intruder within the region, while China believes that her participation within South Asia is legitimate [and] other states welcome the Chinese counterweight to Indian pretensions to regional hegemony.'[60] This is particularly the case with Nepal and Bhutan. These kingdoms occupy the strategic 'commanding heights' of the Himalayan watershed – the so-called 'logical' border between India and China. These states were directly involved in the Sino-Indian cold war that started after the assertion of Chinese control over Tibet in 1959. Nepal established diplomatic relations with China in 1955, and following India's lead on the 1954 agreement over 'the autonomous region of Tibet' has used the five principles of Panscheel to govern bilateral relations with Beijing. Over the years, and especially after the 1962 border war, the degree of flexibility in Nepali-Indian and Bhutan-Indian relations has thus varied considerably under the influence of Sino-Indian relations. Periods of high tension between Beijing and New Delhi have increased the flexibility of these kingdoms although it has never weakened the Indian resolve to retain them as, to all intents and purposes, buffer states.

In 1988, Nepal finally concluded a border settlement with China, based upon the principle that a border inspection will verify the situation on the ground every five years, a telling diplomatic victory that further isolated India as one of the only remaining states yet to settle her borders with China. Since the 1980s Nepal has benefited from a significant amount of Chinese aid. In 1986 it was estimated that China contributed about US $5.9 million to Nepal (twice as much as the 1979 figure, although less than half of the Indian figure) and Chinese experts were working on about twenty or so projects. As already noted, Chinese co-operation on various road-building projects has touched upon Indian security concerns, especially in the sensitive Xianping district which in turn borders on 'Azad Kashmir'.[61]

This said, however, Bhutan and Nepal have broadly accepted their so-called 'special relationship with India'. Their socio-cultural links with India are obvious enough – Nepal is closely associated to India through Hinduism[62] – while Nepal, Bhutan and Sikkim are interlinked in terms of ethnicity and language, especially with spoken Nepali.[63]

The intimacy of these links, as is so often the case within the region, are as much a source of tension within bilateral relations as they are a source of agreement. Moreover, such links tend to extend domestic political traumas in one state into the domestic political arena of another. In 1989 the Nepali community within Bhutan set up the Nepal Forum for Human Rights to defend their culture and political rights against the 1988 'code of conduct' which aimed to discourage the use of Nepali. Such a proclamation is indicative of the ethnic animosity between the Nepali immigrants and Hinduism and the 'indigenous' Drukpa tribes who are Buddhist. Recent attempts to control immigration, and strip descendants of Nepali immigrants of Bhutanese citizenship has led to moments of tension between Nepal and Bhutan and political violence within Bhutan against the monarchy.[64]

The origins of the 'special relationships' between these states and India originated under the British. In 1941 King Jigme Wangchuk of Bhutan extended a previous treaty signed with the British allowing India to 'guide and direct' her foreign policy. Following the agreement between Bhutan and British India in 1911, the Bhutanese Maharaja came under pressure from the Chinese for signing an agreement with the British without first referring it to the Emperor. The British Agent protested against this 'Chinese habit of tentative aggression, which if unchecked is simply escalated'. Since its gradual emergence as a state after 1947, Bhutan has been sure to avoid excessive complications with China, and her implicit use of China to concentrate the mind of the Indian External Affairs ministry has not be as forthright as Nepal's. Following the 1962 war, India and Bhutan undertook to clarify their defence positions over Chinese aggression, tentative or otherwise. Unlike Nepal, Bhutan – probably for reasons of size – is more willing to accept Indian hegemony and the benefits of Indian protection.

In 1950, India and Nepal signed a treaty of 'everlasting peace and friendship', while in 1954 an *aide memoire* issued in New Delhi suggested closer association between India and Nepal on matters of foreign policy, especially in relation to China and Tibet.[65] In 1965 New Delhi and Kathmandu signed an 'arms assistance agreement' which recognised the rights of Nepal to arm herself from anyone, except China, and only when India could not herself provide the weapons. It was this agreement that Nepal had appeared to violate in 1989.

While Bangladesh has the advantages of independent access to the region (and the wider international community) through the bay of Bengal, Nepal, Bhutan (and until 1975 the kingdom of Sikkim) are landlocked political entities that rely almost exclusively upon Indian co-operation for their economic well-being. Apart from a small trade relationship with Tibet, virtually all of Nepal's imports and exports must be transported through India, and India provides by far the largest market for Nepalese goods. In 1989 Nepal imported US $199.20 million dollars worth of goods from India (the next largest market being Singapore at US $66.89 million), while India dominated

Nepalese exports. In 1989 the Indian market absorbed US $55·4 million. Nepal and Bhutan have also received large amounts of Indian aid in terms of both loans and grants. Between 1954 and 1973 India provided Nepal with Rs11049 lakhs, over 80 per cent of total Nepali aid, although this figure decline after 1971 when Nepal turned increasingly to multilateral sources from the IRBD and the United Nations.

With India's economic dominance has also come the charge of political interference within the internal affairs of the kingdoms. That this interference has taken place is impossible to deny, but India claims moral and ideological justifications behind her invitations to support nascent democratic forces.

There are obvious parallels here with the Bangladesh situation, although unlike Bangladesh in both Nepal and Bhutan, authoritarian forces as such are associated not with the military, but with courtly faction and established aristocratic families. In 1950–51, India intervened within the domestic politics of Nepal to rally the pro-democracy movement under the leadership of the monarch against the powerful Rana family, and has since then been closely associated with political developments.

In 1961 India implicitly condemned King Mahendra's decision to ban political parties by offering support to the outlawed Nepalese Congress and a well-organised communist party. As in Bangladesh and Pakistan, India has supported calls for a democratic government, although following the Sino-Indian border clash of 1962 India reconciled her differences with the Nepalese court by curtailing support for the pro-democracy forces from inside India. Just before the border clash King Mahendra had visited Beijing and had been able to persuade the Chinese implicitly to condemn Indian interference, a move calculated to irritate New Delhi.

India resumed the rights of paramount power over Sikkim after 1947, along with the other kingdoms, although an actual agreement was not signed until 1950. Indian involvement with an internal dispute between a popular-based political movement and the *Chogyal* over the degree of democratic involvement resulted in Sikkim's eventual incorporation into India.

The Sikkim Agreement of 8 May 1973 ended a period of internal instability in which both the *Chogyal* and the Indian government 'recognised the need to establish responsible government'. Under the auspices of the Indian Electoral Commission, and a nominated Indian Chief Executive to advise the monarch, Sikkim entered into a new and more turbulent phase of political development, in which the Sikkim National Congress, and some other small parties, pressed for parliamentary government. In 1974, the *Chogyal* was converted into a constitutional monarch presiding over an elected cabinet and was then eventually 'deposed' in 1975. Preparations were then made for popular elections within the framework of the Indian Union.[66]

The integration (or, from an alternative perspective, the annexation) of Sikkim furthered the anxiety in Nepal and Bhutan that India's ultimate policy was to absorb them within the Indian political system. It is also possible that the culmination of India's policy towards Bhutan will end up in her 'integration' into the Indian Union, since the parallels with Sikkim are much more relevant for her than for Nepal. Since 1975, not long after the coronation of King Birendra in 1972, Nepal has redoubled her attempts to differentiate her foreign policy from India by calling for an internationally recognised Himalayan peace zone, recognised by the United Nations, thus ignoring India's stress upon her regional primacy and in apparent disregard for India's strategic obsessions with the Himalayan crests.

The 'yam between two boulders' metaphor is also useful, if less accurate, for an understanding of the Himalayan kingdoms' approach to Pakistan, although Islamabad is much more removed both physically and culturally. Since the late 1980s, with the intensification of regional co-operation, Nepal and Bhutan have been brought closer to Pakistan, Sri Lanka and Bangladesh. Nepal supports Bangladesh's objections to the link canal proposal, while Bangladesh supports Nepal's calls for a Himalayan Peace Zone. Nepali-Pakistan relations have flourished 'at arm's length', with Pakistan encouraging Nepalese independence from India's foreign policy. In 1984 Nepal signed a joint trade agreement with Pakistan in an attempt to diversify her trade relations throughout the region. In 1989 the Pakistani minister for finance promised to step in to the Nepali-Indian breach with credits worth US $1 million.

Sri Lanka

Critics of India's regional policy usually cite the example of Indo-Bangladesh relations, or recently Nepal, as an example of how *not* to win favours with small relatively defenceless states. By the late 1980s some critics were using the experience of Sri Lanka to argue that, far from constructing some durable system based upon Indian hegemony, New Delhi's regional designs merely fuelled anti-Indian sentiment, and further eroded the possibility of long-term regional stability.

In 1987 it was announced that India and Sri Lanka had signed a dramatic accord wherein India would deploy the Indian Peace Keeping Force (IPKF) to assist the Sri Lankan government in solving the 'Tamil problem' through Indian mediation. The Indian government felt it necessary to intervene because the Sri Lankan Tamils no longer trusted the Sri Lankan government (made up of Sinhalese), and because New Delhi was afraid that Indian Tamils living in India were offering support to the rebels without official sanction. Yet, having convened various meetings between the Tamil militants, the parliamentary-orientated Tamil United Liberation Front (TULF) and the Sri Lankan government (the so-called trilateral talks), the Rajiv Gandhi government decided to escalate the level of Indian intervention.

The IPKF was a veritable failure. In 1989, following increased demands from the Sri Lankan President R. Premadasa that Indian troops must withdraw from Sri Lanka by 31 December 1990, India's policy to Colombo was in ruins. On the date of their eventual withdrawal on 24 March 1990, after almost three years in action and three months after the deadline set by the Sri Lankan government, the Indian Army had lost 1,100 men, and had failed to assist the government of Sri Lanka to find a political settlement on the Tamil problem. In many cases the situation was worse than before the Indian intervention.

While both India and Sri Lanka wished to replace the accord with some form of friendship treaty, they disagree profoundly over its contents. India is anxious to retain the recognition of Indian primacy contained within the accord, while Sri Lanka is determined to enshrine the principle of mutual consultation and joint 'co-operation' only. Unlike the case of Bangladesh, the case of Sri Lanka is even more damning since Indo-Sri Lankan relations have traditionally been friendly, based upon a shared commitment to non-alignment, and free of the legacies of either Partition or secession. Yet like the other small states in the South Asian region, Sri Lanka's geographical location is of strategic importance to India and the Indian ocean, and has since the time of the British been incorporated within Indian defence policies.

K. M. Panikkar, in his influential book *India and the Indian Ocean*, noted that Sri Lanka was intimately linked to India's security, although he refrained from spelling out the consequences of this. This geographical proximity is underscored by the clear ethno-linguistic relationship between the Tamil majority province of India (Tamil

Nadu) and the Sri Lankan Tamils. Sri Lankan Tamils make up approximately 32 per cent of the island population, a minority within a predominantly Sinhalese society.

Other minorities include 'Moors' and Eurasians. These ethno-linguistic identities cross-cut religious identities. Tamils are pre-dominantly Hindu, but some are Muslim. Sinhalese speakers are predominantly Buddhists but some are Protestant and Catholic Christians.[67] Again, despite her size, Sri Lanka duplicates the socio-ethnic complexities found throughout the South Asian region. The deterioration of Tamil-Sinhalese relations on the island has had a direct impact upon Indo-Sri Lankan relations.

Sri Lanka is fifty times smaller than India, and is at one stage separated by a mere twenty miles of water. At the time of independence Sri Lanka had no defined maritime border with India through the Palk Straits and had inherited the problem of stateless Indian Tamils in need of repatriation or settlement. While all the above factors did not amount to a very high or imminent 'threat perception' from India, they have encouraged a certain degree of anxiety which notably increased during the 1980s.

Sri Lanka's response to India's physical domination of the region has been to evolve a careful balance of intra-regional relations (with India, Pakistan and China) with wider international links, initially through the Commonwealth. As early as 1947 the Sri Lankan delegation to the South-East Asian Prime Ministers' Conference of New Delhi referred to the dangers of the smaller states falling under the domination 'emanating' from either China or India and stressed the need for multilateralism.[68] Again, as in all the other smaller states, this commitment contrasted with India's growing determination to deal with each state bilaterally.

Indo-Sri Lankan relations were complicated by Sri Lanka's close links with the Commonwealth under her first United National Party (UNP) governments 1947–52, and 1952–6, which opened up the possibility of Sri Lanka offering military bases to western powers. Moreover, Prime Minister Sir John Kotelawala was virulently anti-communist and caused various 'incidents' at the Bandung Afro-Asian conference of 1955, which although they endeared him to the Pakistanis (and the Americans), only served to embarrass Nehru who was still convinced that close Sino-Indian relations could develop with the Chinese in spite of the outstanding territorial disagreement.[69]

Although Kotelawala made several accusations against both China and the USSR for offering material assistance to communist groups in

Sri Lanka, such statements did not rule out a realistic appraisal of China's uses. Sri Lanka recognised China in 1950 (following the British decision) and signed a rubber–rice barter agreement with China in 1952 which enabled Sri Lanka to import cheap rice and bolster up demand from her rubber plantations. Following a change in government after 1956 and the election of a socialist-orientated United Front, Sri Lanka pursued various diplomatic links with the communist powers and established cordial relations with China and the Soviet Union. Typical of Sri Lankan flexibility, following the Sino-Soviet split, Colombo has attempted to balance her relations with the two communist giants.

The 1956–60 socialist government brought India and Sri Lanka to closer co-operation and facilitated agreements over various foreign and domestic issues. The so-called Shastri–Sirima agreement signed in 1964, and the later 1974 agreement between Mrs Gandhi and Mrs Bandaranaike solved the Indian Tamil problem, although it left unanswered the possibility of forced repatriations.[70] 1974 also saw the demarcation of the maritime border in the Palk Straits and some settlement of the wider matter of territorial waters, an issue that had been aggravated by India's unilateral extension of her territorial waters in 1956 and 1957. The matter of extended 'zones' eventually involved a trilateral agreement between India, Sri Lanka and the Maldives that has yet to be concluded, but which is now on the agenda of SAARC. India claims an extended economic zone across the Indian Ocean of 715,000 square miles, and 'primary access' to a further million square miles, and implicit dominance of Sri Lanka's own maritime interests.

Regardless of the vagaries of party politics – and there have been more frequent changes of party government in Sri Lanka than in any other state of South Asia – the one theme that emerges is the theme of balance. At critical moments, when the regional framework has been disturbed by war, Sri Lanka has found herself in a delicate position. A policy of strict neutrality throughout all three Indo-Pakistan wars has led in some cases to charges of being anti-Indian. During the Indo-Chinese war of 1962 Sri Lanka convened a meeting of the so-called Colombo powers to try and bring China and India to the negotiating table. This was in spite of the fact that earlier, the Chinese repression of Tibetan autonomy and the flight of the Dalai Lama had adversely affected Buddhist sentiments on the island, and caused the government to call for a peaceful solution based upon the 'five principles' of Panscheel.

C

During the Indo-Pakistan war of 1971 Sri Lanka would not yield to Indian requests to ban the use of airport facilities by Pakistan, although Colombo insisted that flights were being inspected to ensure that no military supplies or personnel were finding their way into 'East Pakistan'. Sri Lanka was also extremely late in recognising the independent status of Bangladesh for fear of offending either Pakistan or China. It was only after fifty countries had extended diplomatic recognition to Bangladesh that Sri Lanka agreed to do the same on 5 April, 1971 (over four months after India). Even then there was some ambivalence as to how it was to conduct relations with Dhaka until the wider regional patterns had established themselves. Sri Lanka took several more years to establish a residential High Commissioner in Dhaka.

Sri Lanka's relations with India and China have also to an extent been characterised by economic considerations, especially aid. Under the anti-communist proclivities of governments formed by the United National Party, most of Sri Lanka's foreign aid came from multilateral sources such as the Colombo Plan, or direct from western countries. After 1956 Sri Lanka began to receive various economic resources from Eastern bloc countries, and by 1964/5, China was supplying Rs18.4 million, compared to Rs2.4 million from the United Kingdom.[71] Between 1970 and 1976, the socialist government of Mrs Bandaranaike received Rs421.9 million in interest-free loans from China.

Apart from Indian financial resources sent to Sri Lanka via the Colombo Plan, bilateral Indian aid has until recently been in the form of technical assistance under the ITEC scheme, and under a Joint Commission. Since the early 1980s Indian loans and assistance, tied in part to the issues of the Tamil problem, have increased dramatically. Part of the Indo-Sri Lankan accord dealt with financial and technical assistance schemes. Yet, as with the economic dimensions of the pre-1975 Indo-Bangladesh agreements, the extent of these economic and trading incentives have quickly furthered anti-Indian sentiments, especially amongst the violently-inclined Sinhalese nationalist party, the JVP.

The Sri Lankan Tamil demand for Eelam – the creation of a separate Tamil state that would involve the partitioning of the island – has dominated Indo-Sri Lankan relations since the early 1980s. Sri Lankan attempts to deal decisively with Tamil militants through the large-scale deployment of her security forces in the North and around Jaffna led to protests from Tamil Nadu, and accusations within the Indian parliament that Sri Lanka was killing innocent Tamil civilians. Such remarks led to vigorous protests from Sri Lanka. On 22 March, 1984 *India Today* published a report that revealed 'terrorist' training camps in Tamil Nadu, revelations that were subsequently denied by New Delhi. Outraged, the Sri Lankan government purchased vast amounts of the magazine and sent it out to the international community as proof that India was interfering in the internal affairs of the country. Concerns about Indian 'designs' – a curious echo of the Pakistani and Bangladeshi fears – led to the same demands that Sri Lanka must seek external, extra-regional help. This predominantly Sinhalese perception of Indian intentions was again based upon a reading of Indian actions of 1971, and Indian assistance (at first covertly) for the Bengali rebels. How could the island best defend herself against her giant neighbour? Some even pointed to a previous defence agreement signed with the British in 1947 which had never been invoked. Siri Perera QC, former High Commissioner to Britain, hinted that Sri Lanka ought to forge an alliance with her ancient Buddhist associate, China.

Such implied extra-regionalism, leading to the involvement of Israeli and Pakistani intelligence sources, merely compounded the domestic pressure from Tamil Nadu and forced New Delhi to 'act decisively'. Rajiv Gandhi escalated Indian involvement prior to the actual signing of the accord by sanctioning a small-scale naval relief operation and, when this failed, authorising an airdrop of food over Jaffna in blatant violation of Sri Lankan airspace and a provocative display of her new Mirage 2000 jets.

It was probably in such circumstances that President Jayewardene and the UNP decided to invite the Indians in, as opposed to resisting unwarranted interference. It is most likely that the 'invitation', sanctioned by the cordial exchange of letters, was exacted under some pressure. It is not known with any certainty which of the two pressures – fear of domestic entanglements or foreign complications – set New Delhi on the course of mediation. In one of the annexures of the Indo-Sri Lankan Accord, Rajiv Gandhi noted in a letter to the then President of the Sri Lankan Republic: 'Conscious of the friendship between our two countries stretching over two millennia . . . your excellency and myself will reach an early understanding about the relevance and employment of foreign military and intelligence personnel with a view to ensuring that such presences will not prejudice Indo-Sri Lankan relations.'[72] The accord also attempted to ensure that India had a prominent role in the future training of Sri Lanka's security and intelligence forces and attempted to ensure that Sri Lanka would purchase Indian arms and weapons, along lines similar to the Indian-Nepal treaty.

Far from conveying the impression of a benign, non-aligned state, India's action towards Sri Lanka gave the overwhelming impression that India was bullying her neighbours into submission, a situation subsequently supported by the Indian-Nepal crisis. Both Pakistan and Bangladesh supported the subsequent calls by the Sri Lankan government for India to withdraw. The Indian presence on the island became a key part of the 1988 Sri Lankan presidential election campaign. India's apparent refusal to leave, despite continual pressure from the Sri Lankan government, brought Indo-Sri Lankan relations to an all-time low, and isolated India further within the region. Since March 1990, when India finally completed her withdrawal, the Sri Lankan government has resumed massive military operations against the Tamil rebels. In late January 1991, New Delhi dismissed the state government of Tamil Nadu for, amongst other things, close links with Tamil rebels in the north-eastern state.

Summary

In 1988, while engaged in Sri Lanka, India went to the assistance of the Gayoom government in the Maldives following an attempted coup by Tamil militants from Sri Lanka who had put ashore on inflatables. These remote islands, consisting of over 2,500 low-lying coral atolls, of which only 200 are inhabited, were declared a republic in 1967 following the overthrowing of the Sultan. Predominantly Muslim, the political system is presidential, with a cabinet (the *Mahjlis*) constituted at the president's pleasure. The citizens of the atolls elect a lower chamber, while legislation conforms to the concepts of Islamic law laid down in the Shar'iat. As an Islamic republican state without political parties, the Maldives are closer to Pakistan's political traditions, although few links exist between them. Most of the trade links (most of the wealth is based upon tourism and fish) are closer to Sri Lanka and Japan than India. In 1977 Indian Airlines undertook a joint venture to help assist the Maldivian airport company. India has also made a gift of a tuna-canning factory, and other minor technical help has been forthcoming.

Remote from their troubled neighbours, even the Maldives have felt the pull of India. Throughout the 1988 trial of those Sri Lankans involved in the coup attempt, Indian paratroopers remained on the island, and although Gayoom and Rajiv Gandhi held several meetings to assess Maldivian security interests, Gayoom was anxious to secure the return of Indian troops. Thus the Maldives conform to the patterns of trust/mistrust that characterise most of India's relations with her neighbours, and underscore the apparent failures of India in being accepted as a legitimate regional policeman.

There are very few official statements made concerning India's strategic doctrine. Unlike Western Europe at the height of the cold war, there is little public discussion. Yet much evidence exists to imply that the so-called 'Indira Gandhi' doctrine exists, that India supports and has encouraged regional democracy and pro-Indian governments, and that she has increasingly sought to tie up her regional primacy through a series of regional bilateral accords or defence agreements. These policies have caused concern within the region, and disagreements where earlier there was understanding and concord. A good illustration of how, since the 1970s, the smaller states of South Asia have been growing uneasy about Indian intentions concerns the Indian Ocean Zone of Peace Initiative.

Following the British withdrawal in the late 1960s and early 1970s, India expressed concern that increased US naval activity, and especially the presence of the American base at Diego Garcia, would lead to increased Soviet activity and pull the area into the cold war. India was able to find broad agreement with Sri Lanka, and both states called for a 'zone of peace' (ZOP). Both states also favoured declaring the Indian Ocean a Nuclear Free Zone(NFZ).

These initiatives, discussed frequently at the UN (and presided over by a Commission under UN auspices) were rejected by both superpowers on the grounds that such a zone would interfere with international trade and the laws of the sea. Since 1985, however, following changes in Soviet thinking, the USSR has come around to agreeing with the NFZ proposal, only to find that New Delhi is backtracking on the proposal. The reasons behind this change of policy are not hard to find.

The rationality behind India's previous support for the ZOP and NFZ was that they would exclude foreign powers (primarily the superpowers) from the Indian Ocean, but not her own (growing) navy. Since the late 1980s this navy has come to contain nuclear powered submarines. Pakistan and to an extent Sri Lanka, quick to spot the sleight of hand, have continued to express their support for a NFZ, and the ZOP, on the condition that it includes all naval and military deployments, including the regional states. One Pakistani analyst has noted that 'India's advocacy of the demilitarisation of the Indian

Ocean by the superpowers is an essential element of her goal to establish naval supremacy'.[73] and to convert the Indian Ocean into an Indian lake. The remarks of one recent Bangladeshi commentator sum up the attitude of all the small states of South Asia, and even the views of Pakistan: 'Bangladesh realistically perceived that a security system that sought to remove the extra-regional military presences, but left the questions relating to security threats emanating from within the region would not be workable or acceptable.'[74]

The difficulties that emerge from coming to an understanding with India confront even the casual observer of sub-continental affairs. The causes of these problems are internal to the region and are intimately tied with how India has come increasingly to perceive herself. As we shall see, while this does not exclude wider international events from opening up possible channels of mediation and compromise, it rules out the possibility of any externally-imposed security arrangement.

The divisions and mistrust that dominate the South Asia region are historically and *regionally* based. The security complex has not been imposed from outside and, as we shall see, although it has been supported and greatly exaggerated by US and Soviet help, future settlements must ultimately come from some form of political dialogue within the region. The roots of this animosity are perhaps paradoxical. Given the proximity of India to Pakistan, S. Gangal noted sadly that 'India and Pakistan have more in common, river systems, climates, languages, cultures and religion than perhaps any two nations anywhere else'.[75] This is true of all the states of South Asia, even the land of the Thunder Dragon (Bhutan) and the remote Maldives. It is *because* of this commonality that the region is so insecure. One of the many consequences of Partition has been a conventional arms race. Another has been the lack of economic trade and co-operation between India and Pakistan, and within the region as a whole. The odd cricket match apart, surprising little still takes place to bring these states together.

The British placed the Bengali jute fields in East Pakistan while they gave the jute processing plants (situated in and around Calcutta) to India. For a time there was some doubt in the minds of the boundary commission whether to give Lahore to India or to Pakistan. The animosity of those early years (amplified by China and then other 'external powers') closed off various avenues of development, and these avenues remain closed to this day.

Notes

1 M. G. Kabir and S. Hassan, *Issues and Challenges Facing Bangladesh Foreign Policy*, Dhaka, 1983, p. xi.

2 B. Buzan and G. Rizvi, *South Asian Insecurity and the Great Powers*, Basingstoke, 1986.

3 See V. P. Dutt, *India's Foreign Policy*, New Delhi, 1984 for a basic introduction to the literature. See P. Singh, *India and the Future of Asia*, New Delhi, 1966, and O. Marwah and J. Pollack, *Asia's Major Powers*, Boulder, 1978.

4 Nehru, *Letters to the Chief Ministers*, 25 October 1957, Vol. 3, New Delhi, 1988.

5 A. Vanaik and P. Bidwai, 'India and Pakistan', in R. C. Karp (ed.) *Security With Nuclear Weapons? Differing Perspectives on National Security*, London, 1991, p. 263.

6 Cited in Kabir and Hassan (p. 23).

7 The defence breakdown is usually in the order of 70:20:10 for the army, air force and navy respectfully. The navy has always been the most junior of the services. See R. Thomas, *The Defence of India: A Budgetary Perspective of Strategy and Politics*, Lexington, 1978, and R. Thomas, 'The armed services and India's defence budget', *Asian Survey*, 20, 1980, pp. 280–97.

8 See P. Duncan, *Indo-Soviet Relations*, London, 1987.

9 In the mid-1980s India declined Zimbabwe MiG 21s produced by Hindustan Aeronautics for the fear of offending international opinion. See Amit Gupta, 'The Indian arms industry', *Asian Survey*, 29, 1989, pp. 846–61.

10 See R. W. Bradnock, *India's Foreign Policy*, London, 1990.

11 A. Shahi, *Pakistan's Security and Foreign Policy*, Lahore, 1988.

12 Raju Thomas, 'US transfers of dual-use technologies' in *Asian Survey*, Vol. 30, 1990, pp. 825–45.

13 *The Military Balance 1989–90*, London, 1990. Put another way, however, India still spends less on defence as a percentage of her GNP (about 4 per cent) than Pakistan's estimated 7 per cent. There are difficulties in calculating or estimating China's defence expenditure and quotes vary from 4 to 8 per cent. See *Brassey's Asian Security*, RIPS, London, 1989, p. 43.

14 M. Ayoob, *India and South East Asia: Indian Perceptions and Policies*, London, 1990, p. 42.

15 I. Husain. *The Strategic Dimensions of Pakistan's Foreign Policy*, Lahore, 1989. Little or no argument is advanced to support many of the extraordinary statements in this book.

16 See S. Cohen, *The Pakistan Army*, Berkeley, 1984, and S. Ganguly, *War in South Asia*, Boulder, 1986.

17 S. Ganguly, 'Avoiding war in Kashmir', *Foreign Affairs*, 69, 1990–91, pp. 57–73.

18 Carrier-battle groups involve a main aircraft carrier with an air wing and a series of support ships which are capable of sustaining themselves in a combat area relatively autonomously. For an Indian perspective on this see the *Indian Defence Review 1990*, New Delhi, 1989.

19 See H. V. Hobson, *The Great Divide: Great Britain, India and Pakistan*, Karachi, 1985. In the context of South Asia, the term communal usually refers to inter-religious disputes, especially Hindu–Muslim violence.

20 'Pakistan' means essentially 'land of the pure'. India refused to use the name of Hindustan on the grounds that it was a secular polity, and contained a signifiant number of Muslims even after Partition.

21 There has been much recent and outstanding scholarship on Pakistan: see in particular A. Jalal, *Jinnah: The Sole Spokesman*, Cambridge, 1987 and her *The State of Martial Rule: The Origins of Pakistan's Political Economy of Defence*, Cambridge, 1990. See also P. I. Cheema, *Pakistan's Defence Policy, 1947–1958*, London, 1990.

22 Jalal, *Martial Rule*, p. 29.

23 For a fascinating study of the problems faced by the boundary commission see R. J. Moore, *Making the New Commonwealth*, London, 1987. Moore notes that 'the essential conditions of [Radcliffe's] brief [from the government] which he took up on 8 July was that he must exercise independent judgement to bring down the awards by 15 August' (p. 25). It is not surprising that later 'he could never relive the experience by rereading the evidence of which he took account'.

24 The Afghan claims on Pakistan primarily involved the province of Baluchistan. As late as 1969 the Afghan government issued a postage stamp that showed the borders of Afghanistan as incorporating Baluchistan and parts of the Pakistan tribal belt. See M. Z. Ispanhani, *Roads and Rivals: The Politics of Access in the Borderlands of Asia*, London, 1991.

25 Interestingly enough, this issue was settled in 1985 when Bangladesh settled the border with Burma on the basis of an earlier agreement in 1979 to 'prepare a joint survey' of the Nagar hill tracts.

26 Jalal, *Martial Rule*, p. 25.

27 In 1965 India extended diplomatic support to Afghanistan and called for the upholding of the 'legitimate rights of the pashto people' to be given due recognition by the Pakistan government. See Ispanhani, *Roads and Rivals*.

28 Z. A. Khan, *Pakistan's Security*, Lahore, 1990.

29 M. Waseem, *Pakistan Under Martial Law, 1977–1985*, Lahore, 1987, p. 222.

30 R. Gandhi, *Understanding the Muslim Mind*, Harmondsworth, 1987, p. 2.

31 The prestigious bi-weekly news magazine *India Today* reviewed the situation in great detail in an issue entitled 'Are We Prepared?', 15 July 1990.

32 On 26 October 1947 the Maharaja of Kashmir joined India and signed an agreement with New Delhi. Indian troops were dispatched on 27 October. One of the most extraordinary aspects of the conflict was that both the Indian and Pakistani armies were under British commanders and during the initial outbreak of hostilities under a British Commander-in-Chief.

33 G. Rizvi, 'Arms control in South Asia' in G. Segal (ed.), *Arms Control in Asia*, Basingstoke, 1987, p. 121.

34 J. Nehru, *Letters to the Chief Ministers*, Vol. 1, 5 February 1948. New Delhi, 1988.

35 For a discussion of this peculiar involvement of the British Army see Moore, *New Commonwealth*.

36 Sajjad Hyder, *Reflections of an Ambassador*, Lahore, 1988, p. 75.

37 See for example, Rashiduzzaman, 'East–West conflict in Pakistan: Bengali regionalism' in A. J. Wilson and D. Dalton, *The States of South Asia*, London, 1982; L. Lifschutz, *Bangladesh: The Unfinished Revolution*, London, 1979. The most recent account of the event, from both the Pakistani and the Indian side, is L. Rose and R. Sisson, *War and Secession: India, Pakistan and the Creation of Bangladesh*, Princeton, 1990.

38 See P. N. Haksar, *India's Foreign Policies and Its Problems*, New Delhi, 1989. Haksar was a key adviser to Indira Gandhi on the Simla Accord and has often referred to it as one of the crowning achievements of his diplomatic and political career.

39 Editorial 30 July 1972. Cited in M. Ayoob, *India, Pakistan and Banglandesh*, New Delhi, 1975, p. 37.
40 G. Rizvi, 'Arms control'. p. 116
41 Text of communiqué printed in *Keesing's Contemporary Archive*, 1976, p. 27846.
42 For details see D. C. Vohra, *India's Aid Diplomacy to the Third World*, New Delhi, 1980.
43 N. Rengger (ed.), *Treaties and Alliances*, p. 385.
44 *Keesing's Contemporary Archives*, 1976, p. 27523.
45 Under international laws that deal with trans-boundary flows, it is illegal for a country to dam the flow of a shared river resource and prevent a downriver state from receiving a fair share of water. A barrage – defined as a temporary structure that does not obstruct the flow of water – is apparently exempt.
46 This matter is further discussed in Chapter 4.
47 IISA, *The Military Balance*, London, 1989–90. It is noted in the report that spare parts are in short supply and that the serviceability of the air force and the navy is questionable.
48 Hugh Evans 'Bangladesh: South Asia's unknown quantity', *Asian Affairs*, 75, 1988, pp. 306–16.
49 Cited in E. Ahamed, *The Foreign Policy of Bangladesh: Imperatives of a Small State*, Dhaka, 1984, p. 130.
50 Caroline Thomas, 'New directions in thinking about security in the Third World' in K. Booth (ed.), *New Thinking About Strategy and International Security*, London, 1991, pp. 267–86.
51 See Jasjit Singh, 'Indian security: a framework for national strategy', *Strategic Analysis*, 11, 1987, pp. 898–917.
52 Ashok Kapur, 'India's foreign policy: perspectives and present predicaments', *Round Table*, 295, 1985, pp. 230–9.
53 N. Maxwell, *India's China War*, Harmondsworth, 1962. See also A. Ramakant, *Nepal, China and Indian Relations*, New Delhi, 1976, and B. Sen Gupta, *The Fulcrum of Asia: Relations Amongst China, India, Pakistan and the USSR*, New Delhi, 1970. Kuldip Nayar's *Distant Neighbours*, New Delhi, 1972 remains a very readable book on India's early regional policy. See also S. P. Varma and K. P. Misra, *The Foreign Policy of South Asia*, New Delhi, 1979.
54 R. Thomas, *India's Foreign Policy*, London, 1986, p. 59 (emphasis added).
55 Ramesh Thakur, 'Normalising Sino-Indian relations', *The Pacific Review*, 4, 1991, p. 9.
56 B. N. Goswami, *Pakistan and China: A Study in Their Relations*, New Delhi, 1971.
57 P. N. Haksar, *India's Foreign Policy and its Problems*, New Delhi, 1989, p. 56.
58 *World Bank Annual Report*, Washington, 1990.
59 L. Rose, 'India's foreign relations: reassesing basic policies', in M. Bouton and P. Oldenburg, *India Briefing 1990*, Boulder, 1990, p. 63.
60 Thakur, 'Normalising Sino-Indian relations', p. 15.
61 See Wang Hong Wei, 'Sino-Nepali relations in the 1980s' in *Asian Survey*, 25, 1985, pp. 512–34.
62 The Hindu credentials of the monarchy are visible in the fact that the Nepalese King is the only individual – apart from the high priest – who can enter the inner sanctum of the Jagarnath Temple in Puri, Orissa. Priests for the temple of Pashupati Nath, the presiding deity of Nepal, are chosen from Southern India and retain close links with their districts. See M. D. Dharamdasari, *India's Diplomacy in Nepal*, Jaipur, 1976.

63 See L. Rose and J. Scholz, *Nepal: Profile of a Himalayan Kingdom*, Boulder. 1980, and R. Shaha *Nepali Politics*. New Delhi, 1978.

64 See 'Violence comes to Shangri-La', *The Economist*, London, 6–12 October 1990, p. 84.

65 Throughout the colonial period the British recognised Nepal as an 'independent' kingdom, on the condition that she would continue her 'natural policy of isolation' and remain on good terms with the British. In 1923 the British signed a treaty of friendship and co-operation with the King of Nepal. In 1890 the GOI deprived Sikkim's *Chogyal* of all powers and appointed a political officer, although in 1918 the *Chogyal* was restored and Sikkim granted full autonomy as an associated member of British India. Bhutan first encountered the British in the form of Ashely Eden's mission in 1864 which, in retaliation for 'a poor reception and ill mannered porters' annexed some rather crucial border areas which are now compensated for by an annual grant from India. In 1911 Bhutan concluded a paramountcy agreement with British India.

66 India's Sikkim policy has been controversial within India as well as within China. See Datta Ray, *Smash and Grab: The Annexation of Sikkim*, New Delhi, 1984, and R. Rao, *Sikkim: The Story of its Integration with India*, New Delhi, 1978.

67 I postpone a discussion about the politics of ethnicity until Chapter 3.

68 S. U. Kodikara, *The Foreign Policy of Sri Lanka: A Third World Perspective*, New Delhi, 1982, see Ch. 7, 'Sri Lanka and Asian regionalism'.

69 Sir John wanted to condemn Soviet imperialism in Eastern Europe in the final communiqué of the Afro-Asian summit. He also called for the disbanding of Comiform and accused Zhou En Lai of funding Marxist movements within Sri Lanka. See H. S. S. Nissanka *Sri Lanka's Foreign Policy: A Study in Non-Alignment*, New Delhi, 1984.

70 The Sirima–Shastri agreement meant that India would give Indian citizenship to 525,000 Tamils of Indian origin, and that Sri Lanka would give citizenship to 300,000. The agreement was not without problems, and there were various delays that compelled a further settlement. Following the 1974 agreement India and Sri Lanka decided to halve the remaining community – 75,000 to be expatriated to India, 75, 000 to be settled in Sri Lanka.

71 H. S. S. Nissanka, *Foreign Policy of Sri Lanka*, p. 255.

72 Reproduced in Shankar Bhaduri and Afsir Karim, *The Sri Lankan Crisis*, New Delhi, 1989.

73 Cited in P. Duncan, *Indo-Soviet Relations*, p. 60.

74 E. Ahamed, *The Foreign Policy of Bangladesh*, p. 85.

75 S. C. Gangal, *India and the Commonwealth*, New Delhi, 1970, p. 63.

2

The states of South Asia (II): the international setting

To many commentators of the international scene the 1989 revolutions in Eastern Europe, made possible by the dramatic changes that had taken place within the Soviet Union since 1985, mark the end of global bipolarity and the cold war.[1] More importantly, some analysts have argued that the easing of tensions between the Soviet Union and the United States of America will affect Indo-Pakistan relations. Others point to the *rapprochement* that appeared to be taking place between China and the Soviet Union and argued that this will force the Indians to come to some speedy settlement with China, because India has previously relied upon the Soviets to support her position on the border dispute.[2]

The apparent breakdown of bipolarity in which the old landmarks of superpower influence are eroded raises the question of the New World Order and the interests such an order will represent. In the aftermath of the Iraqi invasion of Kuwait the Bush administration has taken the lead in trying to shape the forces that could emerge in the 1990s and beyond, in active co-operation with the Soviet Union. Not surprisingly, South Asia (and a greater part of the Third World) does not seem to take a very prominent part within the New World Order, nor is the region at present in a position to influence decisively the global agenda.

America has often appeared unwilling to trust India fully, and has seen her criticism of US–Pakistan relations as an attack upon US foreign policy generally. The profile that India commands in America is still minute. In the mid 1970s Mellor noted that: 'The US state department included India in its Near East/South West Asia Desk, which [was] under an assistant secretary of state, who [was] almost totally preoccupied with Israel'.[3] More candidly perhaps, Nihal Singh noted that what has continually bedevilled US–Indian relations,

Pakistan notwithstanding, was 'India's putative if not actual power status and the American refusal to acknowledge it'.[4]

Since India considers herself a powerful state with regional (and potentially extra-regional) interests and responsibilities, it is essential that India somehow acquires a higher profile within American thinking, despite her mistrust of Washington's supremacy. While India has much to fear from a invigorated United States, especially one that 'thumps any country that gets out of line, shakes down its rich friends to pay for the mugging, gets a meek go ahead from the cops in the UN and tells the Soviet Union to butt out,[5] she has almost as much to fear from an America reluctant to involve herself in global management, especially in the face of Japanese (and German) reluctance to assume wider international responsibilities. Sisir Gupta commented perceptively that 'new nations have more reason to be afraid of international anarchy than powerful states . . . For one thing, instability may aggravate their domestic problems of nation building.'[6] Global instability, both economically and politically, would isolate India from much-needed industrial and economic resources.

While various overtures have been made to America, including the successful Rajiv Gandhi visit in 1985 and the much-heard themes of 'shared democratic values and democratic experiences', there remain serious obstacles in the way of Indo-American relations. In 1986 Maya Chadda believed that there was still no real basis for any strategic co-operation between India and the United States, regardless of India's commitment to liberalise her trading practices and in spite of the signing of the Memorandum of Understanding (MOU) in New Delhi to open the way for the sales of sensitive 'dual-track' technology, needed for her economic and military development.

Previously such sales have stalled because of India's intimacy with the Soviet Union and the likelihood of her passing on sophisticated systems to Moscow.[7] Without a visible Soviet threat the Americans may well find it difficult to object to technology transfers to India on the grounds of security, but there remain matters of unfair trading, unlicensed duplication, and more seriously, the threat of sensitive technology being used for an Indian nuclear weapons programme.

Apart from reassessing her relationship with the United States, India has also to come to terms with what is happening within the Soviet Union and decide if (and how) these changes affect Indo-Soviet relations, which since 1971 have been of great importance to New Delhi. In 1983 one security analyst set his face against the tide and noted ruefully, 'we should guard against the simplifications of subscribing to the 'doom' theory that portrays the Soviet Union as a declining power'.[8]

The disintegration of the Soviet Union, if the doom theory does come to pass, could well have a profound effect upon India and upon her economic and military capabilities. In 1980 India had signed a US $1·6 billion arms deal with the Soviet Union and in 1989 India signed another trade protocol worth Rs70,000 million, principally to import weaponry. Earlier the Soviets had expressed some irritation over Indian attempts to diversify her arms industry by approaching western firms and pointing out the differences in cost and terms of interest.[9]

Increased financial hardships within the Soviet Union, combined with her own need for scarce 'hard currencies', could soon end the era of cheap arms, especially since cheapness is the main attraction in the face of superior western technology. Moreover, both the Soviet Union and India are attempting – albeit from different premises – to liberalise their economies and in order to do so, both are turning towards the West and the international capitalist economy and away from each other.

Recent developments within US–Pakistan relations have shown the extent to which future co-operation is based upon Pakistan's assurances that she will comply with America's policy on nuclear non-proliferation. On 1 October 1990 the Bush administration cut off a five-year aid package signed in 1987 worth between US $564 and 578 million for 1991 alone, in response to reports that Pakistan was still constructing a nuclear bomb. Early in 1987 the House Appropriations Committee held up an aid package worth US $4·02 billion following Pakistan's refusal to open up some of her nuclear installations to international inspection.

Yet US intervention into Pakistani affairs is not confined to matters of nuclear weapons development. In 1990 a remark by US senator Stephen Solarz about future American aid being conditional on a 'free and fair' election following the dismissal of the Benazir Bhutto government, led to the accusation that Washington was interfering in the internal affairs of a 'friendly yet independent' state. During the Kuwait crisis, General Beg, the most senior officer in the Pakistan army, issued a statement regretting US-led actions against Iraq and referring to Saddam Hussein as an important leader in the Islamic world, distancing himself (and by implication, the army) from the foreign policy of the civilian government. Such comments underscore the divergence that is taking place within US–Pakistan relations. If the 'special relationship' deteriorates, does this mean that Indo–US relations will improve?

The United States and South Asia

It has always been something of a mystery (even to some an embarrassment) that the United States of America should, virtually without exception, find itself on more intimate terms with Pakistan (and invariably Pakistani generals) than with democratically-elected Indian leaders.[10] Why should this be? Raju Thomas has pointed out that one of the problems concerns the 'image' that most Americans have of the Indian political system as one dominated by poverty. Another irritant to American policy towards New Delhi has been India's habit of moralising and pontificating about western responsibilities and obligations to the post-colonial world, and her inclination to take an independent stance on global issues, such as her refusal to join (and her condemnation of) the American policy of containment aimed at the Soviet Union. It is this latter point, expressed through the language of non-alignment, that has caused the greatest amount of consternation for Washington.

Non-alignment has been invariably too clever by half for the Americans, who have perceived it as a piece of muddled logic, or worse an act of calculated duplicity, allowing India to condemn 'power bloc' rivalries and military alliances, while closely associating herself with the Soviet Union and, on various occasions, even appearing to condone Soviet action. India's stand on issues such as the Dutch–Indonesian war (1948–50), the Korean war (1950–1), and the Soviet invasion of Hungary (1956) alarmed American sensibilities further. India's decision to abstain in the UN votes condemning the Soviet invasion of Hungary and Czechoslovakia was met with consternation: did not the act contradict India's professed support for the rules of international law and political independence? How could India condemn Anglo-French actions against the Egyptians at Suez, and yet ignore Soviet actions in Eastern Europe?

For Foster Dulles and his generation of American strategic thinkers, this refusal to uphold the principles of a 'free world', in favour of seeking reconciliation through negotiation, was simply so much hot air. The talk of Afro-Asian solidarity and 'global peace' was even pernicious since it detracted attention away from the real threat to global security and led to 'fraternisation' with rebel states such as the Soviet Union and China.

To the Americans at least, the Sino-Indian war of 1962 was a welcome development, since it appeared to snap Nehru out of his obsession with 'peaceful coexistence' and force him to think seriously about defence. New Delhi's rush for Anglo-American aid – to the tune of US $70 million by 1965 – was further seen by Chester Bowles as opening up the possibility for greater US–Indian co-operation against a common Chinese foe, even if India had been receiving financial support from the Soviet foe since the beginning of the 1960s.

Under the Kennedy regime the basis of good will was extended with significant aid and trade agreements. India was already receiving a significant amount of food under the 1954 Agricultural Trade and Development Act, and would continue to receive large amounts of cheap American grains throughout the 1960s. Between 1946 and 1966 India received US $6,810·2 million from the US in aid, compared to Pakistan's US $3,095 million.[11]

Yet by late 1962 India was also reaching a degree of understanding with the Soviets that would by small degrees of mutual accommodation, strengthen considerably by the beginning of the 1970s. There have been many near agreements between the United States and India, in 1977 between the non-Congress Janata government under Morarji Desai and President Carter, and most recently between Rajiv Gandhi and Ronald Reagan. Nothing has come of them and Indian acts of studied defiance, such as her refusal to sign the Nuclear Non-Proliferation Treaty in 1967,[12] the Peaceful Nuclear Explosion (PNE) in 1974, and her stand on American naval deployments in the Indian Ocean can easily lead to remarks about 'Indian treachery' and result in a consequent deterioration in US–Indian relations.

Certainly India's indifference to the West remains, but there are also compelling reasons why India needs western (US) or Japanese co-operation. India's role in the Kuwait crisis was marginal compared to Pakistan, or even Bangladesh. Throughout, New Delhi was determined to follow her own diplomacy through the Non-Aligned Movement (NAM). The decision by the Chandra Senkhar government to allow American planes to refuel at Bombay during the Kuwait crisis, for example, created an open rift in the cabinet and had to be withdrawn.

Compared to this historical indifference, the US economic, military and technological relations with Islamabad appear well established and genuinely friendly, despite two arms embargoes (1965 and 1971) and doses of pro-Indian sentiment. Throughout the 1950s the US provided Pakistan with US $1·3 billion for 'infrastructural support' as well as US $700 million worth of Patton Tanks.[13] Between 1954 and 1965 US weapons to Pakistan came to US $1·5 billion.

Unlike US–Indian relations, the explanation for the success of US–Pakistan relations is that they have come to share a particular geostrategic view of the world. The fact that Pakistan found the Americans so accommodating was largely coincidental; it could well have been the Soviet Union or even the Commonwealth, since Pakistan approached each one in turn to help her fend off Indian aggression after Partition.[14]

Although the Indians believed that the British were pro-Muslim, the British government had indicated its unwillingness to release foreign exchange to Pakistan for the purpose of buying arms.[15] The western bias within the Pakistani military elite made thoughts of close links with the Soviets difficult but not impossible to contemplate. In the wake of Partition, the Muslim states of the Middle East were too weak and divided to offer much assistance. In 1956 H. S. Suhrawardy, a Pakistani leader, noted that the power of the Arab World could be summarised as 'zero plus zero'.

From 1952 onwards, and in particular after General Ayub Khan came to power in the 1958 coup, the Pakistani elite played consciously on their anti-communist credentials, skilfully combining Pakistan's strategic position (next to the Gulf and part of the Indian Ocean littoral) with notions of Islam's natural abhorrence to the godless Soviet regime.[16] Yet had the Soviet Union actively courted Pakistan after 1947, the relationship could well have been otherwise.

From the 1950s then, the Americans were keen to enlist Pakistan's active involvement in any joint western defence plan for the Middle East, although the British were afraid of India's 'adverse reactions to Pakistan's membership in a Middle East Defence Command and Pakistan receiving additional arms'.[17] Such British sensitivities, made largely irrelevant by British decline after the war, encouraged the Americans to make direct approaches to Pakistan herself. Thus, if India had no place in Foster Dulles's 'northern tier' against the Soviet Union, Pakistan certainly did.

In 1954, Pakistan signed an agreement with the United States and with Turkey and in 1955 Pakistan became a member of CENTO. In 1964 Pakistan signed the Regional Co-operation for Development with Turkey and Iran and further integrated herself into the strategic land bridge that linked Europe to Asia and encircled Soviet Central Asia. The curious location of 'East Pakistan' also invited ideas that would eventually lead to Pakistan's membership of SEATO and direct association with US strategic thinking on the Indian Ocean–Pacific area. By the mid 1960's Pakistan was emerging as America's most 'allied ally'.

The risk that such blatant association with the United States would alienate Pakistan within the then emerging Third World forums was a risk worth taking as long as the United States committed herself to defend Pakistan's territorial integrity. Such a commitment was spelled out in the Mutual Defence Pact of 1954, amid some American reluctance,[18] and was reiterated again in 1959 when the US committed herself to defend Pakistan 'through force if necessary'.[19]

The logic that bound US and Pakistan relations together was mutually beneficial, and while the cold war lasted, pretty consistent. Yet American ties threatened the basis of Pakistan's emerging *entente cordiale* with Beijing after China's 1962 clash with India. Although his anti-communism was very real, Ayub Khan appreciated China's utility as a second front against India, and was anxious not to allow American mistrust of Beijing to spoil his scheme, particularly when the US seemed willing to offer assistance to India against China in 1962. In his autobiography the General noted that Pakistan foreign policy must be guided by 'two sets of bilateral equations, one between Pakistan and the United States, and one between Pakistan and China, which must in turn not be allowed to constrain US–Pak relations'.[20] There was little indication then that these two equations would come together into a veritable Triple Entente.

Yet it was Pakistan's proximity to Beijing that encouraged the Americans to use Islamabad as a go-between to open the way for Nixon's historic visit to China. The Pakistani price for this support was for the Americans to pressurise the Indians as they prepared to assist the Bengalis. American pressure certainly prompted the Indians into speeding up the preparations for the signing of the friendship treaty with Moscow in 1971. Even then, in spite of American misperception, the treaty was 'more than a non-aggression pact, but much less than an alliance'.[21]

In 1980 Van Hollen argued that 'the Nixon–Kissinger geo-political approach to South Asia was flawed both in conception and implementation'.[22] American policy during the 1971 civil war was aimed at preventing Indian designs against Pakistan complicating US policy towards China. To India, the US attitude towards South Asia implied that since India did not fit into Washington's policies, she was expendable, as was the future of an independent Bangladesh.

America's approach to the crisis is an extraordinary testimony to the extent to which the 'view from Washington' and the 'view from New Delhi' not only diverged but actually conflicted. In the various meetings of the Security Council's senior review group Nixon found Mrs Gandhi (referred to by the President starkly as 'that bitch') uncompromising, and Indian policies incomprehensible. In a recent examination of the crisis, Rose and Sisson also highlight the degree to which American calculations over Soviet intentions were wildly inaccurate. The belief that the Soviets were pushing India into a war were simply incorrect. Throughout the August–November period, the Soviets were attempting to constrain India and even seeking to open diplomatic channels to Pakistan.

Raju Thomas has noted that the 'basic problem of Indo-American relations [has been] their divergent security interests and the fact that Indo-Pak rivalry has complicated US global strategy'.[23] Such complications have compelled the US to contain India's regional ambitions. Nowhere is this more clearly illustrated than in the events of 1971. The decision to deploy the USS *Enterprise* into the Bay of Bengal was interpreted by New Delhi as a blatant attempt by Washington to intimidate India and constrain her policy towards Pakistan. It was an act that was (and still is) *deeply* resented by India's political elite.

If Washington and India very rarely seemed to see and talk about the same international system, the basis of US–Pakistan understanding was and has remained circumstantial. Based upon differing premises – on the one hand Pakistan's pro-western leanings and her role within the wider American interests of CENTO, and on the other her vital need of American aid against India – the security arrangement is fragile and in the late 1980s appeared to be slowly unwinding. That the United States proved ultimately unwilling to intervene within the Bangladesh crisis profoundly impressed Prime Minister Bhutto, Pakistan's first civilian leader since 1958, as did the subsequent arms embargo which was not lifted until 1975, but was quickly reimposed following the election of President Carter over the Islamic bomb.

Bhutto had come to power on an electoral programme which involved a commitment to Islamic socialism, and more critically, further links with the Arab Muslim world and with China. One of the first acts that Bhutto did following the secession of Bangladesh was to visit leading states within the Islamic world. Ziring notes in a history of Pakistani foreign policy that Bhutto 'envisaged a foreign policy that liberated Pakistan from American dependence. Pakistan was, Bhutto declared, a Middle East Country, a nation which drew its purpose and identity from the sands of the Arabian peninsula, not from the steaming jungles of the sub-continent.'[24] Bhutto was himself responsible for constructing a powerful myth of US betrayal, which furthered insecurities within the military that Pakistan's defence against India rested on a questionable ally. One consequence of this perceived insecurity – Bhutto's relentless quest to construct a Pakistani nuclear device – has only led to further American pressure.

The degree of mistrust between Islamabad and Washington deepened following the coup of 1977 that brought the military back to power. The successful implementation of *Operation Fairplay* (the code name for General Zia-el-Haq's seizure of power) coincided with the Carter administration's stress upon human rights and democracy, and a fresh round of openings to India. Had not the decrepit Brezhnev come to the rescue by invading Afghanistan, the US–Pakistan security arrangement might well have come undone a decade earlier.[25]

The tragedy of Afghanistan, which has been the subject of several informative studies,[26] is a crucial reminder of how external factors can often come to the rescue of a state's foreign policy and even how it can sustain a particular political regime. Not only did the Soviet action put Pakistan back into the centre of the US global perspective, and convert General (by 1985, President) Zia from being a dictator into becoming a defender of democracy, it transformed an illegal regime into a loyal friend of the West standing alone in the way of the inexorable Soviet march to the Gulf.

The entire tenor of US–Pakistan relations was transformed overnight, much to the misgivings of India, and any possibility of sustained improvements between India and the US was once more closed off. The election of the Reagan administration saw a further hardening of American attitudes towards supporting strident anti-communist regimes, regardless of their particular human rights records.

By 1983 the Americans had waived the Symington Amendment to the US Trades Act that outlawed US aid to 'threshold nuclear states'.[27] After a token gesture of aid, the Americans agreed to give Pakistan a US $3·2 billion aid package, half of which was made up of sophisticated weapons such as the F-16. Further aid packages were announced in 1987 to the sum of US $ 4.7 billion.

Indian denunciations of the US were strident. New Delhi accused the Americans of assisting the Pakistani nuclear weapons programme by exempting her from anti-proliferation legislation, and providing Pakistan with weapons far in excess of her legitimate defence requirements. While Carter had at least tried to square the circle of pleasing both Islamabad and New Delhi, the attitude of the Reagan administration towards India was blunt, made worse by India's apparent condoning of Soviet action, by her own long standing-links with Afghanistan, and by her support for the Soviet-backed Afghanistan government. For the duration of the Afghanistan crisis, mutual US–Indian suspicion returned to the forefront of their relationship.

Having been revived by an escalation in East–West tensions, it follows that the Soviet withdrawal from Afghanistan, and the much more dramatic global disengagement of the superpowers that has taken place since 1989–90, has once more marginalised Pakistan. Yet even during the Afghanistan crisis, there were differences between US and Pakistani objectives, especially over which faction of the Afghan resistance – the Mujahadeen – should be promoted to oust the Soviet-backed regime. Zia was keen to support the Islamic fundamentalist faction led by Gulbadeen Hekbatyar, while Washington – and some domestic critics of the Zia regime – favoured a support for the moderates. Since 1990 there is a distinct possibility that Pakistan will be left out in the cold to face India alone, unless she can satisfy the Americans that she has no real nuclear ambitions. If Pakistan cannot maintain her profile on the US strategic horizon, the effects of such withdrawal would have profound consequences for Pakistan's conventional security. Prior to the suspension of aid in 1990 the United States provided Pakistan with US $230 million worth of arms in one year alone.

America's attitude to any future Indo–Pakistan war would be more like her 1965 response: joint embargoes and pressures on both sides to negotiate. In a recent article, Sumit Ganguly has noted that 'at a time of declining world tensions . . . a war on the sub-continent would divert US attention from on-going attempts to shape the new world order'.[28]

Yet it remains unclear how India (or even Pakistan) fits into these wider American schemes. If Washington were to accept India as the regional policeman, committed to upholding security within the region as a whole, it would open the way for sustained Indian–US co-operation but would terrify Pakistan. Even if Washington was willing to recognise India as a 'rising middle power', it is not clear to what extent India would concur with US hegemony.

There therefore remains the distinct possibility that the 'New World Order' will be as divergent from New Delhi's ideas and instincts as Foster Dulles's northern tier was. India's foreign policy approach to the Gulf crisis underscores the very fundamental differences about the concept of world order. While condemning the Iraqi invasion of Kuwait, India has remained ambivalent towards the role of the so-called 'coalition'. Suspicious of American designs on the Arabs, Indian differences are fuelled by her dependency on oil, her own not inconsiderable Muslim population, and the ideology of non-alignment. As American interests in Pakistan decline, and her interests in India do not improve, the importance of South Asia as a whole could well diminish. And there remains the distinct possibility that Indo-American relations will deteriorate.[29]

If US intervention in Indo–Pakistan relations was dictated through her own geopolitical priorities, what of US relations with the other South Asian states? Sri Lanka, pro-western under the UNP governments and pro-eastern under the SLFP and SLFP-coalition governments, had some strategic weight in the 1960s, offering the US prospects of base facilities in the Indian Ocean. Under Sir John the Americans were permitted to use Sri Lanka to refuel planes on their way to the Korean War. Yet Sri Lanka's somewhat more categorical commitment to non-alignment after 1956, combined with an appreciation of India's security interests, ended all such arrangements, and ended the prospects of extra-regional forces acquiring port facilities in Trincomlee. Given the base facilities available on the island of Diego Garcia however, the strategic relevance of Sri Lanka has declined.

India has always been suspicious of close US–Sri Lankan co-operation. The Indian government believed that J. R. Jayawardene's visit to Washington in 1984 involved a request for military help in the event of an Indian invasion of the island, and as the Indo-Sri Lankan Accord reveals, India remains highly sensitive to potential US designs on Trincomlee. The disagreement apart, since 1977 and the election of the Premadasa presidency in 1988, US–Sri Lankan relations have been particularly cordial, supported by trade and by Sri Lankan hopes for further US investment.

Sri Lanka has also been prominent in the move aimed to make the Indian Ocean a 'zone of peace', both during the United Nations General Assembly in December 1971, and again in 1973 at the summit of the Non-Aligned Movement (NAM). Sri Lanka has also supported similar recommendations for the South Pacific and has supported Nepal's call for a Himalayan peace zone.

The US approach to Bangladesh – remarkably good considering the circumstances of her birth – and US foreign policy approaches to the Himalayan kingdoms generally, have been dominated by aid and economic assistance. The reasoning behind such aid has been to encourage 'Third World' enthusiasm for the United States, and to encourage where possible the adoption of capitalist and world market orientated activities, such as the opening out of domestic economies for US investment. Much of the US aid to Bangladesh has been of a multilateral and humanitarian kind. Importantly, Nepali, Bhutanese and Bangladeshi support for American interests and actions within the South Asia region followed the same compulsions that have figured so prominently in US–Pakistan relations: the need to head off Indian dominance. This is especially true of Bangladesh after 1975. By 1988 the Americans had endorsed King Birendra's plans for a Himalayan 'zone of peace' proposal. China had supported it, while India and the Soviet Union rejected it as 'impractical'.

The Soviet Union and South Asia

It has already been suggested that the Americans have consistently misunderstood the nature of Indo-Soviet relations since the mid 1960s, and especially since 1971. In 1984 it was seriously suggested by one analyst that the Soviet invasion of Afghanistan might well encourage India to 'annexe territory' with implicit Soviet support, the suggestion being that the USSR had informed India about Afghanistan and offered it some share in the action.[30] As with the Nixon–Kissinger view of the 1970s, such a belief can only rest on a complete misreading of events in the 1980s.[31] The first and most important explanation as to why the Indian–Soviet bilateral relationship has been so successful is that Moscow has given to New Delhi the sort of categorical political recognition that she has never been able to secure from Washington. As Duncan notes, like US–Pakistan relations 'the key to the success of the Soviet–Indian relationship is geo-political. The two countries lack a common border, but do have common enemies and adversaries'.[32]

As with the US–Pakistan relationship, the basis of the relationship is a tentative convergence of Indian and Soviet interests that has involved significant amounts of Soviet aid and diplomatic support for each other. Between 1955 and 1965 India received Soviet aid to the value of US $1·5 billion in credits, while at the end of the 1960s she had received US $700 million in military equipment. While lagging far behind US and western aid in terms of value, Soviet aid is less conditional, and has a high military component. Likewise, the Soviets have candidly acknowledged India's influence throughout the non-aligned movement and the Third World and have benefited from the ideological connotations of this support: that the USSR was with the poor and recently decolonised nations of the Earth.

As early as 1954, Khrushchev had addressed the General Assembly in the UN and supported the 'five principles' of Panscheel and the Non-Aligned Movement. Soviet dealings in South Asia were more equitable in the pre-1969 period, when it was possible for the Kremlin to mediate over the 1965 Indo-Pakistan war as an honest broker, and indeed between 1948 and 1969 the Soviets had provided Pakistan with up to US $246 million in general aid. The basis of the Soviet–Indian alliance was definitely secured by the growing links between Islamabad and Washington, and furthered by the close Sino-Pakistan relations in the wake of the Sino-Soviet split. The calculation that the Kremlin ultimately had more to gain from India than from Pakistan was probably completed by 1970, reflecting the Soviet assessment of India's political stability and future military potential in Asia compared to Pakistan, which many expected to disintegrate.[33]

Nonetheless there has always been a tendency to exaggerate the permanence of this accord. India has required Soviet support against China, and against Washington and Pakistan, and has generously received that support both before 1971, and afterwards, but never unconditionally, and always as a process of careful bargaining. Until the onset of the Pakistani civil war, India was reluctant to sign the Soviet Friendship treaty, which had been on the drawing board since 1970, but had yet to be given final shape and publicly acknowledged for fear of domestic and foreign criticism over a so-called 'tilt' in New Delhi's foreign policy. Yet it was at India's insistence that Foreign Minister Gromyko made the trip to New Delhi in August 1971 to conclude the treaty in order to strengthen India's hand within the region, especially against China.[34] Some analysts have suggested that the signing of the Indo-Soviet Friendship Treaty was enough to deter China (and the US) from coming to the rescue of a united Pakistan in 1971.

More generally, India's foreign policy has been more complimentary to Moscow than it has been to Washington. India was one of the first countries to recognise the Marxist regime in Afghanistan in 1978. Following Indira Gandhi's election in 1980, India gave diplomatic recognition to the Vietnamese-backed Kampuchean regime following the fall of Pol Pot. Close relations between India and Vietnam, cemented by common concerns over China, complemented Soviet–Vietnamese links. Much the same can be said of India's policy towards Cuba.

Given the changes of tone in Sino-Soviet relations, and a convergence of Soviet and Indian interests in the West, the geopolitical imperatives that lie at the root of Soviet–Indian relations have lessened significantly. Until very recently, the degree of technical and industrial co-operation between India and the Soviet Union was far more significant and comprehensive than that between India and the United States. In 1965 India was the Soviet Union's largest non-communist trading partner, and on various occasions Indo-Soviet trade has exceeded Indo-US trade. One explanation for the high level of trade with the Soviets is that India has found the offer of concessional trade and barter agreements – the so-called Rouble–Rupee agreements – particularly helpful in times of foreign exchange shortages. In 1989 Indian exports to the Soviet Union were estimated at around US $3,575 million, while exports to America were US $1,883 million.[35]

The limits to Indo-Soviet co-operation concern the determination of New Delhi to isolate the South Asia region from external influence – even that of the Soviets – unless invited in by the Indians (as in 1971) or unless such action is part of a wider agreement that preserves India's premier position in South Asia and her freedom to act outside it. It was these reasons that led India to reject Moscow's advice to sign the Nuclear Non-Proliferation treaty in 1967, the Soviet offer of an Asian Defence pact in 1969 aimed to contain Chinese aggression, and which in 1979–80 led to India's concerns over the Soviet invasion of Afghanistan.

The Afghanistan crisis showed the tensions within Indo-Soviet relations. India had no prior warning about Soviet plans to invade, and appeared genuinely bewildered by the event. Throughout the crisis – potentially embarrassed by her isolation both in the United Nations and the Non-Aligned Movement – India attempted to show solidarity with the Soviet Union while pressurising the Kremlin to withdraw. In the General Assembly debates of January 1980, the Indian Ambassador to the United Nations called for the withdrawal of 'all troops' from Afghanistan and later remarked 'we have no reason to doubt assurances [of a speedy withdrawal], particularly from a friendly country like the Soviet Union with whom we have many important ties'.

India abstained from the UN vote which sought categorically to condemn Soviet action. Yet, on a state visit to Moscow in 1983 Mrs Gandhi again raised Indian objections to the Soviet policy and remarked during an interview that Soviet troops should be with-drawn.[36] In this respect India failed to alter the Soviet agenda in Afghanistan. When it did change, following the rise of President Gorbachev, it did so for domestic reasons.

Concerning the future for Indo-Soviet Relations, there are two sources of visible decline at the beginning of the 1990s. One is the growing trade surplus between India and the Soviet Union. During the early 1980s the value of Indo-Soviet trade increased dramatically. In part this reflects increased sales of Soviet oil to India.[37] In addition it reflects India's growing dissatisfaction with the quality of Soviet goods and technology. The Soviet Union is also less willing now to absorb a high level of Indian manufactured goods that would have difficulty in finding other markets. The other source of decline is the changing perception that the Soviets have of India's position in Asia *vis-à-vis* China. In 1986, following the signing of the joint Indo-Soviet declaration which called for global disarmament and international economic co-operation in New Delhi, Rajiv Gandhi referred to the Soviet Union as an Asian power, firm in his conviction that the Soviets saw India in the same light. Later that year in Vladivostock on 28 July, Gorbachev gave out the Asian version of the earlier European 'common home' speech, and called for an Asian collective security doctrine which, appearing to hinge upon Chinese co-operation and the great future of China, caused some concern in New Delhi.

Subsequent Soviet speeches at Krasnoyarsk (1988) and in Beijing (in 1989) implied that China was not just the subject of a few stray thoughts, but part of a comprehensive rethink of Soviet Asian policy. Should the Soviets move towards a closer association with Beijing, bolstered by trade agreements and arms reductions, to what extent would the Soviets be willing to support India in any future Sino-Indian disagreements? It was widely believed that significant Sino-Soviet improvements on the border question in 1987, especially in the area of the Amur river, pressurised India to seek a political breakthrough by dispatching Rajiv Gandhi to Beijing in 1988, although the Chinese repression of the pro-democracy movement in 1989 has stalled the general momentum.[38]

By late 1987 it was estimated that the Chinese had demobilised around 1 million men, the great majority of them stationed along the Soviet border. Paradoxically, Indian concerns over the ending of the cold war in Asia are probably more profound than if the cold war were to continue. The effects of a Sino-Soviet rapprochement could isolate India in her own private dispute with China and greatly augment China's potential influence throughout Asia. India does not support Gorbachev's call for a Helsinki-style Conference on Asia.

The Afghanistan war ended any real basis for normal relations between Pakistan and the Soviet Union. Islamabad had to deal with over 3 million refugees descending on her sensitive north-western territories, and her support for the Mujahadeen Alliance in their struggle against the Soviet-backed regime led to numerous violations of Pakistani airspace. On 18 June 1984 Pakistan complained to the Secretary General of the UN that Afghan MiGs had violated Pakistan airspace on twenty-eight separate occasions since the beginning of the year, and had even carried out bombing raids against refugee camps.[39] Soviet attempts to secure Pakistan's recognition of the Kamal government by assuring Pakistan that the refugees would return as soon as the situation 'normalised' largely failed, despite the acute ethnic pressures (and violence) that the refugee problem was creating. President Zia's personal attachment to the radical Islamic factions within the Mujahadeen was particularly vexing to Moscow. Surrounded by such gloom, as well as the domestic inconvenience of burying three General Secretaries of the CPSU in as many years, the Soviets were particularly appreciative of Indian support.

Speculation that the dramatic easing of tensions between the Soviet Union and the United States has opened up the way towards improved relations between Islamabad and Moscow fail to take into account the continuing sensitivity that Moscow has for India over Kashmir, and ignores the amount of mistrust that has grown up in Pakistan towards Moscow in the wake of the Afghan war. The continuing survival of the Najibullah regime prevents normalised relations with Pakistan, who is still supporting the resistance. Irredentist pressures and regional unrest still threaten Pakistan's provinces of Baluchistan and NWFP. If frozen out from America, Pakistan may well find some benefits in links with the Soviet Union. Yet Islamabad would get neither the technology nor the diplomatic support to allow her to break the NPT regime.

Soviet links to the rest of South Asia have generally been perceived through the prism of the 'special relationship' with India. Soviet support for Bhutan, for example, is expressed in the general support for India's security doctrine towards the Himalayan kingdoms, and in Indian economic assistance. As such, the states of Bangladesh and Sri Lanka have had little use in deploying Soviet influence and aid as a natural counterweight to Indian influence as the two have tended to be complementary. Soviet–Bangladesh relations reached an all-time low after the 1975 coup, as the Ziaul Rehman regime toyed with China and Pakistan, but relations have improved during the 1980s, with Bangladesh and Nepal responding favourably to the Vladivostock speech.

Like most of the small states of South Asia – and unlike India – Bangladesh stands to gain from Sino-Soviet *détente* by increasing her trading links with both. In 1985 the Soviets extended credit facilities to help Bangladesh build a power station, and plans were announced to build a Russian culture centre in Dhaka. Earlier in 1984 Bangladesh had secured a five-year trade agreement with China worth US $200 million. In 1989 Bangladesh imports from the Soviet Union were worth US $69 million, compared to US $282·2 million from the United States, and they seem set to improve throughout the 1990s.

For Nepal the proximity of Moscow and New Delhi is still something of a problem, stifling her foreign policy initiatives and reinforcing her perceptions of Indian dominance. Nepal has nonetheless been the recipient of Soviet aid in the past. By 1966 she had received US $14 million and has continued to benefit since. Unlike the United States however, and the global financial institutions that are supported by western finance, the USSR's contributions in aid have been small. As noted above, the Soviets do not support the Himalayan Peace Zone initiative.

In comparison to Chinese and American influence, the Soviet Union has commanded a relatively low profile in Sri Lanka, even under the UF–SLFP governments. Relations were obviously soured by the initial anti-communism of the UNP government, and Sir John Kotelawala's virulent outbursts at Bandung. Moreover, the Soviet Union repeatedly blocked the membership of Sri Lanka to the United Nations (twice in 1948 and once in 1949) on the grounds that the island was not an independent sovereign state but a continuing appendage of British imperialism. Soviet objections were only withdrawn when, in 1955, Sri Lanka's inclusion in the UN was based upon a western acceptance of Albanian and Mongolian membership.

By 1956 the Bandaranaike government had initiated various links with the Soviet Union and, along with China, was receiving various grants and loans. Between 1960 and 1964 Sri Lanka's total net receipts in foreign aid from capitalist countries were to the value of Rs51 million, while contributions from socialist countries were Rs67 million.[40] In total, in the periods 1956–65 and 1970–2, the Soviet Union contributed Rs192·8 million to successive SLFP governments in Sri Lanka, compared to the Rs315 million from the PRC for the whole period. During the 1970–76 period, Sri Lanka obtained US $436·3 million from the International Bank of Reconstruction and Development (IBRD), and a further Rs1,748 million in loans from the IMF. Since the late 1980s Sri Lanka has drawn increasingly from the IMF. Again, as with communist aid generally, while small compared to western sources it has the traditional advantage of being at lower rates of interest and less stringently tied to conditions.[41] Unlike India, trade links with the Soviet Union remain weak. Sri Lankan exports to the United States were worth US $400 million in 1989, while exports to the USSR were worth US $26·7 million.[42]

Like the Americans, the Soviets have stood to benefit from the strategic importance of Sri Lanka. The early 1970s were dominated by rumours that the then socialist government was about to lease military bases to either the Russians, or indeed the Chinese. In 1971 the Ministry for External Affairs issued a statement denying that any requests had been made. As would be expected, the Indians would be as concerned about a Soviet base on Sri Lanka as they would be with an American one.

Apart from the bilateral relations between the region and the superpowers, South Asia is closely bound up by a whole web of international diplomatic activity that centres on the United Nations and the Non-Aligned Movement (NAM). Pakistan, Bangladesh and the Maldives, grouped together through common Islamic ties, have participated within various Islamic forums, especially the Organisation of Islamic Conference. The significance of the Commonwealth, in terms of economic aid and of political support, has declined. In the early years, before non-alignment became established, the Commonwealth provided India with an important niche within the international system. Since the mid 1980s, especially during the Thatcher governments of 1979–1990, the Commonwealth has suffered from neglect and political controversy in which India – and not Britain – has led a majority of states over various international issues.[43]

Within these forums, India's diplomatic profile is the highest and the most dominant of the South Asian states with the telling exception of the Islamic Conference. In the other forums she has attempted to forge a regional response to specific issues and has been anxious to avoid open displays of regional division and mistrust on the international stage. Many of the South Asian diplomatic initiatives use all three forums simultaneously: the Sri Lankan proposal to make the Indian Ocean a 'zone of peace' was first raised in the Lusaka summit of the Non-Aligned Movement in 1970, then at the Commonwealth Heads of Government meeting, and then introduced into the United Nations in 1971. India's proposals for disarmament were first brought before the Non-Aligned Movement in Cairo in 1964, and then introduced to the United Nations. Pakistan has brought the matter of Kashmir to the attention of virtually every international organisation of which she is a member.

The United Nations and South Asia

Since the Kashmir crisis of 1947–8, India's attitudes towards the United Nations, and its role within international relations generally, has undergone significant change. Indian foreign policy under Nehru favoured the concept of international equality and the 'rule of law' that was enshrined in the UN Charter. Yet he was the first to appreciate, in the light of the UN debates on Kashmir, the limitations imposed on the organisation by the frustrations and bitterness of the cold war and a hierarchy of great power states.

Following on from the experiences of Kashmir – and forming part of the American mistrust of Indian diplomacy – India has favoured United Nations initiatives with a particularly anti-western bias, while it has come to disregard or criticise UN intervention in the South Asia region on the grounds of unwarranted interference.

India took an active role in the diplomacy surrounding the Korean War (1950–4), and was a supporter of Mao's claim to China's seat in the UN. Throughout the 1980s India was active in the various UN debates against South Africa, and in vigorous calls for global disarmament. While India's commitment to the UN has been ideological it has, like much of India's international diplomacy after the 1950s and the falling out with China, been underscored by political realism.[44] With the ending of the colonial empires (and the west's natural dominance on the UN), India has been clever to use the UN as a forum in which to enhance her prestige and her influence on the newly emerging states of Africa and Asia as a state opposed to the forces of imperialism and neo-colonialism.[45] From 1960 onwards India was active on the Special Committee for De-colonisation, while she has been particularly active in the United Nations Conference on Trade and Development (UNCTAD) created in 1964, which called for global economic reform aimed to assist 'Third World' states undertake economic and social development. The second session of the UNCTAD conference was held in New Delhi in 1982.

In particular, American criticism has centred on India's voting behaviour in the UN which has invariably appeared pro-Soviet. On many occasions India has voted in favour of Soviet moves, such as the attempts to secure the UN seat for Kampuchea as opposed to the exiled 'Cambodian' leadership. As already noted, India has abstained in votes that sought to condemn Soviet action, while she has vigorously condemned US policy in Vietnam and Libya, and the invasion of Panama in 1989.

While critical of the cold war and the effects this has had on polarising United Nations diplomacy, India has relied upon the use of the Soviet veto to shield her from international condemnation. During the Bangladesh crisis the Soviet Union vetoed three peace initiatives sponsored by the United States and Britain which, had they been successful, would have hindered India's execution of the war. One element of the Nehruvian legacy is still present, however: India's political elite remain terribly sensitive to UN opinion, especially the risk of being subjected to an adverse UN resolution. Throughout the 1984–7 crisis in Indo-Sri Lankan relations, there was some concern that the Sri Lankan government would refer the matter of Indian assistance to the Tamils for the Security Council and opened the matter to 'great power' interference.

Since the 1960s India has continued this general support for Third World issues, both economically through the various UNCTAD resolutions, and politically through the call for a New International Economic Order (NIEO) made in 1974 at a special session of the UN General Assembly. Her attitude towards North–South issues is often phrased in radical terminology, and has at times reinforced India's image as a radical power. In 1980 India supported the calling by UNESCO for a New World Information and Communications Order, which many western states believed was 'overtly political' and well outside of UNESCO's charter. Sir Anthony Parsons noted recently that such posturing has led to a malaise within the UN, especially within the UN specialist agencies.[46]

Indian remarks, as part of a general Third World verbal and procedural assault over South Africa, racial discrimination generally and disarmament, have further been construed as attacks against US interests. In a letter to the Director-General of the ILO, Henry Kissinger stated that 'in recent years the International Labour Organisation (ILO) has become increasingly and excessively involved in political issues which are quite beyond the competence and mandate of the organisation'.[47]

In contrast to India's use of the United Nations for principled statements on foreign and international policy, Pakistan has often appeared to be sidelined. Although active on various UN committees, she has not taken such a general involvement in global issues. Her major role in the Geneva talks that brought about the end to the Afghanistan crisis on 1988 were typical of Pakistan's involvement: as a forum to settle matters within the region, and often to settle them at India's expense.

Far from using the UN as a window to wider interests, Pakistan has sought to use the General Assembly as a forum in which to condemn India and to frustrate India's regional ambition.[48] Even as recently as 1984, Pakistan provoked Indian condemnation by bringing up the issue of Kashmir in a discussion on the Iran–Iraq war. In 1989 Pakistan still envisaged a solution to the Kashmir crisis based upon the active role of the UN. In this, Pakistan has much in common with Nepal, Bangladesh and Bhutan, states that have used voting within the General Assembly as a means to signal disapproval to New Delhi rather than to construct wider ranging foreign policy initiatives.

Nepal and Bangladesh have voted with China and with the US on issues aimed to irritate New Delhi. Bangladesh, which became a member of the UN in 1974 has, like Pakistan over Kashmir, attempted to use the UN as a way of isolating India. Sri Lanka's position towards the United Nations has been more in line with India, although she has on several occasions voted against the Soviet Union over the use of force in Eastern Europe and over the Afghanistan invasion.

All of the South Asia states, especially Bhutan, Bangladesh and Nepal, have benefited from the economic and financial institutions of the United Nations, such as the International Monetary Fund (IMF) and the General Agreement on Tariffs and Trade (GATT), as well as the World Bank and its subsidiary institutions, more perhaps than they have benefited from the political and diplomatic dimensions of the UN.[49] On becoming a member of the organisation in 1974, Bhutan was able to move away from her almost total reliance upon India and involved United Nations expertise within her own development strategies.

In the recently published *History of the United Nations*, Evan Luard has noted that the decade between 1955 and 1965 was 'the . . . period when the United Nations came closest . . . to achieving the goals it was set up to accomplish. There has existed no other period in its history when there existed such a widespread willingness to turn to the organisation.'[50]

Between 1979 and 1986 this willingness to co-operate was largely ebbing under increased North–South pressures generated by economic hardships, and following Afghanistan and the first Reagan presidency, renewed cold war tensions. Following the onset of Soviet reforms since 1985, the situation has been revolutionised. It is difficult to realise how recently the UN was perceived as an object of 'disregard and disillusion'. The events of 1989 have removed many of the objections that Nehru made of the organisation's activities during the 1950s, by freeing the international agenda of overt cold war considerations and sensitivities. Yet the question of the future of the United Nations as an international policeman and, more profoundly, the main forum of a new international order, impinge on the previous discussion of Indian–US relations and India's ability to use the UN without appearing to concur to American dominance. Given the possible rise of US–USSR condominium, the role of the United Nations seems set to increase further.

On 15 November 1989, the Soviets and the Americans sponsored a joint resolution (44/21) calling upon all states to support the UN Charter and to take up the 'peace dividends' that were now on offer. While the prospect of greater co-operation won overall approval, India in particular may have reasons to fear the onset of US–Soviet global co-operation, since it could limit her flexibility within the United Nations.

Such 'joint superpower' action (or, more cynically, the realities of a 'uni-multipolar world based upon the US') could well be worse than a United Nations agenda deadlocked and divided over cold war issues. India distanced herself from the American efforts to construct a new world order after the Second World War (of which the United Nations was an integral part). Her attitude towards the wider visions of the Bush administration are cautious, especially with regard to current thinking on environmental pollution, and changes in the UN Security Council.

India did not sign the Montreal Protocol in 1987 to cut back on the global emissions of the primary ozone-depleting gases, on the grounds that it did not recognise the obligations of the 'developed' world to the industrialising countries. Interestingly enough, India and China both couched their objections in the language of Third World solidarity, and supported the same position.

India has consistently argued that the industrial nations must bear much of the costs for cleaning up the environment to the extent of granting to the less developed countries financial help to switch to new, cleaner technology. Throughout the 44th session of the UN (in 1989) India insisted that the discussion on the environment be widened to take into consideration the issue of technological transfers. The USA objected to the demand for the setting up of a fund of US $100,000,000 on the grounds that financial support was already forthcoming through various other UN agencies, primarily the United Nations Environmental Programme (UNEP) set up in 1972.[51] At the November 1990 conference on global warming, India was able to secure some provisions for assistance to the developing countries which went some way to removing some of her earlier objections, but the detailed negotiations over the amount and the 'conditionality' have been postponed until February 1991 and a conference in Brazil in 1992. The USA, along with other western powers, is likely to argue against further financial support.[52]

Indian criticism of the Security Council is based on the simple fact that, for all practical purposes, the UN charter enthrones the permanent members above the General Assembly. In particular India believes that Article Twelve is too restrictive. Article Twelve states that 'while the Security Council is exercising in respect of any dispute or situation the functions assigned to it . . . the General Assembly shall not make any recommendations with regard to that dispute or situation unless the Security Council so requests'.[53] While the General Assembly may return issues back to the Security Council for reconsideration, the Council's decision is final and binding. To India, while the Council consists of fifteen member states, ten elected from the General Assembly, the fact that the permanent members retain the powers of veto is out of line with the emerging realities of the international system. At the moment, the Security Council does not represent the interests of important 'middle powers' such as herself, Brazil, Nigeria, or even Iraq.

There have been various suggestions by New Delhi to increase the permanent members to include India, but these have as yet come to nothing. Because of the degree of insecurity within Indo-Pakistan relations, placing India within the Security Council would have serious and immediate repercussions on Pakistan and would not be supported by China. The current discussions about the inclusion of Japan and the recently unified Germany, premised upon their economic influence, further irritate India, since they approximate once more to the image of 'great powers' as the old colonial powers, and are linked in the minds of India's elites to images of an essentially pre-war order.

India's anxiety to break into the charmed circle of the Permanent Members is tied up with India's image of herself, and especially of her status *vis-à-vis* China. Should India fail to convince international opinion of the need for these changes, she will support the UN, but will be more obstructionist and more inclined to pursue matters through alternative forums, especially NAM. And there will be the growing mistrust within India that the 'international society' of the next century will be as exclusively European as the previous one.

D

The Non-Aligned Movement and South Asia

India has never reserved her international diplomacy solely for use within the United Nations. Much has been written on the Non-Aligned Movement (NAM) and the ideological underpinning of Nehru's support for it. In much of the Indian literature, Nehru is given the extraordinary status of statesman–philosopher, and the ideological emphasis of much of the writings gloss over Nehru's appreciation of India's access to, and influence over, the emerging states of Africa and Asia. In 1983, U. S. Bajpal noted that: 'while exaggerated notions of India's strength and influence have to be eschewed, we cannot and should not conceive of ourselves as just another developing country'.[54] Nehru's view of India's status and 'calling' were just as candid, although they were disguised by a rather Edwardian style of delivery. The Bandung Conference – held in April 1955 and heralded as the 'first inter-continental conference of the so-called coloured peoples' – confirmed to Nehru the importance of India, and an Indian 'third way' of foreign policy that would steer through the East-West divide.

NAM is important not just to the international politics of India generally, but to an understanding of her relationship with China. The ideas of non-alignment and Third World solidarity have been one of the main manifestations of Sino-Indian rivalry. NAM grew out of the Bandung conference as a smaller, compact body of states who were not members of any military alliance, who had not allowed foreign bases on their territory, and who were committed to both conventional and nuclear disarmament, and to ideas of Third World collective security.

China's views on Third World' solidarity differed from India's, especially concerning the role of nuclear weapons and collective security. In 1964 India raised the matter of China's nuclear weapons programme at the NAM summit at Cairo on the grounds that it significantly threatened Indian security. China's call for Afro-Asian summits of the Bandung variety throughout the 1970s were resisted by India who believed that they were merely attempts by China to challenge India within her 'Third World niche' by radical proposals of international revolution and reform. Significantly, China has in the past portrayed India's role and influence within NAM as 'hegemonic'.

During the 1971 diplomatic build-up to the Bangladesh crisis, India played her connections with the Third World with consummate skill, ensuring that subsequent military action against Pakistan would not be followed by outrage and criticism within NAM. The signing of the Indo-Soviet treaty led to some condemnation, but India had been careful to ensure that the treaty's significance was down-played, and anxious to portray it as an economic and cultural agreement. The Americans were quick to point out the apparent contradiction between professed Indian non-alignment and the Indo–Soviet treaty.

Initiated at Bandung, the Non-Aligned Movement was founded at Belgrade in 1961, and took the 'five principles' – the Panscheel – as its rationale. India claims (as to a lesser extent does Sri Lanka) the role of intellectual founder behind the Non-Aligned Movement. The prime function of NAM was to stabilise the existence of post-colonial states from either US or Soviet interference, and allow them to deal with all their numerous problems of irredentism and 'secession'. It followed that the movement was at its most coherent when the cold war was at its height.

The institutional structures of NAM have evolved from the infrequent summits of 1961, 1964 and 1970 to regular meetings at foreign ministers level and to the setting-up of a co-ordination bureau. The states of India, Sri Lanka and Nepal were all active members in 1961 and have remained committed members since. Bhutan and Bangladesh joined in 1973. The Maldives joined NAM in 1976 with India's support and encouragement. Pakistan was excluded because of her membership of SEATO, and CENTO only applied to join in 1974 following Bhutto's reorientation of her foreign policy and her decision to quit CENTO. Pakistan was finally admitted in 1979 amid serious Indian reservations as to her credentials, but did not attempt to resist the move.

Pakistan's decision to seek readmission was part of a genuine attempt to widen the scope of Pakistan policy towards the Third World, and more significantly towards the moderate Arab states of the Middle East, especially Saudi Arabia. The presence of the Arab League at the various NAM summits have allowed Pakistan to pursue her links with the Islamic world on a bilateral basis. While India has been aware of Pakistani overtures in the Gulf and South-West Asia, she has tended to concentrate on East Asia, using NAM to extend her bilateral relations with Vietnam, and through supporting Vietnam, to reaffirm her commitment to contain China.[55] More generally, as in the fifty-four page political declaration after the 1983 Delhi conference, India has reaffirmed, at some length, her ideological commitment to the old Nehruvian agenda, even if to western observers the tone of the declaration seemed particularly antediluvian.

India and Sri Lanka have been closely bound together in their common stand against the cold war, the various peace zone initiatives, and the calls for nuclear disarmament, and NAM has greatly complemented their bilateral relations. Sri Lanka was head of NAM from 1976 until 1978 while India presided from 1983 to 1985.

Since the 1975 summit at Lima, Peru, NAM moved away from the earlier concerns of military security based upon calls for global disarmament, towards the more broader issues of economic development and global economic reform. This widening of the agenda brought NAM closer to the UN and its various affiliated institutions. The call for the NIEO, for example, was discussed both at Lima and then at the special session of the UN General Assembly.

As the agenda widened, so too did the membership. By 1981, the original twenty-five states had grown to ninety-three full members. By 1989 these had grown to a further 102 countries, with two affiliated organisations (the PLO and SWAPO). With this increase in size has come new problems of leadership and agreement. Such an increasing membership – that has paradoxically approached China's preferred format of Afro-Asian conferences – has brought difficulties of leadership and consensus and some dilution of influence.

One of the problems that beset the Non-Aligned Movement in the late 1970s was the rise of the so-called 'radical thesis', forwarded by Cuba, that urged NAM to move closer towards the USSR as a bulwark against American 'imperialism'. Both America and China protested over Cuba's hosting of the sixth summit in 1979 because of its obvious Soviet links, and their suspicions seemed confirmed following Castro's anti-American speech. Yet India sided immediately with the 'moderate states' of Yugoslavia and Saudi Arabia in opposing such a move and in retaining the 'no-bloc' principle. The dispute was complicated by the Soviet invasion of Afghanistan – a member of NAM – which embarrassed Cuba and India. As with her policy within the UN, India would not openly condemn the move within NAM – a position that immediately played into the hands of Pakistan and the United States – but merely called for the upholding of the five principles and the withdrawal of all foreign troops.

There can be no doubt that India's role within the Non-Aligned Movement has given her prestige and status. It has also enabled India to take part in various global initiatives. In 1981 it was agreed that India would assist the PLO in an attempt to mediate the Iran–Iraq War, and in late January 1991 India was involved in various attempts within NAM to try, with Iranian help, to open up a dialogue between Iraq and the US-led coalition forces.[56] Although many western commentators have dismissed NAM as being a sort of ideological 'critics' forum without weight or real internal consensus, it has provided many South Asian states – particularly the smaller countries – with the scope for extending their bilateral relations outside of the region, in terms of trade and economic assistance.

The Afghanistan crisis occurred during India's presidency of Non-Aligned Movement, as did the Kampuchean/Cambodian issue which was still unresolved from the time of the Colombo Summit in 1976. In 1976, both the ousted Pol Pot regime and the Vietnamese-backed Heng Samrin regime sent delegates to attend the summit. In 1983 India caused some political embarrassment by issuing an invitation to the Heng Samrin government and not representatives of the exiled Khmer Rouge. Eventually, after much discussion, India agreed to an 'empty seat' solution. Significantly Sri Lanka has consistently refused to accept the legitimacy of the Heng Samrin government in both NAM and at the UN Special Conference on Kampuchea in 1981, on the grounds that the government had been installed by a foreign power: 'to accept the principle of intervention or to give it legitimacy in any form would be to make all small states vulnerable and powerful states belligerent...'[57] Such an argument has obvious parallels to Sri Lanka's relationship to India and were made with such parallels in mind. Sri Lanka rejects the Indian doctrine that the Heng Samrin government is legitimate because it has 'effective control' since such a doctrine would legitimate the invasion and control of Sri Lanka.

The increasing divergences within NAM, and throughout the various forums of the Third World, reflect the different degrees of success countries have had in dealing with the problem of nation-building and economic development. As the ideological cohesiveness of 'anti-colonialism' has receded, the movement has become more fragmentary. The language of aggressive anti-imperialism can still be heard, and often it is still ideologically linked to the 'radical thesis' that ties NAM to the Soviet Union. In the 1986 summit in Harare, Col. Gadaffi returned to the earlier themes of the 1970s, implying that several NAM members were 'puppets of the imperialists' and should therefore be expelled. Critical of NAM's failure to come to Libya's side during the US bombings, Gadaffi called for some curious military alliance to declare war against the 'West'. Such language was seen by India and the other states of South Asia as being increasingly archaic.

Without the cold war, what will happen to the ideology of non-alignment? One possible answer is that it will move away from a singular concern over disarmament towards the broader North–South debates over economic and environmental issues, such as those of

UNCTAD and NIEO. Such a move will not automatically complement Indian foreign policy, for her interests in economic development are – more so than at any time since her independence – towards the North and not against it, but it may compensate for Indian disenchantment with the UN.

The 1989 Belgrade Summit was marked by a 'new sense of realism' of shorter, less rhetorical communiqués and more practical, limited calls for economic and political reforms aimed at sharing technology and dealing with environmental degradation. At the Belgrade Summit of 1989, Rajiv Gandhi, the then Prime Minister of India, called for the setting up of a planetary protection fund, paid for primarily by the West. It is unlikely that the West (or more specifically, the Americans) will agree. With the ending of the cold war some states commented on a 'loss of direction', with differences between the small African states and India over the degree and type of economic assistance, and significantly, disagreements over collective security and nuclear weapons.

The Commonwealth and South Asia

Alongside the Non-Aligned Movement and the United Nations, the main states of South Asia all share membership of the British Commonwealth of Nations. Again, as with NAM, Pakistan started off as a member following Partition, left in 1972 (following the decisions of the United Kingdom, Australia and New Zealand to recognise Bangladesh) and was readmitted in 1989. Indian objections to Pakistan rejoining were removed following the election of a civilian government in Islamabad in 1988.

With little constitutional or institutional support the Commonwealth can (and has) been too easily dismissed as an antediluvian association, a curiously British concept without function or focus. Although it has a secretariat, and convenes regularly in summit format every two years, it has long been summarised as an institution beset with division and family disagreements. The 1989 Kuala Lumpur summit had ended with a row following subsequent British disclaimers to a joint communiqué which condemned apartheid and South Africa. Indian criticism about 'British hesitancy' over sanctions against South Africa was prevalent throughout the 1980s. Britain's isolation has given rise to some speculation in the Delhi press that she should leave the Commonwealth! Yet the strengths of the Commonwealth have been to provide member states with a relatively small and informal arena in which to address international issues. The fact that the Commonwealth contains states such as Canada, Australia and New Zealand also means that it does not duplicate other Third World organisations.

Of all the states of South Asia, India's links with the Commonwealth have been the most important and yet the most problematic. India's commitment to the Commonwealth after 1947 has been crucial to its survival. Had Partition not created two states in animosity to each other, and had Nehru not taken such a principled stand on foreign policy against colonialism, it is likely that British ideas over the shape and form of the Commonwealth would have favoured a more centralised, alliance-based structure to uphold Britain's position East of Suez after the end of the war. India and Pakistan's refusal to enter into any common agreement scotched these ideas from the beginning, as did the speed of Britain's decline after 1949.

India's support for the Commonwealth idea opened the way for the African states formed in the late 1950s and early 1960s to seek membership: 'to India belongs the singular credit of opening the Commonwealth door to the Republics'[58] and overcoming the constitutional difficulties of republics associating themselves with a monarchy. Had India withdrawn it is likely that the Commonwealth would have either collapsed or consisted entirely of the old White Dominions

India's subsequent support has tended to follow the ups and downs of Anglo-Indian relations, with New Delhi extremely sensitive to British support towards Pakistan, and wider anti-British feelings expressed within NAM or the UN over South Africa. During the Suez crisis of 1956 Nehru came under direct pressure from within the Congress Party to withdraw in the wider interests of Afro-Asian solidarity. In 1957 India was outraged by British support for a Pakistani resolution calling for the holding of a plebiscite over Kashmir. During the Falklands war, India found her historic association with Britain awkward.

Yet, like so much of India's policy, ideological vision has been combined with clear national interest, and the Commonwealth, for all its idiosyncrasies, has been particularly useful for India. Like the Non-Aligned Movement, the Commonwealth provided India with an area in which to establish close links with African and East Asian countries at a critical time in their struggle for independence.

By the mid 1960s India was providing technical know-how to thirty countries, a majority of them within the Commonwealth, providing aid to the Commonwealth secretariat as well as receiving it through the

Colombo Plan.[59] One analyst has noted significantly that: India at present [1980] is at once the recipient of the largest quality of foreign aid from the advanced countries, and a donor of massive assistance to other developing countries.'[60] No other South Asian state has used the Commonwealth link so effectively.

It could be argued that Pakistan failed to take advantage of the Commonwealth links because she allowed the Kashmir issue – and her perception that both the British and the Dominions were pro-Indian – to dominate her foreign policy to the exclusion of everything else. At the Commonwealth Prime Ministers' meeting in London in 1950, Liquat Ali Khan, the Pakistani Prime Minister, threatened to stay away because the Kashmir issue had not found its way on to the agenda. The issue was resolved through 'informal' discussions outside the framework of the main conference. Such incidents tended to improve India's image of moderation and flexibility to the general detriment of Pakistan.

Since 1989 Pakistan has seen the Commonwealth links as a conduit to other states and not simply as an arena in which to criticise and isolate India. Like her earlier decision to seek admission to NAM, her return to the Commonwealth reflects both a restoration of earlier pre-1954 policies and a profound change in outlook about the importance of the US link to the detriment of all other contacts. Although India accepted British mediation in the April 1965 Rann of Kutch incident, India saw the Commonwealth as just another ruse for Pakistan to internationalise bilateral issues and has rejected it. Should Pakistan return to this policy, it is remotely possible that India would once more seriously entertain the idea of pulling out.

South Asia and the international politics of the Muslim world

Under Zulfika Al Bhutto, and dictated in part by the need to reconstruct a new state after the loss of East Bengal, Pakistan pursued an active 'Islamic' foreign policy that brought financial and political dividends, especially from Saudi Arabia. By 1974, between 1 and 1·5 million Pakistanis were working in the Arabian peninsular, and between 1975 and 1980 these workers returned US $2 billion home in remittances. In 1980, following the invasion of Afghanistan, on a state visit, Crown Prince Fahd said that Saudi Arabia and Pakistan were 'now closely associated in terms of security and defence'. Pakistan's support for the Mujahadeen opposition in Afghanistan, and President Zia's insistence that a settlement in Afghanistan involved the entire

'Muslim world' also bound Pakistan close to the Islamic community of states within the Middle East. While these links were not new, they have re-emerged at the centre of Pakistan's quest for security and national identity from the 1970s onwards.

After US aid to India 1962, and as part of the new 'balanced' approach to foreign affairs that opened up close links with China, Ayub Khan began to involve Pakistan within the various Islamic forums, attending an Islamic summit in Jakarta in 1965, and another one held in Rabat in September 1969. These various summit meetings, which drew Muslim countries from the Middle and the Far East, resulted in the founding of the Organisation of Islamic Conferences in 1971.[61] The founding of this set of Islamic institutions and specialist bodies coincided with Prime Minister Bhutto's general disillusionment with the US and with the reliability of the West in general. Moreover, following from the establishment (and obvious influence) of OPEC, it no longer appeared that the Middle Eastern states were a 'string of noughts' within the global power equation. Pakistan was instrumental in getting the Islamic states to set up the Islamic Development Bank, to which Saudi Arabia and Iran gave substantial collateral.

Z. Bhutto pursued active bilateral relations with the Kingdom of Saudi Arabia, the Shah of Iran, and even Gaddafi of Libya, although relations between them were to cool somewhat under pressure from the Shah. This involved taking a high profile in condemning Israeli aggression against the Arab states, and in numerous calls by Pakistan in favour of the setting up of a Palestinian state.[62] In return, Pakistan expected not just material and financial help, but diplomatic support against India over the Kashmir issue, which it duly received.

Apart from the remittances, there was also the prospect of trade, especially in manufactured goods to the Middle East in the form of textiles. Moreover Pakistan was to acquire a particularly useful relationship with the Saudi military in supplying military expertise and training. Saudi Arabia was the first Islamic state to offer Pakistan financial assistance to deal with refugees from Afghanistan: US $25,000,000 at the Islamabad meeting in 1980. Pakistan was also to pursue much-needed trade links with Libya and, prior to the 1978 revolution, with Iran. Significantly, Pakistani policy towards the Middle East complemented her earlier links with the US Both Saudi Arabia and the Shah were linked to Washington with various defence and economic agreements.

As a secular state, India did not give any particular emphasis to Islam within her foreign policy, despite being the fourth most populous

Muslim state in the world. Yet at times, such as the case of the Rushdie affair, India has shown a particular sensitivity to her Muslim subjects. India was the first South Asian state to ban *The Satanic Verses* on the grounds of blasphemy, and on several occasions she has shown some interest in joining in the politics of the Muslim world. Here, perhaps not surprisingly, she has run up against Pakistani objections.

The reasons for Pakistan's anxiety are not hard to find. Within the ICO, 'Pakistan did not have to compete with India . . . whereas in the third world movement India remained a formidable force'.[63] Pakistan's sensitivity on this matter cannot be overestimated. In 1969 India had been invited to attend the summit of Islamic states at Rabat but in the face of Pakistani protests, and the threat to withdraw, Saudi Arabia felt sufficiently pressured into withdrawing its invitation. India has never been invited since.

Following this diplomatic coup, Pakistan has held various summits and Foreign Ministers' meetings of the Islamic Conference, in Karachi in 1970 just prior to the founding of the Conference, at Lahore in 1974, and at Islamabad in 1980. Pakistan has played a role within the Islamic conference almost identical to India's within the Non-Aligned Movement. In 1977 Pakistan called for the setting-up of nuclear free zones in the Indian Ocean and the Middle East, and in 1980 Pakistan voted in favour of a resolution that called upon Islamic states to deny military facilities to 'foreign powers'. After 1980, Pakistan cut a very high profile within the ICO over the Afghanistan crisis (part of a clear policy of embarrassing New Delhi's support for the Kabul regime), while the Islamic Conference provided the forum for Pakistani diplomatic initiatives such as the mission to try and mediate over the Iran–Iraq war in 1980.

Pakistan's Islamic foreign policy has brought fewer dividends to her relations with East Asia. Under Ayub Khan, Pakistan moved closer to Malaysia and Indonesia. During the 1965 war with India, Indonesia even offered to provide Pakistan with military help, and to 'seize the Andaman and Nicobar islands' so as to detract India from Kashmir. Pakistan continues to enjoy close relations with Indonesia, although the affinities between these two states has less to do with Islam that with a shared threat perception of India's stratagems in the Indian Ocean and her attempts to 'augment [her] naval power and acquire a power projection capability in the vicinity of the sub-continent'.[64]

The importance of the Islamic world to Pakistan is very significant. By 1989 there were over twenty-one subsidiary organisations associated with the Islamic Conference covering areas such as Islamic jurisprudence, economic and technical development, as well as trade and heritage foundations, and Pakistan was actively associated in most of these: in 1989 Pakistan was involved in discussing the importance of the Rushdie affair to the relations between the Muslim world and the West.[65]

Embarrassed by the 1969 fiasco, India has tried to play down her exclusion from the Islamic world by Pakistan, while expressing concern over Pakistan's relationship with Saudi Arabia and, prior to 1978, the Shah. As in the case of China, New Delhi was concerned that arms sales to the Middle East would be diverted into Pakistan, and that technical co-operation and assistance with Middle Eastern states may well assist Pakistan military rearmament programmes after the loss of the East wing. India was particularly concerned that the modernisation of the Shah's army would give Pakistan another powerful, extra-regional ally against India, or even technical help – via the US – for Pakistan's bomb.

India's attempts to pursue Pakistan into the Middle East by adopting close bilateral ties with Iraq and Syria have not been very successful since they had tended to support, with the exception of Libya, those Arab states closely associated with the Soviet Union and opposed to Saudi conservatism. Thus, as with Pakistan, India's support for Egypt, Iraq and Syria mirrored her own bilateral association with the Soviet Union. Her historical links with Iraq were one of the reasons for India's mute support for the recently-concluded Coalition forces deployed against Hussein.

Against the backdrop of international change and transition since 1989, these sets of relations, Indo-Middle Eastern and Indo-Soviet, and Pakistan-Middle Eastern and Pakistan-US will lessen. Moreover, Pakistan's ability to pursue both an Islamic/pro-USA policy has, like so much of Pakistani diplomacy since the 1980s, been largely co-incidental, and there is the growing possibility that Pakistan may well have to choose between them. American–Pakistan relations seem likely to be the first major victim of America's growing problems in dealing with the instability within the Middle East. The Americans have themselves become more sensitive to the consequences that might follow from Pakistan's wider identity with apparent US policy *against* Muslim states: a State Department travel warning issued on 14 January 1991 said: 'Non-essential government personnel and all dependants have been ordered to depart Jordan, Mauritania, Sudan, Yemen . . . Algeria, Pakistan and Tunisia. American citizens should consider deferring all travel to all of these areas'.[66]

More critically, the future scope for Pakistani relations within the Middle East is therefore not necessarily plain sailing, since it depends on the overall degree of consensus within Arab politics: 'through the mid 1980s, the success of Pakistan's Islamic foreign policy is that it has tended to become limited by the divisions within the Islamic world itself'.[67] While Pakistan has been anxious to avoid the internal and factional strife that has so often characterised the relations of conservative-radical Arab states, relying upon Saudi Arabia, it has not always worked, and has often been in itself a source of tension.

The Iranian revolution and the rise of a fundamentalist Shi'ia regime caused particular concern for Pakistan. Like Saudi Arabia, Pakistan is a predominantly Sunni society, but contains a small Shi'ite minority. Throughout the early 1980s Iran denounced Pakistan, along with the USA and Saudi Arabia, and Iranian accusations against CIA involvement in the seizure of the Grand Mosque at Mecca in 1979 led to the burning down of the US embassy in Islamabad.[68] The assassination of President Zia in 1988 was linked to possible domestic discontent amongst the Shi'ite community over the codification of Shar'iat law. Significantly, however – and perhaps a sign of Islamabad's overall success in forging close Islamic links – Pakistan has a good (and growing) share of Middle Eastern trade, more than India.

While Sri Lanka has pursued good relations with the Middle East, she has not given the area any particular priority, although she has a small Muslim minority (about 6 per cent). Mrs Bandaranaike's decision in 1970 to break off diplomatic relations with Israel gave Colombo a favourable press, but – like India – she has pursued Islamic links either bilaterally or through the workings of NAM. Sri Lanka's exports to the Middle East are generally low: US \$243·6 million in 1989, compared to US \$392·6 million with the EEC, and largely unchanged throughout the 1980s.[69]

While the Himalayan kingdoms of Bhutan and Nepal have virtually no direct links with the Islamic world and poor bilateral relations with the Middle East – relying upon India's particular diplomacy – both the Maldives and Bangladesh are members of the Islamic Conference. The Maldives have participated in all the Islamic summits, but their main aim has been to use the wider Islamic Conference as an arena in which to develop links with Pakistan and Bangladesh. The Maldives have virtually no trade with the Middle East, and have concentrated on Sri Lanka, Thailand, Singapore and Hong Kong. Isolated from the subcontinent, the Maldives are characterised more by the maritime Islamic traditions of East Asia, which serve to isolate it from Islam within South Asia and within the Middle East as well.

As in Pakistan, the influence of Islam on Bangladesh foreign policy has been intimately linked with the long internal search for an Islamic domestic identity that began after 1975. Under Ziaul Rehman and Mohammed Ershad, Bangladesh pursued its links with the Islamic world to even out India's influence, and to bring about a rapprochement with Pakistan and assure access to oil.

Initially, several Muslim states withheld recognition of Bangladesh for fear of offending Islamabad. It was two Muslim South East Asian states – Malaysia and Indonesia – who acknowledged Dhaka first. Yet it was to be within the framework of the Islamic Conference that Pakistan would finally extend her own recognition of Bangladesh , at Lahore in 1974. At the seventh summit of the Islamic Conference Pakistan called upon other Muslim states to support Bangladesh in her dispute with India over the Ganges River. Yet Islam to Bangladesh has a specific East Asian dimension as well, involving her in close relations with Malaysia and Indonesia. Bangladesh's attempts to use the Islamic Conference to gain access to finance has been largely disappointing, although she has secured good relations with Saudi Arabia and has had access to the Islamic Development Bank on concessional terms.

In 1988 President Ershad declared Bangladesh to be an Islamic republic, but although the event was noted in the Middle East, it was directed mainly at a domestic audience. Lacking Pakistan's military expertise and economic size, Bangladesh has nonetheless succeeded in cutting some profile within international affairs through the offices of the Islamic Conference. In 1987 Bangladesh hosted the Islamic Conference Organisation's Foreign Ministers' meeting.

Summary

A regional analysis of superpower relations with India and Pakistan reveal not how India and Pakistan have furthered the strategic aims of the USA or the USSR, but how the superpowers have furthered the strategic interests of New Delhi and Islamabad, both towards each other, and towards the international system generally.

The exact sets of relations which have evolved between the states of South Asia and the superpowers have had more to do with degrees of practical flexibility than ideological interest: in this respect there is no surprise why, for so much of the post-war period, the Soviets supported a democratic regime and the Americans supported an oligarchy. Other forums, such as the United Nations, NAM, and the

Commonwealth, have been used by Pakistan and India to display the extra-regional dimensions of foreign policy free of superpower involvement, but with an eye to superpower response and accommodation, and with the hope of embarrassing each other in wider global councils. Of the other states, only Sri Lanka has managed to pursue a wider foreign policy free of Indo-Pakistan rivalries, and has been the most genuinely non-aligned of NAM states.

As this chapter has shown, global events since 1989 are having a profound influence upon the options and flexibility that the states of South Asia have in dealing with each other and with differing parts of the world: but since the cause of the Indo-Pakistan dispute is regional, wider international events may have little influence on the state of their bilateral relations. These events could well make matters worse. A disengagement of the US–Pakistan relationship could heighten Pakistan's insecurity and weaken her economy, while a disengagement between the USSR and India could seriously increase India's costs in laying claim to a 'middle power' status.

Moreover, within the context of the so-called Pacific century, the states of South Asia have started to turn increasingly towards East Asia, to the states of Hong Kong, Taiwan, Singapore, South Korea and Japan. Irritatingly for India, she has come late to the Japanese banquet, discouraged by the strength of the US–Japanese special alliance, and later by the degree of Chinese interest in Japan and Japanese technology. While there has been some technical co-operation between India and Japan dating back to 1958 (the so-called 'yen loan'), Japanese–Indian relations are bedevilled by a series of political misunderstandings.

These misunderstandings are found, to a lesser degree, with the other South Asian states generally. India's association with Japan cooled following her normalisation of relations with China in 1972 through the Zhou–Tanaka communiqué, and following the signing of the Sino-Japanese Friendship Treaty of 1978. Moreover, in 1978 Japan suspended aid to Vietnam, a close ally of India and the Soviet Union, in apparent deference to Chinese sensibilities. Sri Lankan–Japanese relations remain cordial, in part because of some shared Buddhist traditions, and because the Japanese were impressed by Sri Lanka's decision in 1948 to forgo Japanese reparations and to 'confront hatred with love'. Japanese funds to Sri Lanka, to Bangladesh and to the smaller Himalayan kingdoms and the Maldives are relatively small in an area that does not command much interest within Japanese foreign policy. In 1989 Bangladesh, India, Sri Lanka, and Pakistan were respectively fifth, sixth, seventh and eighth in the top ten of Japanese aid-receivers, with the first four all South-east Asian states.

As will be discussed in chapter four, there are economic reasons why South Asia's share in Japanese bilateral foreign aid remains small – 16·1 per cent (US $1·091 million) in 1989 compared to 32·8% earmarked for South East Asia. The states of ASEAN received 31·5 per cent.[70] India's V. P. Singh Government announced in the wake of the 1989 elections that it gave Japan a particular priority in its foreign policy agenda, but it was not clear that this interest was reciprocated. This 'image problem' for Pakistan and India persists, especially as Japan remains distracted by Chinese and now Soviet overtures.

Notes

1 Ken Booth noted triumphantly, 'The Cold War is over, and we have won it. The West is secure and its societies enjoy considerable material comfort.' K. Booth and J. Baylis, *Britain, NATO and Nuclear Weapons: Alternative Defence versus Alliance Reform*, London, 1989, p. 3.

2 See the final chapter of P. Duncan, *Indo-Soviet Relations*, London, 1987 and Ramesh Thakur, 'Normalising Sino-Indian Relations', *The Pacific Review*, 4, 1991.

3 J. W. Mellor (ed.), *India: A Rising Middle Power*, Princeton, 1978, p. 359.

4 Nihal Singh, 'Can the US and India Really be Friends?', *Asian Survey*, 23, 1983, p. 1024.

5 'On top of the world?', *The Economist*, London, 9–15 March 1991, p. 3.

6 Sisir Gupta, 'Great power relations, world order and the Third World' in M. Rajan and S. S. Ganguly (eds.), *Selected Essays*, New Delhi, 1981.

7 Notable disagreements in the 1980s have involved Indian attempts to purchase a super-computer, and her desired purchasing of TOW anti-tank missiles with night sight capabilities. See Dilip Mukerjee, 'US weaponry for India', in *Asian Survey*, 27, 1987, pp. 595–640. Duncan points out that India has always taken somewhat excessive precautions to ensure that western defence technologies do not fall into the hands of Soviet advisers, even to the point of having separate dockyards and worksheds.

8 U. S. Bajpal (ed.), *India's Security: The Politico-Strategic Environment*, New Delhi, 1983, p. 18.

9 The Soviets are alleged to have asked why, if India could afford to spend between US $18 and 20 million cash on the Mirage 2000 jet fighter, they should provide her with cheap credit over seventeen years at 2.7% interest? See S. N. Singh, 'Why India goes to Moscow for arms', *Asian Survey*, 24, 1984, pp. 707–740.

10 India – and South Asia as a whole – have tended to be merged into a greater Asian identity dominated by Beijing and South East Asia. Alan Romberg's review of Washington's priorities in the mid 1980s, entitled 'New stirrings in Asia', did not even mention India once: *Foreign Affairs*, 64, 1985, pp. 515–38. Kreisberg's assessment of India following the death of Mrs Gandhi noted the failure of the US to award India a place in America's strategic thinking: 'India after Indira', *Foreign Affairs*, 63, 1985, pp. 871–91.

11 S. P. Varma and K. P. Misra, *Foreign Policy of South Asia*, New Delhi, 1969.

12 This matter is discussed in Chapter 6.

13 Raju Thomas, *India's Security Policy*, Princeton, 1986.

14 The Soviet view of India was not particularly favourable until the mid 1950s. Stalin believed that Nehru and the Indian middle class were essentially the 'running dogs' of US imperialism.

15 A. Jalal, *The State of Martial Rule*, Cambridge, 1990. The author cites a memo from the then Secretary of Commonwealth Relations regarding Anglo–US differences over Pakistan which stated: that 'Let's talk with the Americans, but for heaven's sake don't let's be rushed into some paper guarantees [to Pakistan's territorial integrity] . . . India's friendship is very important and must not be jeopardised' (p. 126).

16 See in particular Ayub Khan's autobiography, *Friends, Not Masters: A Political Autobiography*, London, 1967.

17 Sultana Afroz, 'Pakistan and the Middle East Defence Plan 1951', *Asian Affairs*, 75, 1988, pp. 170–79.

18 See P. I. Cheema, *Pakistan's Foreign Policy*, London, 1990, p 168.

19 S. Afroz, 'Pakistan and the Middle East', p. 174.

20 Cited in B. N. Goswami, *Pakistan and China: A Study in their Relations*, New Delhi, 1971, p. 79.

21 P. Duncan, *Indo-Soviet Relations*, p. 2.

22 Van Hollen, 'The tilt policy revisited', *Asian Survey*, 20, 1980, p. 355.

23 Raju Thomas, 'Security relations in southern Asia', *Asian Survey*, 21, 1981, pp. 689–740.

24 S. Burke and L. Ziring, *Pakistan's Foreign Policy: An Historical Analysis*, Karachi, 1991, p. 417.

25 T. P. Thornton, 'Between the stools: US policy towards Pakistan during the Carter administration', *Asian Survey*, 22, 1982, pp. 959–70.

26 B. Buzan and G. Rizvi, *South Asian Insecurity*, Basingstoke, 1985. See also A. Shahi, *Pakistan's Security and Foreign Policy*, Lahore, 1988 and Z. Khalizad, *Security in South West Asia*, Aldershot, 1984.

27 G. Quester (ed.), *The Politics of Nuclear Proliferation*, Baltimore, 1973.

28 S. Ganguly, 'Avoiding war', *Foreign Affairs*, 69, Winter 1990–91.

29 The question of economics will be addressed in Chapter 4.

30 P. Duncan, *Indo-Soviet Relations*, p.51.

31 W. Anderson, 'The Soviets in the Indian Ocean', *Asian Survey*, 24, 1984, pp. 910–53.

32 Duncan, *Indo-Soviet Relations*, p. 12.

33 B. Sen Gupta, *Soviet Perspectives on Contemporary Asia*, New Delhi, 1982.

34 See R. Sisson and L. Rose, *War and Secession: India, Pakistan, and the Creation of Bangladesh*, Princeton, 1989.

35 *Direction of Trade Statistics*, IMF, Washington, 1990, p. 534.

36 Robert Horn, *Soviet-Indian Relations: Issues and Influences*, London, 1982.

37 There are difficulties in comparing Indian and Soviet trade because of the way in which the figures are calculated. Duncan notes that Indian imports often exclude arms sales and thus show a Soviet trade surplus as an Indian one. Nonetheless the trends in trade have become increasingly clear throughout the 1980s, with the Soviets less keen to import poor manufactured goods, and with India less interested in antiquated technology.

38 It has even been suggested that the Indians deliberately contrived the border crisis at Sumdurong Chu to test Soviet, not Chinese, resolve. See Leo Rose, 'India's foreign relations' in M. Bouton and P. Oldenburg, *India File: 1990*, Boulder, 1990.

39 *UN Year Book*, Geneva, 1984.

40 H. S. S. Nissankar, *Sri Lanka's Foreign Policy*, p. 256.

41 A. J. Wilson, *Politics in Sri Lanka 1947–1979*, London, 1979, p. 263.

42 *Direction of Trade Statistics*, IMF, Washington, 1990, p. 524.

43 For a discussion of this see M. Lipton, *The Erosion of a Relationship: India and Britain since 1960*, Brighton, 1975.

44 For an interesting study of the early years of Indian diplomacy on the UN see the Indian Council of World Affairs report on *India and the United Nations*, New York, 1957.

45 For evidence of this see M. Brecher's political study entitled *Nehru*, London, 1959.

46 The specialist agencies of the United Nations Organisation consist of the following: the International Atomic Energy Association (IAEA), the International Labour Organisation (ILO), the Food and Agricultural Organisation (FAO), the United Nations Educational Scientific and Cultural Organisation (UNESCO), the World Health Organisation (WHO), the International Monetary Fund (IMF), the International Bank for Reconstruction and Development (IBRD), the International Finance Commission (IFC), the Universal Postal Union (UPU), the International Telecommunications Union (ITU), the World Meteorological Organisation (WMO), the International Maritime Organisation (IMO), the General Agreement on Tariffs and Trade (GATT) and the World Intellectual Properties Union (WIPU).

47 Douglas Williams, *The Specialised Agencies and the United Nations*, London, 1987.

48 See the report prepared by the Pakistan Institute of International Affairs, *Pakistan and the United Nations*, New York, 1957. The report contains a useful discussion of Pakistan's involvement with the United Nations over Kashmir.

49 The financial relationships of the South Asian states are discussed in Chapter 4.

50 Evan Luard, *A History of the United Nations, Volume Two: The Age of Decolonisation, 1955–65*, London, 1989, p. 514.

51 See J. Rengger (ed.), *Treatises and Alliances of the World*, London, 1990, p. 53.

53 *UN Year Book*, Geneva, 1990.

54 U. S. Bajpal, *India's Security: The Politico-Strategic Environment*, New Delhi, 1983.

55 M. Ayoob, *India and South East Asia: Indian Perceptions and Policies*, London, 1990.

56 *Guardian*, 11 February 1991. It is important to note that a great deal of NAM is simply ignored by the western media. Just a brief glance at an Indian or Pakistani English daily will reveal not only the fact that global events are reported from different regional angles, but that entirely different events are reported altogether.

57 Foreign Minister's statement to the UN conference, cited in S. U. Kodikara, *Foreign Policy on Sri Lanka*, New Delhi, 1982, p. 155.

58 S. C. Gangal, *India and the Commonwealth*, New Delhi, 1970, p. 15.

59 In 1975 India contributed 7 per cent of the Commonwealth Secretariat's funds for multilateral assistance, see C. Vohra, *India's Aid Diplomacy and the Third World*, New Delhi, 1980.

60 Vohra, p. 70.

61 For an further discussion of the processes behind the formation of the Islamic Conference, see Hasan Moinduddin, *The Charter of the Islamic Conference*, Oxford, 1987.

62 Shirin Tahir-Kheli, 'In search of an identity: Islam and Pakistan's foreign policy', in A. Dawisha, *Islam and Foreign Policy*, Cambridge, 1983, pp. 68–83.

63 Shirin Tahir-Kheli, 'In search of an identity', p. 72.

64 Ayoob, *India and South East Asia*, p. 42.

65 The slight irony here is that India was the first country on the sub-continent to ban the book, representing a heightened concern over her Muslim minorities, and her vulnerability to criticism within the Islamic world.

66 State Department text supplied by the US Information Service, Grosvenor Square, London.

67 Burke and Ziring, *Pakistan's Foreign Policy*, p. 463.

68 The Americans took a firm stand on this issue, demanding compensation and guarantees, but modified their position considerably following the Soviet invasion of Afghanistan.

69 *Direction of Trade Statistics*, IMF, Washington, 1990. Within the Middle East, Egypt is the leading importer of Sri Lankan goods, while Sri Lanka imports a significant amount from Iran: US $97·7 million, more than any other Middle Eastern Country in 1989.

70 Figures taken from Shafiqul Islam (ed.), *Yen For Development: Japanese Foreign Aid and the Politics of Burden Sharing*, New York, 1991.

3

The domestic politics of South Asia: state–society relations and regional stability

The late 1980s have witnessed a curious convergence of domestic instability within India and Pakistan that will probably add to, rather than detract from, regional instability. 1988 saw the restoration within Pakistan of the principle of party-based elections and civilian rule, after a long period of military control and limited popular participation. The electoral victory of Benazir Bhutto's Pakistan People's Party (PPP) in 1988 was, however, seriously restricted by the legacies of military rule under president Zia (1977–88) and the presence of a powerful presidential figure – Mohammed Ishaq Khan. Moreover, since the PPP failed to win an overall majority in the National Assembly it could not amend the constitution to try to limit further the powers of the presidency, or limit the influence of the army. The Benazir government also faced sustained opposition from some of the states, including the Punjab, over issues of national policy.[1] Baluchistan, for example, refused to implement the PPP's National Works Programme.

Amid rumours that the military leadership under General Beg was not reconciled to the full restoration of civilian rule, and constrained by a coalition based upon volatile ethnic and regionally-based constituencies,[2] the Bhutto government faced growing domestic criticism over alleged corruption and poor economic performance. In terms of foreign policy the army were also critical of her handling of the Kashmir crisis with India, the handling of the Afghanistan resistance to Najibullah (especially in the wake of the so-called Jalalabad fiasco),[3] and Pakistan's policies in the Gulf crisis. Following significant policy disagreements with provincial governments in Sind and Punjab, Bhutto was dismissed in August 1990. Fresh elections were held in November 1990 and resulted in the victory of the Islamic Democratic Alliance under Nawar Sharif, which won 105 seats out of 207.

At the same time that Benazir Bhutto was being criticised for being 'soft' on India, the Indian coalition government of V. P. Singh was also entering its terminal phase. Since defeating Rajiv Gandhi in November 1989, the National Front government had been unable to deal with growing Hindu–Muslim violence within the northern states of Uttar Pradesh and Bihar, nor prevent caste violence over job reservations for so-called 'backward castes'. The government also failed to deal with terrorism within the Indian Punjab and the Kashmir valley, issues that it had inherited from the previous Congress government under Rajiv.

Like Benazir Bhutto's government in Pakistan, V. P. Singh's government relied for support upon a combination of secular and religious, left wing and right wing forces within the national assembly (the Lok Sabha). In the wake of increased communal violence, this elaborate combination could not be sustained.

The involvement of the Hindu-based Bharitya Janata Party (BJP) in the Ayodhya Temple dispute – the attempts by fundamentalist Hindus to demolish a mosque and build a temple to commemorate Lord Ram's birthplace in the state of Uttar Pradesh – brought down the government in November 1990.[4] After a few days of indecision, Chandra Senkhar was appointed as a caretaker Prime Minister, but his attempts to lead a 'minority of a minority' failed in March 1991 when the Congress Party withdrew its support in Parliament.

Redefining national security

In the introduction it was noted that the realist conception of international relations, which stresses the importance of the state and the interactions of sovereign states within an anarchical environment, directs attention away from the internal structures of states. Realism fails to conceptualise the ways in which internal politics shapes and directs the foreign policy agenda. Caroline Thomas has recently noted that: 'the state-centric geopolitical approach to international relations is inadequate for conceptualising the third world security environment'.[5] Buzan has also noted the tendency in the past to treat 'third world national security problems . . . as a mere extension of a systemic level dynamic', that is, as a function of superpower or great power rivalry without any reference to internal politics.[6]

The political processes that link the state to society and dominant social interests have traditionally been of little interest or relevance to the realist school. By contrast, what are sometimes referred to as the behaviouralist school of international relations stresses that core values and national interest are sociological and psychological terms; they arise from within a particular type of society and political culture. As such, they recognise that images of the international system (and the location of a state within it) are held by specific elites and are subject to specific forms of historical or cultural misperceptions.[7] The advantages of a behaviouralist-inspired approach for a study of South Asian security – compatible as they are with the main characteristics of the 'security complex' – lie in the fact that they stress the historical and sociological roots of foreign policy within South Asia. Given the degree of social diversity within the region, and the political instability and dissent within all the societies of South Asia, the so-called 'core values' of the realists are neither self-evident nor, more importantly, systemically determined by the dynamics of an international system. They are produced, reinforced, or discarded within the domestic political arena, and the domestic problems of one state quickly become projected into the domestic arena of another. Any approach to the security of South Asia that ignores or discards the primacy of domestic politics would be seriously deficient.

The view of the state as a 'homogeneous' entity is of limited use for understanding the interactions of *weak* states in which political elites face various levels of domestic dissent, either in terms of cultural and ethnic demands for political decentralisation, or in terms of broad-based secessionist movements. In the recent past, in Pakistan, Bangladesh, Nepal and even Bhutan, the institutions of state power have been controlled by small elites with little or no access to wider societal support, who have faced challenges from broad-based social movements. In all the states of South Asia, including India and Sri Lanka, social elites also face competition from *within* the state structure, from bureaucracies and military personnel over the allocation of resources and the implementation of policies.

Of all the states of South Asia, only India and Sri Lanka can lay claim to being democratic states, in which regular and generally fair political elections take place for national office. In both states, governments have been defeated and removed from power, and have done so with decorum and honour. Yet both states have witnessed delays in elections through constitutional 'states of emergency', in India between 1975 and 1977 at the national level, and quite frequently at the state level. In India as well as Sri Lanka, political parties have been banned, and opposition leaders detained. More interestingly, both declarations of 'national emergency' (India in 1975, Sri Lanka in 1972) were closely identified with particular prime ministers – Mrs Gandhi and Mrs Bandaranaike – who both faced threats of prosecution from new governments when they finally lost access to state power. Throughout the region, only India, Nepal and Bhutan have been free of attempted or successful military coups. Even in the Maldives, with a small population, there exists an Islamic underground movement known as the White sharks.

These high levels of domestic instability not only limit a state's ability to act authoritatively within the international community; they limit its ability to act upon domestic society with any legitimacy.

Economic change and political instability

One of the most important components of national security for the states of South Asia involves the need to create continued economic growth and industrial development. Each South Asian state in turn has attempted to carry through an industrial revolution to end poverty, create gainful employment, and to increase trade. The process of political and economic change – collectively (if not still teleologically) referred to as development – keeps the positions of elites within the state precariously balanced even as it legitimates their right to rule.

What is sometimes referred to as the wider 'developmentalist' notion of state security has been stated by K. Subrahmanyam thus: 'anything that comes in the way of development, either *internally or externally* is a threat to India's national security'.[8] Amongst the many criticisms levelled at the political leaderships in India, Pakistan, Nepal and Bangladesh, and which eventually replaced governments in all of them from 1989 to 1990, was the charge that they had failed to improve economic wealth, significantly reduce poverty, or retain political order. This chapter is concerned with the primacy of political violence throughout the region and reasons for its dramatic increase since the 1970s.

Developmental strategies generate internal instability by either failing to meet popular expectations of material advancement, or by failing to distribute the benefits of development equally. Urbanisation and industrialisation lead to the differentiation of social identities, change the nature and extent of various political and social demands, and question and redefine particular values.[9] In Pakistan the economic success of the Ayub Khan years were a major contribution to the military coup that removed him from power. In India, the state of the Punjab is one of the wealthiest states in India and also boasts one of the most virulent terrorist movements in the region, with a small but vocal section of the Sikh community determined to secede from New Delhi and create a Khalistan – a Sikh state.

Political scientists writing in the 1960s assumed that economic growth would lessen instability, that it would introduce so-called 'modern values' of consensus and pluralistic behaviour into these societies and that these values would prevail over so-called traditional identities. To an extent this was true, but only partially. In South Asia, socioeconomic change has helped to construct a westernised middle-class elite; it has also augmented and exaggerated the more indigenous non-western elements of social organisation, often redefining them and granting them greater political significance than they previously enjoyed.[10] Earlier, somewhat simplistic theories of modernisation failed to grasp this process entirely.

It was not to be a question of the so-called 'developmental' state overcoming the political crisis of modernisation through a gradual change in political identity, in which 'modern' forms of behaviour and attitudes overcame 'traditional' and 'irrational' forms of association such as caste and religiously-sanctioned customs. The process has been much more traumatic and bloody. The forces of 'obscurantism' – the South Asian term for competing claims of religious and linguistic sub-nationalism that stand in opposition to 'Indian' or 'Pakistani' identity – appear to have multiplied over time, thrown up by the onset of western values and the use of western political organisations.[11]

For every single Tamil group in Sri Lanka that has been willing to discuss a constitutional settlement with Colombo, three others have declared themselves as determined secessionists. For every tribal leader who strikes a deal with New Delhi to co-operate within the federal structure of India, several new groups unite to fight against the political centre and the state elite. In India the challenge is between a so-called 'modern' secular polity and the various core values of a so-called traditional Hinduism. In Pakistan, the dispute involves (at its extreme) a variant of moderate Islam and a fundamentalist Islam committed to a theocracy. Within Sri Lanka, the fight is between secularism and a particularly virulent form of Sinhalese Buddhist nationalism. In Bhutan, the issue is how some form of culturally pure tribalism can be preserved from the contamination of the developmental process, and the immigration of Nepalese, Indian and western ideas.

Until recently, the two competing political frameworks within which the elites of South Asia attempted to manage the 'development crisis' were Indian democracy and Pakistani authoritarianism, based respectively upon a secularist state and a so-called Islamic order.

However simplistic, these two conditions provided the poles of a spectrum of political control and operation within the region. Since the mid 1980s this regional spectrum has become more complex and interrelated. At the time of writing all the states of South Asia contain a component of direct elections, and all of them face a profound socioeconomic and political challenge to the basic structure and ideologies of state power.

Pakistan and the Islamic state

If India and Pakistan were based upon two separate and competing ideologies, confessional and secular,[12] they were also based upon two quite separate political discourses which would in turn sanction and legitimate different domestic political systems. The languages of secularism and the language and symbolism of Islam provided both elites with different institutions, in short, differing *capacities to rule* their respective societies and to structure their respective states.

In the absence of any one accepted definition of Islam, and given the lack of any shared cultural perceptions of an Islamic identity between the provinces of West and East Pakistan before they formed the state of Pakistan, the question asked almost immediately was: 'Whose Islam'? Who would define Islam and uphold it, and who would reconcile any differences over the lineages of the Islamic state?

While there are well-established historical lineages of the secular state (even if they are essentially western in conception), the ideas of an Islamic state remain vague and contradictory: was it democratic or authoritarian, pluralist (and federal) or unitary and hierarchical, civilian or military? Adeed Dawisha asks, 'is there really something specifically definable called Islam . . . a monolith in terms of structure and behaviour?'[13]

Differences of opinion over the political outlines of the Islamic state can be traced back to the pre-Partition period. Two separate strands of Islamic thinking took shape in the nineteenth century: one based around Aligarh, and another based about Deoband.[14] The Aligarhist strand was revisionist and liberal, committed to reworking the ideas of Islam so as to be relevant both to the socioeconomic and political imperatives of pluralistic societies which contained differing ethnic and cultural minorities, and to the economic and technological demands of an emerging (predominantly western) modern world.

In terms of this Aligarhist spirit, Islam did not stand in contradiction to the organisational principles of the nation-state or of parliamentary democracy, despite the frequency of this claim by the mullahs and the religious clergy.[15] Jinnah and the founders of the 'Pakistan' movement drew their inspiration on Islam from this particular tradition. Just before his death in 1948 Jinnah had outlined his version of a future Pakistan based upon a parliamentary system of government in which 'Hindus, Muslims and Christians could become good citizens of Pakistan'. With such little explicit reference to Islam within the 1956 constitution, cynical eyebrows were raised both in New Delhi and within Pakistan herself.

The second tradition (associated with the seminary at Deoband) concerned itself with an essentially medieval, hierarchical view of Islam based upon the powers of the clergy (the mullahs). It saw the Muslim community as a whole, immune from other divisions and competing loyalties and from the artificial identities and symbols of the nation-state. Initially many of the Deobandian scholars rejected the calls for a Pakistani state on the grounds that the ideas of national exclusiveness stood in contradiction to pan-Islamic identity. Maulana Azad, a liberal Muslim who remained within the Indian Congress Party and served in the government of independent India, opposed Pakistan on the grounds of his faith. He noted in his biography that 'it is one of the greatest frauds on the people to suggest that religious affinity can unite areas which are geographically, linguistically and culturally different'.[16]

Having reluctantly accepted Partition, the Deobadian tradition came to dominate the Islamic political parties – the Jamaat–i–Islami (JI), the Jamait–ul–Ulema–i Islam (JUI), and the Jamiat–ul–Ulema–Pakistan (JUP). These organisations, with differing emphases and slightly differing policies, took up the task of creating a real 'Islamic society' based upon the codification of the Shari'at, and the sanctioning of religious authority through the teachings and tenants of Sunni orthodoxy with regard to language (the use of Urdu), punishments for adultery, homosexuality, and theft, and Islamic ideas on interest, taxes and economic development.

Significantly, the Deobadian view of Islam stressed the conception of the Islamic community that was quite separate from the western discourse that stressed elections and a 'numerical' logic of representation.[17] The resulting stress upon the special rights of the Muslim community as a whole immediately raised questions about the role and prospects of differing minorities within Pakistan, differing sects of Muslims (such as the small Shi'ite community, a community of Muslims referred to as the Ammayyides), and the role of women.

What would fundamentalist Islamic political institutions be like? How should such a state be established, and how would it mediate the links with the wider international political and economic systems of a primarily non-Islamic world? Fundamentalists have neither commitment to provincial institutions or federalism, nor commitment to the holding of regular elections. The JI has consistently rejected talk of party-based politics, capitalism or even socialism as being western and intrinsically un-Islamic.

Recent writings on the lineages of an Islamic state have stressed the complexity of the Islamic discourses on political authority. Even the Aligarhist and Deobandian schools of thought are cross-cut by differing interpretations between an urban literati which was essentially more moderate, and a basically rural population in which concepts of Islam are either more aligned with the thinking of the mullahs or variants of *Pir* or tribal mysticism. Mohammed Waseen has recently conveyed the sheer complexity of the so-called 'Islamic tradition' by defining the 'great' and the 'little' traditions, both of which contain elements which are superficially labelled as fundamentalist in the West.[18]

The complexities of this Islamic debate were made infinitely more difficult because it took place within an elite who were so obviously separate from the communities that ended up constituting the territories of Pakistan, and because this elite could not, like India's, arrive at a consensus through a democratic system. Unlike the Indian Congress Party, the Muslim League was a foreign import, staffed by Mohijjars – the name given to the Muslim immigrants who had migrated to Pakistan from India. These immigrants, committed to the two-nation theory, displaced local provincial elites in local and national government, especially in East Pakistan. The only local elites who were able to gain access to the emerging national institutions was an essentially Punjabi one, well represented within the army and the bureaucracy. Apart from a small section of urban, Urdu-speaking Bengalis, Bengali speakers were excluded from the political structures of the Pakistani state, despite the fact that they constituted over 54 per cent of the population of the two-winged nation.

At the time of her creation, few if any Pakistani leaders openly entertained the idea of an authoritarian, theocratic state. Yet lacking access to a broad social consensus or the required prerequisites of party organisation, many leaders stressed the dangers of open democracy, which would hand over power to provincial and district leaders and risk the disintegration of the state. What *was* necessary – and this point was conceded by Jinnah – was to create a Pakistani nationalism in which the unifying symbols and language of Islam could be deployed without handing the state over to the mullahs, without excluding non-Muslims from access to, and protection under, the Pakistani state, and which would align Pakistan with the Muslim world.

Where were these symbols to be had? The answer appeared to be in a reformist, Muslim discourse that, freed of the fear of Hindu domination, could be essentially Muslim without being Islamic. The adoption of Urdu, on the grounds that one national language would speed up the creation of a national identity, and with the added bonus that is was an essentially Islamic language, caused immediate provincial violence, especially in Bengal. Only 8 per cent of the Pakistani population spoke Urdu, and subsequent attempts by the state to repress provincial languages (especially Sindhi and Baluchistani) have caused deep-seated resentment against the central government.

The 1956 Constitution

Pakistan's refusal to legitimate regional languages and dialects, part of a complicated threat-perception of subversive 'sub-nationalist' movements, has had a direct impact upon domestic stability, since demands for linguistic autonomy – accommodated in India within a federal system – have been seen by Islamabad as essentially secessionist and anti-national.

Centre–provincial friction, of which the agitations over language are just a part, have bedevilled Pakistan since its inception. Even before the first military coup in 1958, Pakistan was beset by a desperate search for an internal order sufficiently robust to stand up within the regional and international environment. It took from 1947 to 1956 to create a constitution that lasted just under two years. Various draft constitutions had been rejected because of the Mohijjar-Punjabi prejudice against East Pakistan, and the fear that, as a majority within Pakistan, they could possibly outvote the states of the Western wing and put the Punjabis under Bengali control. The 1956 Constitution gave no recognition to the provinces as political entities. It did not guarantee them any legislative primacy in areas such as agriculture and education, nor did it assure them that their governments would be free from central interference. Moreover, the 1956 Constitution sanctioned the setting-up of a unicameral legislature at the centre, from which state representation (a common feature in federal states) was completely excluded.

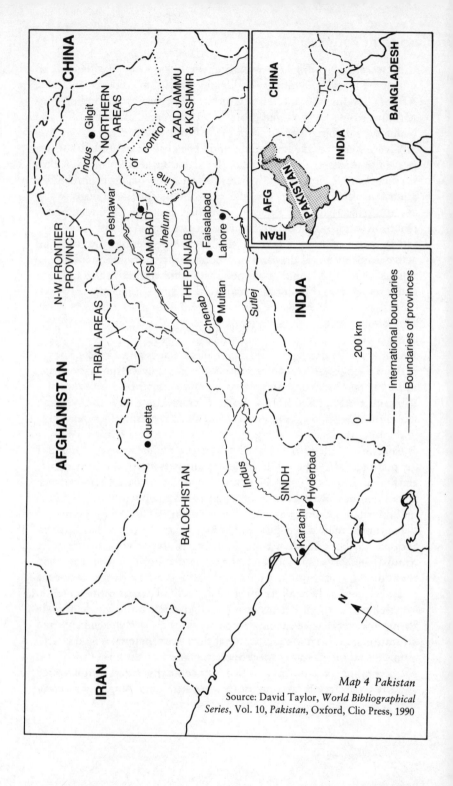

Map 4 Pakistan
Source: David Taylor, *World Bibliographical Series*, Vol. 10, *Pakistan*, Oxford, Clio Press, 1990

Between 1947 and 1958 seven prime ministers rose and fell in Karachi, brought down through intense intra-elite factional rivalries. Without any general election to link 'national' parties to particular programmes of socioeconomic development, horse-trading within the National Assembly made and unmade government majorities, while provincial politics was chaotic and increasingly violent. Jinnah's death in 1948 removed Pakistan's leading statesman, while Liquat Ali Khan, a competent prime minister with whom Nehru negotiated over Kashmir, was assassinated in 1951.

Into this vacuum stepped the Governor-General. The holder of this office – in contrast to the evolution of the office of the President in India – rather than becoming a mere adviser to the prime minister, took an active lead within the political process, dismissing the constituent assembly in 1955 because of 'factionalism' and convening another one, and frequently dismissing the prime ministers.

Such instability confirmed fears of internal disintegration, fears that were underscored by the severity of the regional security environment. In the context of weak (and weakening) party politics, these fears led to demands for strengthening the bureaucratic and military institutions of the state, and for extending the powers of the government.

Rather than stress the Aligarhist links between a reformed Islam and a Pakistani democracy (that was federal and, however paradoxically, secular in outlook), it became essential to rework the emphasis on Islam by either discarding any reference to it at all (which risked causing internal offence within the theocratic and orthodox sunnis, and the popular sentiments of mohijjars) or to stress the non-democratic, hierarchical roots of an Islamic discourse. General Ayub Khan, the architect of the second constitution, adopted the former.

This sleight of hand was made easier by the risks of internal political chaos that seemed to be overtaking the country. In 1954, the Muslim League had been defeated in the Eastern Wing by a coalition of regional and linguistic forces. The new United Front government was committed to a programme of greater autonomy for Bengal, and had ironically used as its election manifesto the Pakistan Resolution (1940) which called for a federal Pakistan. Popular demands for decentral-isation risked encouraging the smaller provinces in the West to press for more freedoms and jeopardise the very foundations of the state.

The situation was only saved through the emergency powers of the state governor, authorised by the Governor-General, and the dismissal of the newly-elected East Pakistan assembly just over three months after it had come to office. From 1956 onwards it became increasingly

clear that the interests of the mohijjar–Punjabi alliance would not be
furthered within a parliamentary, democratic state. Hence their
support for the military coup of Ayub Khan in 1958 and the subsequent
abolition of the 1956 Constitution.

The 1962 Constitution

The new Pakistani state, undemocratic and elitist, seemed much better
equipped to face off the security problems of the region, and secure
some consensus within Pakistan's troubled elite. Yet from the onset
until its collapse in 1970, the Ayubian state was perceived as being
domestically illegitimate, an institutional framework without domestic roots or loyalty, and increasingly incapable of providing the
benefits of real independence to anyone other than a small, unrep-
resentative bureaucratic elite.[19] Initially sanctioned by the need for
order, Ayub Khan found himself between a rock and a hard place,
unwilling to start any significant internal debates about democracy or
about the role of Islam within Pakistani society, and yet afraid that
stifled debate would further undermine his credibility.

At first, following the declarations of martial law in 1959, Ayub
Khan approached this dilemma with all the consummate vagueness of
Jinnah. The constitution was laid out without any explicit reference to
Islam at all. In the face of a public outcry, Ayub Khan finally included
the term 'Islam' and 'Shar'iat' in the preamble. Furthermore, he set up
a Council of Islamic Ideology that would attempt to ensure that the
civil code of Pakistan coincided with Shar'iat laws. Both were without
influence or relevance until the coming of General Zia. The Islamic fig-
leaf aside, the main purpose behind the 1962 Constitution was to set up
and sanction a non-democratic political system.

General Ayub Khan replaced the 1958 Constitution with a novel
political format in which political parties were banned, and in which
the executive office of President was indirectly elected through a series
of tiered councils.[20] Promulgated in 1959, and codified within
Pakistan's second constitution in 1962, Basic Democracies (BDs) were
an elaborate institutional device based upon election and nomination.
They were devised to cross-cut provincial identities by conceding
powers to the district and sub-district levels, and to use predominantly
rural constituents to checkmate urban areas.

As such the system deliberately underrepresented those 'forces of
political disintegration and conspiracy' (a growing middle class and a
small but articulate working class) on the grounds that they were

difficult to manipulate politically. Basic democracies provided the ideal political framework within which the mohijjar–Punjabi alliance could press on with their particular construction of 'a strong Pakistani state', with an economy geared to export-led growth and US investments, and the development of the armed forces.

Because of the BD format, the 1962 Constitution made no reference to the provinces or provincial rights for the simple reason that they had been politically emasculated. Ayub Khan's belief in a durable state–society link was that, if circumstances proved favourable (a telling condition), political participation could be encouraged, but only along the lines favoured by the centre.[21] Firm central direction would also provide a period for the gradual emergence of Pakistani nationalism and the basis for sustained economic growth. The Islamic rationality behind the state's existence was downgraded altogether within the context of domestic policies. In terms of foreign policy, attention still fell firmly upon Kashmir and the 'thousand-year war' with India as a convenient and necessary piece of rhetoric.

The economic performance of Pakistan throughout the 1960s was unprecedented, and is only partially explained by the weakness of the economic and industrial base before 1962. Central rule enabled reorganisations in planning and administration, and stability encouraged significant amounts of foreign investments.[22] That the Ayub Khan system had merely ignored (as opposed to accommodated) political dissent was apparent following the failure of *Operation Gibraltar* in 1965. Zulfikar Bhutto, the architect of Pakistan's balanced equation with China and the USA, resigned as Foreign Minister in 1967 because of Ayub Khan's acceptance of the Tashkent agreement with India.

Following this, Zulfikar Bhutto emerged as a bitter opponent to Ayub Khan, and combined an anti-Indian foreign policy with a radical redefinition of the Islamic state through his talk of Islamic socialism. The reintroduction of Islam into the political system – this time from the left – began a violent urban-based agitation that returned the issues of mass participation to the centre of Pakistani politics and finally brought down the BD system in 1969.

The socio-economic basis of the Bhutto regime

The industrialisation of Pakistan had greatly increased the urban-based middle classes, and had thus strengthened the one constituent of Pakistani society that was deliberately underrepresented within the

Basic Democracy format. The period of greatest Punjabi-mohijjar ascendency had further alienated the Bengalis, who were under-represented in both the army and the bureaucracy. There is considerable economic evidence that suggests that East Pakistan was treated as an 'internal colony', providing raw materials for export, while capital and machine goods were imported to develop the infrastructure of the Western wing. It has been estimated that between 1959/60 and 1969/70, the disparities of per capita production between the Eastern and the Western wings increased from 4 per cent (in favour of the West) to 61 per cent.[23] It has been noted that 'there is little doubt that these increasing inter-wing disparities which generated growing socio-political tensions were largely the consequence of Pakistan's economic policies and her allocation of resources for development'.[24]

The domestic roots of the 1971 civil war

Ayub Khan was removed from office by another military coup, but unlike the 1958 drama, General Yahya Khan resumed the office of Chief Martial Law Administrator to hand power back to a civilian government. The reasons behind this apparent modesty are crucial to any understanding of contemporary Pakistan: the mohijjar–Punjabi elite, beleaguered by the demands from newly emergent sections of society for popular and democratic politics, especially and most systematically from the East Wing, changed tactics in an attempt to reach some form of accommodation with the local and regional elites, opening the way for Pakistan's first – and last – national election.

In December 1969 Yahya Khan announced the holding of a general election, as well as elections within the four provinces. Political parties would be legalised. More importantly, Yahya Khan issued an ordinance known as the Legal Order Framework (LOF), a new constitutional blueprint which set down important preconditions for any future political order: that the national assembly had to frame a constitution within 120 days, that any agreement would require the consent of the President (i.e. the military) and that it would have to be parliamentary and federal.[25] Significantly, the LOF also made reference to the fact that any subsequent constitution would have to be in keeping with the tenets and keepings of Islam.

The important point – especially in the light of provincial demands and the need to ensure some form of stability – was the mention of federalism. Many commentators have argued that the army still envisaged a role for itself within the political framework of Pakistan, especially in the likely event of an indecisive outcome and the formation of a weak coalition government of the kind witnessed in the 1950s. The outcome was, unfortunately for the military, to be quite different, and the circumstances so violent that the army itself was to be largely discredited.

Over seventeen national parties campaigned in the winter of 1970. In the West wing, Bhutto and the PPP had received the support of the predominantly urban-based coalition that had been behind Ayub Khan's downfall, attracted by talk of democracy and Islamic socialism. In the East wing however, the political forces of the Awami League – the basis of which was a middle-class Bengali-speaking elite in a complex coalition with left-wing students and radicals – had laid the basis for a secular Bengali nationalism free of any references to Islam at all. The Awami League campaigned in the 1970 elections on the basis of the so-called 'six points'[26], which dated back to the policies of the United Front government of 1954 and expressed a desire for a weak federal Pakistan giving large areas of legislation to the the East wing. The Awami League did not field any candidates in the West wing. To many sections of the League, the six points were a charter for secession from the moment of its inception; to others they were points to be negotiated with a new civilianised Pakistan, and which had been mentioned within the LOF.

The elections revealed that Jinnah's version of Pakistani nationalism had simply failed to appear. The Awami League won 151 seats out of 300, all of them in the East. The PPP won eighty-one seats, none in the East, with sixty-two from the Punjab alone. The provincial elections, held at the same time, revealed a complex mosaic of competing political identities, with the Awami League clearly established in the East, but with the PPP only in control of two provinces: Sind and Punjab. In reality, the worst fears of the Mohijjar-Punjabi elite had been realised, a Bengali-speaking politician had won an election in Pakistan. The JUI won four seats in the national assembly, while the JUP won seven.

This interaction of provincial and national forces was a new experience for Pakistan. It required significant decentralisation and democratisation of the state's political structures. Yet despite an early announcement by Yahya that he welcomed 'Mujib Rehman as Pakistan's new Prime Minister', there would be no subsequent deal over the six-point programme. By March 1971 Bhutto had rejected the logic of sharing power with 'anti-national' forces. Bhutto was also insistent that the Awami League was receiving help from India, and had been doing so throughout the late 1960s. Meanwhile, Mujib's attempts to renegotiate the meaning of the six points (always vague) led to the further radicalisation of his own student wing and the possible accusation of compromising with the military.

The calculations of the military remain somewhat of a mystery. While Yahya convened several meetings between Bhutto and Mujib, the military were anxious to co-operate with Bhutto once they had accepted the 'fact' that any settlement with the Awami League would jeopardise national security. The responsibility for the decision to 'crack down' on the League and arrest Mujib Rehman in March 1971 lies presumably with Bhutto who was by then *de facto* prime minister.[27] Yet clearly he was supported by the instincts of the military.

Once force had been used (and, as we shall see, this is a valid point in India and Sri Lanka as much as it is for Pakistan), the option of a political compromise within a particular state structure was ruled out. Had the basic democracies been abolished earlier, or had Pakistan adopted within its first constitution provisions for the use of local languages, or the retention of provincially-raised revenues, the situation may well have been different. Had some form of framework existed – had a political language of federalism existed in which the provinces could make demands without implying that they were secessionist – the dialogue between Mujib and Bhutto might well have led to some solutions.

Pakistan under Z. Bhutto, 1971–77

The experience of the Bangladesh war opened up a new phase of state and nation formation within Pakistan. The humiliation of the army greatly strengthened the possibility that Bhutto and the PPP government would break with the 'martial law state', and as a Sindhi, shift state control away from the mohijjar–Punjabi axis. The new state of Pakistan would not be bedevilled by problems of internal 'parity'. She might even be consoled that, having lost the loyalty of the Bengali, Pakistan society was better suited to the tasks of nation-building than at any time since independence.

Confronted with an acute national identity crisis in the wake of the Bangladesh war, Bhutto attempted to re-establish democracy and civilian rule based upon a revivalist notion of Islam: looking back to the ideas of Jinnah and the inspiration of Aligarh. Yet Bhutto's attempt to rework a reformist Islam into a modern state was potentially more radical than Jinnah's. Drawing upon socialist and radical thinking,

Bhutto's combination of Islamic socialism was both a commitment to an Islamic Pakistan and one in which rapid socioeconomic development would overcome rural poverty and lead to sustained industrial growth.

There was virtually no room for any fundamentalist, Deobandian elements within Bhutto's early thinking, and thus no obstacles to the participation of the secular left within politics. Initially, Bhutto was willing to reopen the questions that had been in part been addressed by Jinnah, but basically ignored by Ayub: 'What aspects of Islamic belief in practice are immutable, and what areas are open to reconstruction and reinterpretation in order to respond to new social and historical conditions?'[28] To the right-wing religious parties the term 'Islamic socialism' was both oxymoronic and heretical; it contradicted the virulently anti-socialist, anti-communist slant given to Pakistan's domestic and foreign policy during the 1960s.

Bhutto's particular stress upon Islam was the point of departure for a new domestic order. Moreover, Bhutto's encouragement of Arabic within the school curriculum brought immediate benefits to her foreign policy from the Middle East, even at the same time that it engendered a wide debate within Pakistan as to her real national identity. Domestic talk about socialism also helped cement the close ties between Pakistan and China. Both domestic and foreign policy was supported by anti-Indian rhetoric, despite the commitment of the government to uphold the Simla agreement.

High on the domestic agenda, however, was the legacy of the bureaucratic–military framework and the need to defend the new democratic state. Bhutto began to restructure the army, promoting those individuals who he believed were free of any political motivation, and establishing the principle of civilian authority. At the same time he sought to appease the high command through increasing the defence budget and stepping up arms procurement. Between 1971 and 1975 defence expenditure rose from 5 per cent to 6·5 per cent of GNP (although its share in the government budget fell). The size of the armed forces increased from 365,000 to 502,000.[29] Bhutto also tried to free the bureaucracy from its predominantly colonial mind set, through changes in the entrance exams and through a proliferation in differing and state-based services.[30]

The culmination of all these policies was the 1973 Constitution. Significantly, however, the opportunities to set the record straight on provincial rights and central obligations was effectively missed.[31] While the constitution recognised the importance of provincial autonomy it did not specify those rights, or seek to safeguard them, by authorising either the supreme court or the national parliament to oversee the dismissal and removal of provincial governments by the misuse and abuse of presidential power.

By 1975/6, what gains had been achieved were clouded by Bhutto's own emerging temperament as a leader who took political rebuke badly, and who increasingly feared the extent to which his control of the political process could be undermined by the left wing within the PPP, by fundamentalist Islamic agitations from the mullahs and the Ulama, and by non-PPP governments in the provinces. By late 1973 Bhutto had refused to compromise with the National Awami Party in Baluchistan on the grounds that it had secretly embarked upon negotiations for secession (the so-called London plot), and he dismissed it from power. Faced with serious provincial violence, Bhutto deployed the army to deal with the Baluchistan crisis and to prevent the province 'doing a Bengal'. For Islamabad, the national security was almost as acute as in 1971, with possible Afghan assistance and almost certain Indian diplomatic encouragement.

Disagreements within the PPP over the handling of this crisis, as well as over the scope and direction of government economic policy, persuaded Bhutto to dismiss various left-wing ministers from his government in 1974. By 1974–5, Bhutto was also bedevilled by various allegations of personal corruption. The growth in urban violence against his regime led him to attempt from 1975 onwards to ditch the social coalition that had brought him to power, away from the urban middle class–students–working class combine, towards a fundamentally rural combination that had, in an earlier and more substantial form, provided the electoral base for the Muslim League.

Bhutto's decision to call a general election in May 1977 took place at a time when the political basis of the Bhutto regime was at its weakest. Part of this weakness was, as it had always been, a failure to establish a deep domestic consensus over the form of legitimate activity. The election, in which the PPP faced a combined opposition called the Pakistan National Alliance (PNA), was marred by violence, especially in the cities, and the electoral verdict in favour of Bhutto was put down to vote-rigging and widespread corruption.[32]

Bhutto's refusal to conceded to demands for a fresh poll led to a rapid deterioration in law and order within metropolitan Pakistan. In June 1977 General Zia, a commander picked by Bhutto himself for his apparent commitment to the civilian control of the armed forces, launched a coup, *Operation Fair Play*, for very much the same reasons that Ayub Khan had in 1958. From the viewpoint of the military, political democracy was unpicking the sinews of the nation, destroying earlier hopes for sustained economic development, and making Pakistan 'a laughing stock throughout the world'. Significantly, Zia was also a mohijjar.

The 1977 declaration of martial law put Pakistan back almost twenty years, scrapped the 'Islamic socialist' route towards a democratic federal state and backed the political system into a sustained dialogue with the fundamentalist Deobandian Muslims. Those who came to support and sustain General Zia's 'Islamisation of Pakistan' programme, that started in 1979, did so with some apprehension, and some (the JUP) were to break with Zia when they believed that he was less committed to Islam than he was to power. Zia's view of the Pakistani state ensured a role for the army within a state sanctioned by Islamic erudition. Zia tried, like Ayub, to establish a controlled system of participation, without political parties, linked to the two pillars of the old political order – the military and the bureaucracy – but this time much more explicitly sanctioned by religion. Zia carefully turned Pakistan towards an interpretation of Islam that was conservative and hierarchical, in which the symbols of Islam were more emphatically deployed, but without religious meaning or content.[33] It is what Omar Noman refers to as a view of military theocracy.

While the military sponsored various debates about the role of Islam, and invited comment from prominent fundamentalists, they were careful to ensure that dissent from the right (as much as the left) was censored or downplayed. Superficially at least, Zia accepted the view that the Islamic community was more than just a sum of individuals; it had a totality and a representative function in its own right, sanctioned by religious traditions that could not be reduced to the numerical arithmetic of elections and political mandates.[34] This was pure fundamentalism of a kind associated with JI and teachers like Maulana Maldudi, whose view of politics was essentially one of religious authority and symbolism.

Zia appeared willing at times to accommodate this symbolism to an extraordinary extent. He introduced Islamic banking and finance practices in which the charging of interest was made illegal, despite genuine concern by a Pakistani middle class that this would affect their businesses. Zia introduced the collection of *Zakat*, a tax aimed to eliminate poverty and to fund social welfare programmes. The Jaamat had long noted that: 'an Islamic economy has to conform to the dictates of the Islamic Shar'iat, in which the clear prohibition of interest is beyond doubt . . . Inflation [too] is incompatible with the goals of an Islamic economy, so too are prolonged recession and unemployment.'[35] Conservative dress codes were encouraged for both men and especially for women, as were Islamic punishments – the basis of the Hudood Ordinances of 1979, such as whippings and amputations.[36] Since traditional definitions of crime involved theft, murder, rape, etc. and not fraud, embezzlement and political corruption, the weight of such punishments fell increasingly upon the rural poor. Attempts to codify the Shar'iat led to serious religious violence with Pakistan's small Shi'ite community. Linked to the wider turmoil within the Islamic world following the Iranian revolution, Zia moved quickly to exempt the Shi'ite community from any obligations imposed upon them by religious policies they did not accept.

The 'civilianisation' of the regime (heralded after a whole series of local, presidential and national elections and one referendum) was completed in 1985, by which time the 1973 Constitution had been heavily amended but not totally replaced. It had created a powerful executive president (Zia) working over a bicameral assembly, where a prime minister was nominated by consensus. Without parties, the main basis for a prime minister was presidential patronage.

Although the outlines of the four provinces and the federal system were retained, the federal system functioned through the offices of the central government. And always, despite the hanging of Bhutto in 1979 and the attempts to isolate and undermine the PPP, there remained the possibility that the language of Islam could well return to a more radical, libertarian mode as with the case of NWFP and Baluchistan. This would raise the possibility of wider political associations outside the state of Pakistan altogether.

Why did Zia believe that an Islamic state could not sanction political parties? Was this interpretation self-evident from a casual reading of the Koran? Did his views command widespread support throughout Pakistan, or within the Islamic political parties with which he frequently consulted? The answer, if it is of any use, is no.

By late 1987 Zia was in disagreement with a whole series of domestic and foreign policy views of Prime Minister Junejo, a man effectively picked by him after the 1985 elections. Even before Zia's assassination, there is enough evidence to suggest that Zia's military theocracy had arrived at the end of another political cul-de-sac. In August 1988 the President dismissed Junejo, dissolved the national assembly and called for fresh elections. Before these could be held, however, Zia was killed in a mysterious plane crash, along with the American ambassador. In a

curious testimony to the 'special relationship', they had been in-
specting a Pakistani military installation equipped with American
arms.

1988 and the restoration

Zia survived longer than many of his critics believed possible. The
Soviet invasion of Afghanistan was of profound significance not just
for Pakistan's external orientations, but for sustaining the legitimacy
of a particular leader. Afghanistan gave Zia an external outlet through
which to bolster his domestic regime: both policies were linked to the
shibboleth of the 'pure' Islamic state. His death revealed both the
fragility of his regime and the enduring contradictions that have
remained within Pakistan since its inception.

Free of the overt personalised emphasis upon Islam that characterised Zia's regime, and weakened by the elections of 1988, the
bureaucratic–military framework remains in an uneasy truce with
popularly elected governments (both those of Benazir Bhutto and the
current Naswar Sharif administration). In this respect, the situation is
not unlike that experienced between 1971 and 1977. These governments are hemmed in by powerful military figures such as General
Aslam Beg, and powerful institutions from which popular support is
excluded (such as the Inter-Service Intelligence Unit which is alleged to
monitor both internal and external affairs). The powers of the
president can still in many ways be described as vice-regal. Gulam
Ishaq Khan has on various occasions held up decisions made by the
prime minister, and has ruled that only he can make senior appoint-
ments to the army.

With Zia's death, the ban on political parties was relaxed in both the
1988 and the 1990 elections, but until these political parties solidify,
weak national coalitions will probably come and go with predictable
frequency, brought down in many cases by political violence at the
provincial level. Such a process is unstable and precarious, and risks
giving military leaders the old-established excuse to intervene. In terms
of centre–state relations, current events within Pakistan bear an
uncanny relationship to those of 1955–57. After Zia (and Ayub) it is
not clear what the legitimate basis would be of a military government
to justify the centrality of the state, except the continual reference to
provincial instability and the continuing security threat emanating
from India. That such centralisation has caused provincial instability
has rarely occured to Pakistan's elite. Kemal Faruki has recently stated

that: 'The future of Pakistan ... seems almost inescapably linked to the reassertion of the Aligarh spirit and [a] reformist Islamic movement. Pakistan's problems require *ijtihad*, (disciplined judgement and reinterpretation) of a convincing and wide ranging nature.[37] This would require a democratisation of the state and an allowance of real participation at regional level. In an updated version of his book on Pakistan, Noman remarks: 'The Pakistani elite, civil and military needs pressures imposed through accountability . . . Elected office at various levels of power, larger allocations to the social sectors to produce a more healthy and educated population, and measures to curb the arbitrary use of powers are necessary conditions for the emergence of a less fractious and fragile nation-state.[38]

Such a mission requires not just a new domestic consensus, free of past mistrust and provincial suspicions, but a new political dialogue in which Islam is not a simple ruse for ignoring (or rigging) a federal system. Pakistan also needs, desperately, a stable regional environment in which the threat perceptions of India recede into the background. Yet Indian attempts to reassure the Pakistani government after 1988 have faltered amid sustained domestic violence in Kashmir, and the vulnerabilities of coalition governments. While a stable and deeply democratic Pakistan is vital to regional security, it requires assured regional security to succeed.

State–society relations in Bangladesh

The dilemmas that Pakistan has faced over the exact relationship between state and society have also worked themselves out within the context of Bangladeshi politics. Since its inception, Bangladesh has moved from being a secular Bengali state to an Islamic state under the auspices of the military. Since November 1990, the state has returned to a more secularised view of politics under the Bangladesh National Party. The political system remains in flux, however, with many of the constituent parts of the Ershad regime still in power. With presidential politics scheduled for some time in 1991, the possibility of further military intervention into the political system cannot be ruled out.

This apparent duplication of Pakistan's experiences after Bhutto is extraordinary given the apparent strengths of Mujib Rehman and a Bengali-speaking vernacular elite in the late 1960s. Of all the regional states, with the possible exception of the Maldives, Bangladesh is often cited as the most homogeneous culture, the nearest thing in South Asia to a nation-state. The breakup of Pakistan had removed the Mohijjar-

Punjabi elite and undermined their alliance with the minute percentage of Urdu-speaking Bengalis who had been committed to the 'two-nation' theory.

Even where divisions remained, such as the 20,000 or so Bihari speakers and the small percentage of Hindus, the resulting degree of social cleavage seemed to be much less significant than in India and Pakistan, where clearly separate regional and district identities remain, defined or bolstered by different languages or religions.

For Bangladesh, the imperatives of decentralisation raise issues that have less to do with federalism than with local and district representation, and given the relatively low percentage of urban Bengalis, rural representation at that. Why then has the identity of Bangladesh been so elusive, and the benefits of independence so poor? If the civil war was fought on the grounds that East Pakistan's intrinsic domestic identity and political culture were subject to external domination, why did that identity not emerge in a strong enough form to survive the first five years of independence? To answer these questions, the liberation struggle needs to be located within both a regional and a domestic setting.

In 1971 there were three versions of the Bangladeshi state–society relationship on offer, and three different sets of political symbolism and language that could be used as the basis to create a modern, independent state. The first version was that of a radical, almost Maoist republic in which a predominantly agrarian-based society would construct a stateless social structure based on communal and local power.[39] Such a programme was articulated by the left of the Bengali movement, predominantly students and intellectuals who combined an apparent tradition of Bengali radicalism with a then current enthusiasm for Mao Tse Tung's writings and the successes of the Chinese state. This ideological enthusiasm existed despite the fact that China had played such a negative role throughout the civil war, and despite Beijing's attempts to block Bangladesh from joining the United Nations. The Bengali left were also profoundly anti-Indian and contemptuous of Indian bourgeois democracy.

These views were popularised during the civil war itself through the activities and views of the *mukti bahini*, in which 'peasant armies' were encouraged to resist not simply the Pakistani army, but the forces of 'institutionalised' authority. The *mukti bahini* opposed the organisation of a professional army within Bangladesh after independence on the grounds that it would be used as the repressive arm of the state against the people it was alleged to defend. Those who were eventually enlisted (or infiltrated) into a professionalised Bangladeshi army took many of their radical ideas with them. Thus the civil war not only deeply and profoundly politicised Bengali society, it also politicised important sections of the national army.

The second version of Bangladesh was a bourgeois liberal view of the state, in which the institutions of parliamentary democracy would knit together a strong national identity based upon secularism. This was the view most closely identified with Mujib Rehman and the main faction of the Awami League. The disagreements between this liberal position of Bangladesh and student radicalism were submerged during the actual war, but emerged into the open once the fighting stopped. Rather like Bhutto, left-liberal divisions would force Mujib Rehman not only to expel left-wing ministers from the cabinet in late 1973, but to eventually close down the parliamentary political system under the rubric of a national emergency.

The third view – totally absent during the civil war itself but smuggled in later as part of the remains of the Pakistani phase – was what in the context of Pakistan has been referred to above as the Deobandian, theocratic, hierarchical view of an Islamic state. This vision of an independent Bengal was essentially treasonous to the causes of the civil war and many who openly proclaimed it, such as members of the Islamic religious parties, who had contested the 1970 elections, and members of the Pakistan civil service, were either charged with collaboration, banned, or dismissed from office. Yet the pro-Islamic forces regrouped following the repatriation of Bengali officers and soldiers detained in West Pakistan following the outbreak of the crisis, men who had not experienced the radicalising experiences of the civil war.

Staunch supporters of the role and value of a professional army, and tinged with Ayub Khan's belief in their domestic value, the 'repatriates' quickly found themselves in ideological disagreement with the 'freedom fighters', whose values and language they believed to be deeply subversive, and the civilian leaders of the Awami League. Initially the least popular of the three state–society blueprints, since it was a continuation of the logic of a united Pakistan, it gradually gained ground as the liberal and left-wing versions of Bangladeshi nationalism effectively eliminated each other. This victorious version of the state was as exclusive and repressive as the Zia system was to be, linked to a controlled political process in which parties would either be controlled or banned.

How do we account for the mutual destruction of a middle-class/

radical secularism? With the moderate Awami League in exile in India, and Mujib Rehman imprisoned in West Pakistan for the duration of the war, the leadership was cut off from the radicalising effects that the fighting had on the civilian population. Once installed by the Indian government, a liberal state could only be constructed once civil society had been depoliticised and put back into the grooves of a passive 'representative' system. Attempts by Mujib Rehman to co-opt the left in such an enterprise, difficult at best, were seriously weakened by the international help and assistance given to the Awami League by India, and by serious disagreements over economic policy, especially with respect to the emerging aid relationship with America.

Part of the pressure upon Mujib Rehman was what New Delhi wanted Bangladesh to look like. The government in New Delhi recognised a potential naxalite movement when it saw one, and was anxious to help the Mujib government to 'deal with the left'. Radical Maoism in Bangladesh – involving some unthinkable Chinese connection – was to be avoided at all costs, but Indian support did not help build a strong state. On the contrary, it weakened the state by discrediting the social elite who were trying to construct it as being pro-Indian.

The attempts by Mujib Rehman to put the revolutionary genie back into the bottle were further undermined by the acute socioeconomic difficulties faced by Bangladesh after the civil war and – like Bhutto in the West – by charges of political corruption. The growth in political parties after 1972 quickly reduced the Awami League to a state not dissimilar to the Muslim League: a faction-ridden spoils machine with little ideology, a mere ladder to state power. Coupled with Rehman's policies towards the civil service, again curiously imitative of Bhutto's, the ability of the government to act decisively was seriously weakened. Deprofessionalised, the civil service was undermined at the same time that it was made in charge of a growing public sector, sanctioned, like Bhutto's policies, through the language of socialism. Moreover, many competent civil servants were further purged because of their association with the previous regime.

Rampant inflation seriously limited the degree of support than the middle class were willing to give Mujib Rehman and extend to a parliamentary government. Although the failure of the Rehman government to deal with the agricultural sector was only partially to do with negligence, the possibility of sustained famine destroyed the credibility and legitimacy of his government in the rural areas as well.

Faced with a series of deep-seated, basically ideological divisions,

Rehman attempted to assert the autonomy of the state over all the main sections of Bangladeshi society, except the members of his own family.[40] Rehman's decision to set up a private paramilitary army in 1974, along with his decision to suspend parliament and create a one-party state, lost him the support of both the right and the left, both within the civilian parties and within the military.

The 1975 coups

Much has been written about the drama of Bangladeshi politics since the murder of Mujib Rehman.[41] The most important point to note about the general crisis that overcame the state was that it involved *intra-elite* disputes, taking place without any direct reference to urgent societal needs such as the elimination of poverty, and without much popular support. The coup that killed Rehman created a vacuum in which the army disintegrated into proto-Islamic and socialist groups and in which the secular, urban middle class were leaderless and dispirited.

The eventual rise of an army officer to power – Ziaur-Rehman as president (assumed 1976, confirmed by referendum in 1977) – was a piece of constitutional innovation inherited from the earlier political discourse of Pakistan. Superficially, Ziaur-Rehman seemed to represent the rise of the pro-socialist factions, since he had been an active member of the *mukti bahini*, ironically the man who had announced the birth of Bangladesh to the world from the Chittagong military cantonment in 1971. Yet the political trend of his regime was to be back towards Islam in both domestic and foreign policy, and away from India and secularism.

In 1978 Islam was introduced into the preamble of the constitution, while the term Bengali (printed on passports and on permits as proof of citizenship) was replaced by the term Bangladeshi. Ziaur also unbanned the role of the Islamic parties, and reinstated many civil servants. In foreign policy Ziaur constructed an anti-Indian strategy and a commitment to regionalism with the founding of SAARC. Ziaur also organised a rapprochement with Pakistan within the Islamic Conference Organisation, and further close ties with the US and China. Paradoxically, but with some success, Ziaur-Rehman was also careful to follow up on Mujib Rehman's commitment to the Non-Aligned Movement.

The military leadership in Bangladesh faced exactly the same problem that General Zia faced in Pakistan: how to cement a state–

society relationship that preserved the interests of a factionalised elite with reference to Islam, but without losing out to the Islamic political parties, and how to civilianise a military government enough to ensure that the military would not intervene to remove him. Ziaur-Rehman's first moves were to try and professionalise the army, a policy that involved the widespread hanging of left-wingers within the army command. As with Bhutto, Rehman ensured that the army budget was maintained in order to keep them in the cantonments, while officers suspected of radical sentiments were frequently rotated around command posts to prevent them establishing regionalised support.

Within the domestic arena, the possible strategies for legitimating power was either to forge close links with pre-existing political parties by offering them clear access to state spoils, or by constructing a party from scratch which would hopefully become the vehicle for controlled participation. Ziaur-Rehman adopted the latter – the Bangladesh National Party (BNP) – as an attempted to goad the other parties (including the Awami League) into participating within his presidential system.

Between 1978 and 1981 various attempts were made to rebuild the state, but almost all of them failed. Like Pakistan's numerous 'official' versions of the Muslim League under Ayub Khan and Zia, the BNP failed to free itself from the accusation that it was a mere creature of the central executive. Foreign policy successes – and there were several, including Bangladesh's election on to the Security Council of the United Nations – did not detract attention away from domestic failings and the weakness of Bangladesh's political institutions.

The assassination of Ziaur-Rehman in 1981 was the result of an obscure plot by a group of left-wing army officers without support within the army. In a scene somewhat reminiscent of *Julius Caesar*, the assassination took place in the vague hope that Ziaur-Rehman's death would lead to a general rebellion throughout Bangladesh and within Bengal, and restore the lineaments of the Bangladeshi state to its pre-1973 radicalism. After a few days of studied silence within the ranks, and careful manoeuvrings by High Command in Dhaka, some coup leaders were allowed to leave while one of them, General Manzoor, was killed.

For a while the state fell by default into the hands of an interim civilian administration, with the tacit support of the military under the leadership of General Mohammed Ershad. The popular election of President Sattar in November 1981, previously Chief Justice of the Supreme Court, under the auspices of the BNP was an extraordinary achievement given the circumstances, yet the large number of political parties attempting to contest the subsequent assembly elections hampered both the rule of the civilian leadership and any attempt to reconvene a constituent assembly in order to arrive at a new degree of political consensus. Sattar was unable to establish control of the army, and was finally replaced in a bloodless coup in 1982, when General Ershad assumed control of the state.

Ershad was a repatriated officer and had not experienced the violent and radicalising influences of the civil war. Like General Zia, he was closely associated with Islam, and continued the policies started by Ziaur-Rehman. From 1982 until 1990 Ershad has followed Zia in an attempt to synthesise a Bangladesh nationalism that is Islamic, and in which political participation is controlled by either banning parties or ensuring their registration before election. There were several false starts in which dialogue with the political parties failed, and in which a created official party in 1983 (the Jatiyo Dal) had been unsuccessful in broadening support for the regime. His attempt to build a viable political system also involved various local and district government initiatives.

In 1985 Ershad called a referendum in an attempt to bypass the civilian leadership entirely and in order to locate Islam at the centre of both domestic and foreign policy, and to legitimate his claim to personal rule. The referendum asked for general approval for Ershad's attempts to found a new, strong government, and called upon the opposition for general support. The official turnout was 72 per cent, with 94 per cent of the vote in favour. Foreign observers put the turn out as low as 15–20 per cent. Unperturbed, Ershad then called for local elections in 1985 as the next phase in state formation. In 1986 Ershad called parliamentary elections (which a large number of opposition parties boycotted) and presidential elections. Again, the programme is comparable with Zia's ending of martial law, which also took place in 1985.

Yet, like President Zia in Pakistan, while Ershad managed to civilianise his regime he could not establish a political consensus within domestic politics free from army support. In 1987 a decision to extend the appointment of army officers into district and local councils led to sustained opposition. The declaration of an Islamic state in 1988 did not provide the formula needed, since it ignored the cultural Bengali matrix within which Bangladeshi Islam was set.[42] While it assisted furthering Bangladesh's links with the Gulf states, it could not sanction a viable internal structure.

In 1988 Ershad held fresh parliamentary elections. The opposition parties boycotted the poll and called for Ershad's resignation. Amalgamated into two basic coalitions led by Sheikh Mujib (Mujib Rehman's daughter) and Begum Zia (General Zia's widow), the political parties continued to proliferate and limit areas of potential co-operation between them – except the overall opposition to Ershad and his regime. The ideological content of the parties remains to some extent vague and confused, although the BNP emerged committed to socialist policies and a more revisionist stance on Islam. Both coalitions contained Islamic parties.

The resignation of Ershad in November 1990 was made possible by the army's decision to distance itself from his political fate in the wake of a broad-based student revolt which was quite separate from the parties themselves. The acting President Mr Shahabuddin Ahmed oversaw elections in late February 1991 in which Begum Zia and the BNP won. It would be tempting to conclude that, as if from nowhere, the Bengali secular state has re-emerged, but the socioeconomic basis for such a state remains as weak as ever. The future of Bangladesh will be dominated by the army and the army's attitude towards instability. By themselves, there appears little to show that the parties can organise and define a clear political agenda for the country.

The state–society relationship in India

The search for the political identities of the Pakistani and Bangladeshi state have been conducted within a religious idiom that has remained problematic. The attempt has failed because the institutional structures of an Islamic state have not provided the kind of political participation desired by a particular elite. While it has provided useful and purposeful links with outside powers – especially financially – it has not so much defined the national interest as supported the interests of a small sectional elite.

India provides a striking contrast to Pakistan in terms of her stability and the apparent breadth of her political consensus. If scholars of Pakistan have spent a great deal of their time explaining why democracy collapsed, Indian scholars have spent much of their time explaining why it succeeded. It took the Nehru government just a few years (1947–49) to agree upon a constitutional document that is still essentially in existence today.[43]

At the time of independence, India's elite consisted of a multiethnic middle class who were joined together through a multilingualism based upon the English medium, the use of Hindustani (and after independence, the use of Hindi) and the local vernacular languages. They were further united through their commitment to a secular ideology and political democracy, despite the fact that a majority of Indians were Hindus (over 80 per cent). The Indian National Congress Party ensured that this elite could manage national politics by relying upon a complex set of patron–client relations that reached right down to the provincial and district level, combining numerous political cultures and idioms of power. Thus political participation, although very real, was controlled by a well-established hierarchy that recognised the rules of the game as set by New Delhi.

The entire basis of India's constitution and laws was to provide a national framework within which the rights of religious communities would be protected (Article 14), but one in which the language of religion – even that of the Hindus – would not be legitimate. All would be answerable to the same authority of the state and the state laws. The 1950 Constitution not only recognised the existence of the provinces, it granted to them important areas of legislation such as agriculture, education, and some limited revenues.

Moreover, state identities were even strengthened by national politics, and not weakened. After 1956 the states were increasingly reorganised along linguistic lines and served to strengthen national and regional identities in a way quite unthinkable in Pakistan. Articles 14 and 19 of the Constitution list a charter of individual rights of religious and political expression. Nehru survived long enough as India's first prime minister (1952–64) to establish the principles of cabinet and parliamentary responsibility, and to prevent presidential power – the modern governor-generals and viceroys of India – from taking an active part within the political system, even though India inherited the same emergency powers as Pakistan, along with a centrally-nominated governor acting within each province.

In 1952 India embarked on a series of elections which kept the Congress in power in 1957, 1962, 1967, 1971, 1980 and 1984. In 1975 and 1989 the Congress was defeated by national coalitions.[44] Provincial elections have been held throughout India's federal structure (now numbering twenty-four states) with frequent changes of government at all levels of the political system.

The language problem in India was resolved relatively easily given the fact that secularism had no association with any particular language (such as that alleged to exist in Pakistan between Urdu and Islam). India adopted a three-language formula (Hindi, English, and one of the recognised fifteen national languages) and placed them within the constitution. India even recognised Sindhi and Urdu as national languages as well. Although it recognised Hindi as the national language, the decision to retain English, and to encourage and support the vernacular languages, was to prove extremely flexible.

While claims of political exclusiveness could not be made in terms of religion, language provided a flexible basis for the incorporation of elites into nation-building on the basis of claiming special ethno-linguistic identities.[45] Yet by far the most flexible basis for nation-building was paradoxically democracy. Given India's regional diversity, the electoral significance of minorities and the need to accommodate coalitions of differing minorities became crucial for winning national elections.[46] Key minority groups, especially the Muslims, were courted and grouped together into significant vote banks within the Congress, and retained by patronage and access to state power at differing levels of the federal system.

This flexibility of 'rainbow coalitions' was essential to the success of Indian nationalism and to the success of the Congress Party. Any system that ignored this, or stressed the exclusiveness of any particular community, would shatter the nation. Thus, unlike Pakistan or Bangladesh, political disagreements within India have not taken place within an authoritarian or religious idiom in which elections have been the exception rather than the rule, or in which provisional autonomy has been mistaken for rebellion. In India the idiom has being profoundly democratic, even if it initially relied upon a few key political operators situated throughout the federal system to deliver the vote.

The reasons for Indian strength thus appear obvious: a secular polity within which various identities can coexist with apparent equal legitimacy within the territorial state, a much more clearly defined and institutional federal structure,[47] and a well-knit national party that was not uprooted by Partition. Throughout the 1950s and the 1960s these institutions continued to respond to rapid social change, and co-opt differing sections of society into an inclusive political elite. Moreover, when non-Congress parties began to form governments in the provinces after 1967 they were not immediately seen as being anti-national, although the central government was quick to outlaw or restrict those political parties who couched their policies in secessionist terms.

Yet in the 1970s and 1980s the mediation of mass voting by elites became more problematic as the elite itself began to change and disintegrate through socioeconomic change, and other sections of Indian society became more active and far-ranging in their demands. These new interests, associated with the so-called middle-caste identities, often brought non-Congress state governments to power.[48] This decentralisation of the Indian political system and the breaking-up of established parties into factions, although part of the success of the experiments with democracy and nation-building, coincided with a complex political centralisation within the Congress Party following the 1971 elections and the rise of Mrs Gandhi. These changes made the party less likely to respond to increasing diversities, and less inclined to co-opt these new and more volatile elites, who increasingly turned to their own parties or their own factions.

In a situation in which the number of political parties grew and the strength and distinctiveness of party organisation progressively weakened, the political system became increasingly competitive at the same time that it became disorganised and fragmented. If democratic politics has failed to institutionalise itself in Bangladesh and Pakistan, in India its very success has possibly led to the 'de-institutionalisation' of India's party system.[49] In a recent article on Bihari politics, Atul Kohli has noted that: 'The government of Bihar has simply stopped functioning. The levels of mobilisation along both caste and class lines are so high that nearly all the groups are fighting each other, often with their own private armies.'

How could the Congress centre appeal to what were, in reality, mutually exclusive interests working themselves free of a patron-based system of mediation? Two deceptively simple answers suggested themselves, both based upon the need to find a common denominator. One was a commitment to socialism, that characterised the Indira Gandhi government after 1967, the other was a commitment to Hinduism. Yet would the language and symbolism of Hinduism, which appealed in theory to over 80% of the population, deliver the votes? This problem was compounded by the fact that not all who subscribed to Hinduism subscribed to the same values, in just the same way that not all the Muslims of South Asia subscribed to the values of Pakistan. The myth of the Hindu majority is borne out by an examination of caste and *jati* variations, especially between the sudra (lower castes) and upper caste groups. Brahmanical Hinduism, which is heavily textual and drawn from the Vedic and Aryan scripts is quite alien to lower caste cults throughout southern and south-eastern India. Many Hindu movements are in themselves anti-brahmanical.[50]

Moreover, even if the use of Hinduism could ensure that a new

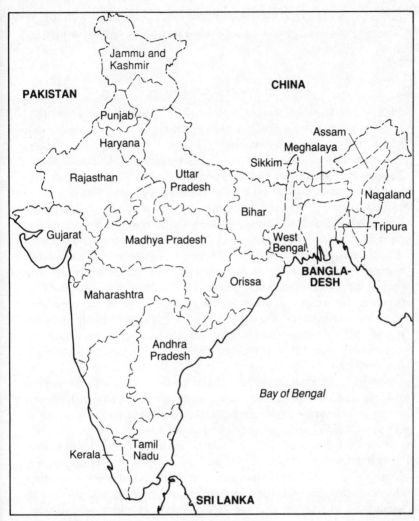

Map 5 India
Source: John R. Wood, *State Politics in Contemporary India*, 1984

coalition of interests could be built to ensure a national government security of electoral tenure, what about the non-Hindu minorities? The answer to this was to try and deploy the language of minority rights simultaneously, indeed even on occasion to create anxiety within the minorities about the Hindus, in order to enlist their support, and even legislate in their interests, but not to the point where the Hindu majority would react adversely. The result of these two paradoxical strategies was the same: religion became paramount to a political process that was once secular.

The rise of the Hindu vote

The political use of Hinduism is associated with the rise of Indira Gandhi as a national but authoritarian figure, who increasingly mistrusted political opponents and saw them as part of some Pakistani–CIA conspiracy against India. Indira Gandhi's similarities to Zufikar Bhutto in this regard are quite remarkable. Not only did she mistrust non-Congress state governments, she was mistrustful of sections of her own party, especially after the Congress split in 1969. Between 1972 and 1975 a large number of state governments were dismissed from office through the powers of the governor, a post nominated by and acting under the centre. Numerous regional parties accused the centre of ignoring the provisions of the Indian constitution that limited the emergency powers of the governors to 'serious' breakdowns in law and order. Non-Congress parties also accused the government of abusing the powers of the prime minister's office, and of misallocating government funds for private and party purposes.

The claim that the opposition parties were in league with 'enemies of the state' can also be seen in the first few years of the Rajiv Gandhi government. Playing on the concern of national unity and the fears of disintegration following the assassination of Mrs Gandhi in 1984, one of the main campaign slogans ran, 'Do You Want India's Borders to Come to Your Door'?

As within Pakistan and the Islamic parties, the political use of Hinduism by the Congress involved some risk that the Hindu parties themselves, of which there were several both before and after independence, would come to prominence on the coat-tails of Congress's Hindu rhetoric. In 1947 various Hindu fundamentalist parties called for the creation of a Hindu state on the grounds that the 'majority of Indians are Hindus'. Moreover, linked to the success of specific minorities within a federal India, Hindu parties were, from the mid 1960s onwards, emphasising the apparent 'belief amongst Hindus in India that since minorities have been better able to deliver blocks of votes, political parties have pandered to their whims against the interest of the majority.'[51] Since the mid 1980s there has been much talk of a 'Hindu India' in which minorities, especially Muslims, will become subject to Hindu laws.

Political support offered to the Hindu fundamentalist parties (such as the BJP) is very small (less than 10 per cent), although in the 1989 elections the BJP did surprisingly well in seats, but mainly because of the success of seat adjustments. In some particular localities (such as Bombay and Jaipur) Hindu chauvinist parties can get higher shares in the vote, but nationally these parties are electorally insignificant. Their position is almost exactly similar to that of the many Islamic religious parties within Pakistan and Bangladesh. But where is the possible threat to secularism from what amounts to a mere cynical and symbolic use of religious symbolism?

The threat comes from the attitudes of the major parties, especially the Congress, towards a growing cultural assertion of Hinduism which it has itself helped to encourage, but which it is no longer able to control. The apparent complicity of the Congress under Indira Gandhi in the use (and abuse) of Hinduism as a political vote-catcher allowed the fundamentalist parties, almost for the first time, to alter the agenda of the Congress and to seriously weaken its appeal to the minorities.

Since the mid 1980s, organisations such as the Vishwa Hindu Parishad (VHP) and the All India Nationalist Forum have gained greater access to the Congress, and have sought to reintroduce the symbols of Hinduism within Indian life. This revival involves the public holding of 'punjas' – religious festivals and ceremonial processions – often through Muslim strongholds and past mosques, with the deliberate intention of provoking communal violence. The political policies of these organisations include the abolition of the various constitutional provisions safeguarding minority rights, clear priority accorded to the army and the armed forces within India, and the declaration of India as a Hindu state.

Muslims in India

Since the mid 1980s, the Congress's attempts to use both Hindu and Muslim symbols to ensure political loyalty has merely divided Indian society further. An interesting example of this is the Shah Bano case, which can be described as being about 'a fundamental disagreement over how differing communities perceive the concept of justice and a just system of laws'.[52] The Congress's support for the Muslim Marriage Act (which exempts Muslim women from India's civil code and allows Muslims to undertake religious legislation) enraged Muslim moderates and women's groups, and further offended the Hindus who had themselves accepted a secular code on marriage and divorce in the mid 1950s. Muslim moderates – rather like their Aligarhist cousins in Pakistan – find themselves in the middle of a difficult and dangerous debate since they appear to sanction adherence to a secularism that is effectively Hindu.

The inability of the Congress leadership to take a decisive stand against communal forces lost the support of many of the minority vote-banks in the 1989 elections, particularly the Muslims and resulted in a historic national electoral defeat, its second only since 1977. V. P. Singh, an erstwhile cabinet minister of the Congress, had united the opposition and come to power in order to oppose government corruption, and to take a stand in favour of the Muslims and other minorities, but even the new government was forced to confront the realities of a growing Hindu lobby.

The National Front electoral manifesto made specific references to the crisis within Indian nationalism and criticised the Congress for introducing communal themes into politics. They were particularly critical of Rajiv Gandhi's decision to start his campaign at Ayodhya. The election results of 1989 produced almost exactly the same situation as the 1988 elections produced in Pakistan: a minority government containing an extraordinary combination of parties drawing upon radically different support. The Janata Dal party had to go into coalition with both the communists and the communalists.

It was within this context that the Babari Masjid/Ram Janambhoomi crisis at Ayodhya became so central to the survival of the government and the relevance of a secular polity. The structure at the centre of the dispute is a mosque that many Hindus believe was once a temple and the birthplace of Lord Ram, an important Hindu god. They argue that the mosque was built after the Moghul invasions and that, since the Moghuls have gone (to *their* state of Pakistan), the temple should be restored by the Indian government.

Subsequent demands to demolish the mosque and reinstate the temple have surfaced throughout the British period, and periodically since 1947. From 1987 onwards, Hindu political parties agitated for the demolition of the mosque and the construction of a temple and organised various religious ceremonies in and near the mosque that significantly heightened the communal temperature throughout India. In 1989 the Rajiv Gandhi government dithered between its fear of offending the Hindus and its fear of loosing the Muslim vote. The result was a political impasse into which the fundamentalist parties took the initiative. Muslim moderates fear that the end of a secular state will destroy their economic and political status, while more fundamentalist (and rural) Muslims fear that events at Ayodhya are the beginning of a concerted drive to 'integrate' the minorities into Hindu culture.

Many religious sites in India are shared sites, many mosques are alongside or close to Hindu temples, and both – despite Pakistan – are part of a sub-continental culture. The factual debate about the authenticity of the temple site have become irrelevant – as specious as the attempts in Sri Lanka to trace the lineaments of a 'Tamil' kingdom that pre-dates the Sinhalese, or viceversa. If Hindu claims to Ayodhya are endorsed and the mosque is pulled down, the secular state will enter into a protracted and potentially fatal crisis. Attempts to satisfy the political demands of two defined communities will alienate the Muslim minority and the Hindus, since part of these demands concerns their exclusivity and primacy within the state as a whole. Each 'round of concessions' will have a ratchet effect on subsequent demands. The Nehruvian concept of secularism was not simply that the state would accommodate differing religious demands, but that the language of religion was illegitimate within national politics. It had been on this basis that he had so opposed the creation of an Islamic state of Pakistan. An alteration in the 'core values' of India from a commitment to secularism towards some notion of Hindu fundamentalism is not inevitable, but it is a trend that has been encouraged by the weakening of political parties and a reduction in their ability to resist fundamentalist pressure.

The Muslims are an important and growing minority within India. They number just over 10 per cent of the population. Relatively secure within the framework of a secular state, recent increases in communal violence have exposed not merely their vulnerability, but the inability of the state to defend them. Of particular concern is the failure of the police force to deal with domestic violence; in some cases they have actually joined in or instigated communal rioting. Pakistan has condemned recent incidents in India, such as the outbreaks of violence in Hyderabad and Agra.[53] Such events appear to bear out the long-held Pakistani prejudice that India is in reality a Hindu state.

The Sikhs of India

The crisis of the secular state in India not only concerns the Muslims, however. The assassination of Indira Gandhi in 1984 by her Sikh bodyguard, and the resulting pogrom of Sikhs by Hindus, brought to a head a much more curious communal divide between two communities who are directly related and have much in common in terms of religious and social practice.[54] The killing of Hindus by Sikhs sharply redefined the ethnic identity between the Sikh and Hindu communities.

All of the Hindu fundamentalist parties define Sikhs as part of the Hindu community. Yet the very proximity of the Sikh identity to mainstream Hindu culture, and the degree to which the Punjab has been economically integrated into India, has precipitated a cultural crisis that has threatened to undermine the community's exclusiveness.[55] In response, sections of Sikh society, and the Sikh political party, the Akali Dal, have demanded greater autonomy within India, while some extreme sections have called for the creation of a separate state altogether.

As with Hinduism generally, ethnic identities have been subject to exaggeration by political parties in search of electoral gains. Both 'moderate' Sikhs and 'moderate' Congress officials have throughout the 1980s used the threat of terrorism (and even the terrorists themselves) to pursue elections to state or national office. The result has been an escalation of violence and the splintering of Sikh opinion as to the core of their cultural identity, and what place this identity has within a federal, secular India. In response to the killing of Hindus, the 'majority' attitude has hardened in support of 'firm action' against minorities – which was part of the Congress's national election campaign in the 1984 and 1989 elections. Factionalising parties, and the suspension of the normal political process in Punjab since the mid 1980s have led to a sense of crisis and drift, which have in part been used by the Congress to play on the fears of the Hindu majority to vote for the Congress to ensure national unity. In 1990 it was reported that large parts of the Punjab were being run by Sikh separatists, enforcing the use of Punjabi, and enforcing dress codes on the women.[56]

Punjab occupies an area of strategic significance to India along the western border with Pakistan. Despite Sikh complicity in the anti-Muslim violence in 1947, the Indian government claims that the Pakistan government is supporting the terrorists' demands. These claims are periodically backed up with exhibitions of Pakistani-acquired American or Chinese weapons dumps, or 'evidence' of Pakistani training camps for Sikh terrorists along the border. Not only has this affected India's relations with Pakistan, it has affected her links with Canada, the US and Britain, in which sizeable Sikh minorities agitate for a 'Khalistan' without restriction. Calls for an independent Sikh state are situated at the heart of the regional stand-off between

India and Pakistan. The secession of Punjab, should it ever come about, would further weaken the ideological basis of Indian nationalism.

Prospects for India

One of the obstacles in the way of a fundamentalist Hindi state is the predominantly urban-based Indian middle class: like Islam in Pakistan, Hindu values are stronger within a rural, agrarian setting than they are within the capitalist environment of the cities. Secularism was not just an ideological commitment, it was a route to status and power for a middle-class elite within the party and, through the party, the state. It was also a route to nation building. Should the government's language and ideological orientation change, the middle class could possibly move towards some endorsement of a politicised Hinduism simply as an attempt to guarantee their continued access to power, despite the possibility that long-term contradictions between Hinduism and the material foundations for a capitalist system could endanger the entire future of the middle class.[57]

Of more immediate concern are the problems associated with the idea of the 'Hindu majority' and the existence of minorities within India. Given the size and complexity of India's political structure, the risk of alienating the minorities is a risk of alienating the nation. India has aptly been described as the land of minorities: 'Muslims are not the only religious minority, for every religious community, and every linguistic group faces a minority situation in one or more states of the Indian Union.'[58] Sanjib Baruah has noted in the context of Assam that 'the label Assamese can be either inclusive or exclusive, depending upon the exact political use behind the definition: politics constitutes and reconstitutes these categories. An "ethnic group" is in reality an ethnic coalition potentially divisible into many smaller groups.'[59]

If the concept of a 'minority' is relative and fluid, so is the concept of a majority. Rajendra Singh, political leader of the Rashtriya Swayamsevak Sangh (RSS) party, a communal organisation with substantial links to the present Bharati Janata Party, noted recently that the goal of the RSS was to create a Hindu nation: 'our society should be homogenous, let India be a Hindu commonwealth'.[60] The belief that there can exist a Hindu nation is, however, a political fiction, since Hinduism as a religious identity is heavy subsumed by differing languages and local custom. That 82·6 per cent of the Indian population are Hindu is merely academic, as much as the 'two nation theory' that led to the creation of Pakistan is academic. Of the 82·6 per cent of Hindus, less than 40 per cent speak Hindi, and Hindi contains various dialectical differences from region to region. How would a religious state settle the language issue, the legitimacy of the fifteen recognised national languages, if it assumed that spoken Hindi must be given priority within a Hindu state?

The inflexibility of a religious discourse to deal with the diversity of a democratic, federal India is self-evident. If economic issues are considered, then the divisions between dominant and lower castes within Hindu society become even more obvious. In 1990 intra-Hindu violence was sparked off by the announcement that the Indian government would increase the number of job reservations for 'backward classes' – a category that is defined with reference to economic and not ascriptive notions of backwardness. What appeared to be culturally homogeneous (i.e., even Hindu sudra castes) potentially disintegrated under economic pressure. Even if there were subscribed Hindu institutions laid down within an equivalent of the Koran, a Hindu state will not be a strong state, it will not overcome the problems that have been 'caused' by secularism. It will not give the state access to a ready-made nation. It is not even clear that it could build a state. As yet, attempts to construct some form of religiously sanctified monarchy, such as that witnessed in Nepal, has not been started or even suggested.

State-society relations in Sri Lanka

For the pessimists who have written off the 'great Nehruvian' adventure with secularism as a long delusion, a form of Hindu reformism, Sri Lanka is seen as the end-game of a multi-ethnic society caught within the tensions of the unitary state. A detailed resumé of the civil war in Sri Lanka is unnecessary and many have now been presented.[61]

Put bluntly, what is at issue is the long-felt economic and cultural grievance of a Sinhalese Buddhist 'majority' against an articulate (and indigenous) Tamil minority who, as a minority, have apparently fared far too well both under the British and after independence. As in India, the myths of the 'pampered minority' are the reverse side of the claim that the majority have somehow been suppressed and silenced. What makes this situation even worse is that the Tamil minority make up an overwhelming majority – 95·6 per cent – of one province, situated on the Jaffna peninsular, and also constitute significant minorities in the district of Trincomalee (33 per cent) and a large majority in Batticoloa (70 per cent). Both of these districts lie in the eastern province. While the distributions of economic wealth and employment make up much of the grievances felt by both sides, what is also at issue is the role that cultural and religious symbolism plays within Sri Lankan society and within the structures of the state.

The economic development of Sri Lanka has been essentially mixed. Sri Lanka has since independence been committed to a welfare state, and has managed to achieve remarkably high scores on the Physical Quality of Life Index (PQLI).[62] Government policies on education, food subsidies and basic health care has ensured that 'development in Sri Lanka (has) created conditions that are conducive to continuing public participation in the decision-making process'.[63] This success, which is no small achievement, is nonetheless part of the process that has sowed the seeds for sustained ethnic conflict within the island.

As with India, Sri Lanka presents a whole series of cross-cutting social cleavages that have, at various times, been openly courted by political parties. The first series of cleavages are linguistic. Sinhala is spoken by the majority of the island (74 per cent) followed by Tamil (about 18 per cent). Members of Sri Lanka's political elite (comprising initially westernised Tamils and Sinhala speakers) often speak English as a first or second language. These cleavages are overlaid by religious ones.[64] 69 per cent of Sri Lanka's population is Buddhist, and an overwhelming majority of these speak Sinhalese; over 15 per cent are Hindus, while 7 per cent are Muslims. A further 6 per cent are Roman Catholics.[65] The Tamil language has tended to unite, until quite recently, Hindus with Muslims, and has incorporated some Christians, although many Christians are Sinhalese speakers. The Muslim community is split between those of Indian, Sri Lankan and Malay origins.

If these sociolinguistic divisions are not enough, they are further broken down by general cultural differences between highland Sinhalese (who provide the backbone of the Buddhist-Sinhalese majority) and lowland Sinhalese, differences that were in part encouraged (and further developed) by the British and British colonial policy. It has already been noted that the Tamil language could not unite the Sri Lankan Tamils with the Indian Tamils, although this situation began to change after 1983 when, following widespread anti-Tamil violence, Indian Tamils sought protection in the Tamil majority areas.

Ideological issues, rising out of the rapid socioeconomic transformations since independence, have also left their mark on various communities, with both Sinhalese and Tamil ethnic extremism being associated in part with left-wing or Marxist fundamentalism. The language of socialism (and more, of Maoism and radical Marxism-Leninism) is used to further the interests of both Tamil and Sinhalese chauvinism. The radical JVP movement is both pro-Sinhalese and Marxist, and both ethnic communities have stressed their ideological identities to gain financial support from the communists (either the Soviet Union or China). In 1971 the JVP launched an insurgency against a government that was already identified with pro-Sinhalese policies.

The genesis of the crisis

In rough chronological terms, since 1947 the Tamil minority have felt increasingly excluded from national politics. Between 1951 and 1970 Tamil politicians demanded some form of federal arrangement to guarantee Tamil rights and interests. Yet in 1976, Tamil political parties representing Sri Lankan Tamils, and united under the title of Tamil United Liberation Front (TULF) spoke in terms of a separate Tamil state of Eelam consisting of both the northern and the eastern provinces. This demand has been made following alleged attempts by the Sri Lankan Freedom Party (SLFP)–Left coalition under the first republic (1972–78) to destroy the Tamil language, to limit Tamil access to the universities (and hence government jobs), and to enshrine Sinhalese Buddhism as the national religion.

If Sinhalese national identity is problematic, based as in Pakistan upon an elusive link between language and religion, the concept of an independent Tamil state is even more so. Language has failed to provide the basis for agreement within the Tamils, even though it has provided the basis of opposition against the Sinhalese majority. What has characterised the pattern of communal violence in Sri Lanka's eastern and northern provinces since 1983 has been the killing of differing Tamil groups on the grounds of their ideological orientation, or simply through the escalation of factional competition. Moreover, Tamil-speaking Muslims have complicated the matter by recently demanding significant autonomy for their own community. Under the terms of the 1987 Indo-Sri Lankan Accord, the Indian government adopted and supported a rival group of Tamils, the EPRLF (Eelam Popular Revolutionary Liberation Front) which with Indian support contested provincial elections in 1988. Following the Indian withdrawal, EPRLF faced the wrath of the Tigers and most of them left with the Indian Peace Keeping Force.

The Tamil Tigers are just one of many Tamil groups strung between those committed to the creation of an independent Tamil state and those who are still committed to decentralisation and autonomy through some form of federalism. Each successive attempt to deal with the Tamil problem has spawned another set of Tamil parties and interests that have been opposed by other Tamil interests. The real tragedy of Sri Lanka is that, like East Pakistan in 1971, the chance to deal within the framework of the state has probably now passed.

It is necessary to underline several comparative points that link the identity of the Sri Lankan state and the crisis that has beset nation-formation with South Asia as a whole. The first point is that the influence of party-based political competition on redefining ethnicity in terms of 'vote banks' and political agendas, as in India, cannot be overestimated, for it was the '[P]olitical competition between the Sinhalese political parties, united Sinhalese fronts and Sinhalese Buddhist movements [that] prevented an easy solution to Tamil demands'. It also actually furthered the alienation of Tamils, and shaped the nature of the demands that the Tamils were putting forward themselves.[66]

At the beginning of independence Sri Lanka's political elite were closer to those of India than Pakistan, a multiethnic and multilingual elite united in their use of English and their commitment to western values. Smaller than their Indian counterparts, they were at one remove from the many local and regionalised idioms of the island's politics.

Although communal tensions were certainly not absent during the British period, political elites delivered votes through patronage. Such a system worked indirectly, in spite of the existence of a universal franchise since the 1930s, since between Colombo and the Provinces were situated tiers of local interests that did not impinge upon national politics. Under the Soulbury Constitution that came into effect in 1947, Sri Lanka was secular and parliamentary, with legislation to defend the minorities in the form of Section 29 (and the various sub-clauses that defended the freedom of religious practice). Although it has nine provinces and twenty-four districts, these have been administrative as opposed to political units. The British envisaged a unitary state based upon a variant of local governments as practiced in Britain.

While Sri Lankan Tamil opinion was critical of a relatively centralised state that made no concessions to regional and local districts, Tamils retained their links with national power through the Tamil section of the westernised political elite. While demands for a federal state were a common part of the Tamil agenda (especially among the Sri Lankan Tamils), demands for a separate state were made outside the main social elite and did not impinge upon the political language of the unitary state until a crisis of identity set in within the first generation of this westernised elite itself, and the breakdown in the structure of political mediation occurred.

Political independence after 1950, coupled with broad-based socio-economic change within Sri Lanka, deepened popular participation and brought local and national idioms together for the first time. Part of this resurgence was a demand for a Buddhist, Sinhalese-speaking state. To the first generation of Sri Lanka's elite, such as Don Senanayake (1947–52), Dudley Senanayake (1952–3) and Sir John Kotelawala (1952–6), the importance of Buddhism to Sri Lanka was almost as obscure as was the importance of socialism. Yet to other politicians the symbols of language and religion struck a chord, especially since they held out the promise of political power.

The SLFP, formed by Solomon W. R. D. Bandaranaike in 1950, was an offshoot of the UNP. It was caused by personal intra-elite differences over party positions, and a disagreement over the role that Buddhism was to play after independence. From 1950 until its first electoral victory in 1956, the SLFP both responded to, and directed, popular agitation in and around the central Kandyan areas to give Buddhism a primary place within independent Sri Lanka. In 1953, the All-Ceylon-Buddhist Congress had issued a wide-ranging report entitled *The Betrayal of Buddhism*. The report criticised the western, apparently pro-minority government of the UNP, and its rhetoric and values found their way into the SLFP manifesto of 1956.

This commitment, part of a concerted effort to make inroads into the UNP's electoral majority, also involved a commitment to the Sinhalese language. Active in the agitations (focused through the 2, 500th anniversary of the birth of the Buddha) was the *bhikku*, the Buddhist clergy who deployed the idiom of a religious community as part of the wider claims in favour of the Sinhalese language and the Sinhalese race. The *Betrayal of Buddhism* had noted: 'the history of Sri Lanka is the history of the Sinhalese race. Buddhism is the golden thread running through the history of the race and the land.'[67]

In 1956 Mr Bandaranaike passed legislation that made Sinhala the only official language for the island. The result was widespread rioting in the Jaffna peninsular (the heartland of Sri Lankan Tamil identity).

Under pressure, Bandaranaike compromised and formed a pact with the Tamil leader of then Tamil Federal Party, S. J. V. Chevanayakam. This pact ensured that the government would legislate for the 'reasonable' use of Tamil through the Tamil Special Provision act. The result was Bandaranaike's assassination by a Buddhist cleric in 1959 for failing to uphold the interests of the Sinhalese. In 1960, the UNP was returned on a bare minority of seats and in a subsequent election in the same year was defeated by the SLFP, led by Mr Bandaranaike's widow. Faced with such an electorally successful strategy, the UNP also started to issue statements and policies that would appeal to the Buddhist-Sinhalese majority, recognising the electoral futility of supporting the minority if the result of this was to hand over a Sinhalese majority to the opposition.

As ethnic identities sharpened, the Tamils demanded various constitutional reforms that would preserve their identity, especially in the Jaffna peninsular and in key districts of the eastern province. The obvious formula was either a federal state, or some form of local government scheme involving a significant degree of autonomy and access to state funds. By the mid 1960s, with both UNP and the SLFP governments tied to a volatile Sinhalese vote, attempts to meet Tamil demands through political devolution led to increased radicalism on behalf of the Sinhalese Buddhists.

Forced to compromise for fear of losing the 'majority', and driven from behind by a radical Marxist pro-Sinhalese movement, both UNP and SLFP government indecisiveness merely hardened Tamil opinion and Sinhalese demands. The turning point came in 1983. V. Pranhakaran, the leader of the Tamil Tigers, detonated a land mine that killed thirteen Sinhalese soldiers. Throughout the island the Sinhalese retaliated by killing Tamils. Over 60,000 Tamils were displaced from their homes during the violence. As in India in 1984, government attempts to secure Tamil lives appeared to some to be half-hearted and even negligent.

Political devolution and reform 1983–90

Attempts to satisfy demands from both the moderates and extremists within both communities squeezed out the middle ground: in this case the ability of Tamil demands to be settled within a federal constitution and for the Sinhalese majority to accept a significant degree of political devolution. It is this dynamic that can be traced within Pakistan during the period 1966–71, and which may well be working out within India now. What has made matters worse for Sri Lankan attempts to deal with the Tamils is that Tamil agitation has taken place within a region dominated by India, and the belief that India was both training and funding Tamil terrorists.

Three attempts have been made to devolve power to the provinces and to restore internal consensus to Sri Lanka. The first attempt, the so-called 'Development Council' plan of 1982, failed to satisfy Tamil demands because it was based upon district – not provincial – autonomy. Rather like Ayub Khan's Basic Democracies, this was partially in order to prevent ethnic solidarity coalescing at the provincial level, but partly in recognition that the ethnic make-up of the provinces (especially the key eastern province) did not reflect the ethnic make-up of particular districts. The Tamils also objected to the level of central supervision in the setting-up of the councils and the appointment of the district minister.[68]

The second attempt was an integral part of the Indo-Sri Lankan Accord of 1987 which gave significant powers of devolution to the provinces, and more critically, merged the northern and the eastern provinces into one. This policy, seen as part of India's policy to 'invade' Sri Lanka, was bitterly opposed by radical Sinhalese and the JVP as well as members of the government, including Premadasa. For the duration of the Indo-Sri Lankan Accord, the JVP launched campaigns of terror against the Sri Lankan government, appearing to have successfully infiltrated the government's security forces, and to have forced the government on to the defensive in the more prosperous southern areas.

The Indian government was neither capable of negotiating on behalf of the Tamil Tigers, or with them. The Tigers' boycott of the provincial elections within Jaffna undermined their legitimacy and descredited those Tamil groups who were willing to co-operate with the government and the Indian Peace Keeping Force (IPKF). With the Indian withdrawal, the Premadasa government annulled the merger of the northern and eastern provinces in deference to Sinhalese sensitivities.

The third attempt follows from the government's recent decision to embark upon a plan to 'copy' the Indian federal system and grant the nine provinces 'significant' powers of devolution – although it remains unclear what these powers entail and which Tamils actually support the initiative. At the same time, throughout 1990, the government resumed the job of the 'all-out offensive' in Jaffna and the north against Tamil terrorism, and in the south against the JVP insurgents.

Summary

All the states of South Asia are weak and dominated by serious domestic conflict that wastes resources and endangers bilateral relations. Lawrence Ziring, a well-known commentator on Pakistani affairs, has recently noted that 'both India and Pakistan have internal problems that they cannot solve and which are likely to intensify with the passage of time'.[69] The consequences of this for Indo-Pakistan relations is important.

Given the degree of domestic instability and flux, and given the sheer degree of cultural overlap that exists between the states of South Asia, it is clear that issues and concepts of national security must be based upon an assessment of domestic politics, and the nature (and flexibility) of their political systems. There is an old fashioned, essentially western prejudice that democratic societies do not go to war with each other. This view has often been expressed by India about Pakistan. Within South Asia, where increased levels of democracy open up levels of direct political competition, the resulting insecurities, on behalf of both emerging and disintegrating elites, could well imperil regional security.

The ability of the various political elites within South Asia to deal with social tensions is a function of their ideological and institutional strengths. The argument has been in favour of secularism, but secularism requires a political elite who are committed to it ideologically and who benefit from it economically. Even this is not a guarantee that the nation-building project will succeed and that, one fine day, the states of South Asia will reach the fine sunlit uplands of modernity. This is a cruel paradox. In the context of South Asia, strong states are legitimate states, well integrated within a democratic and economically viable nationalism. This is a long-term goal for India, Pakistan and Bangladesh as much as it is for the small Himalayan kingdoms of Bhutan and Nepal. Yet the demands (and the disturbances) of development may weaken the state in order to strengthen it.

The degree of internal instability – a key factor of the region's insecurity – cannot be overcome through socioeconomic development *alone* since the pace of transition is contributory to the problem. While growth must be ensured, it requires imaginative political management with an elite that is under constant pressure from below. While in terms of military and economic performance, states like India are 'middle powers', in terms of social development they are still very much part of a volatile 'Third World'. This is a serious – and continuing – weakness.

F

Notes

1 Omar Noman, *Pakistan: Political and Economic History Since 1947*, London, 1990, Ch.6. See *The Economist*, 27 October–2 November 1990.

2 The PPP government entered into a coalition with the Mohijjar Qaumi Movement (MQM), which was based in the urban centres of Sind. Serious ethnic violence between the Mohijjars (Urdu speakers) and Sindhi speakers has been a characteristic of Karachi and Hyderabad since independence, but the level of ethnic violence reached almost endemic proportions in the early 1980s and again in the mid 1990s.

3 The Pakistani Inter-Services Intelligence Unit (ISI) recommended in January 1989 that the Mujahideen be persuaded to fight an open 'set' battle to take the city of Jalalabad, and move away from its earlier patterns of guerrilla fighting favoured before the Soviet withdrawal. The battle failed and led to attempts by the civilian government to remove the head of the ISI – General Hamid Gul. See S. Burke and L. Ziring. *The Foreign Policy of Pakistan*, Lahore, 1991, p. 472.

4 For a discussion of the Ayodhya see N. Nugent, *Rajiv Gandhi*, London, 1990. The Temple/Mosque dispute has surfaced several times since independence. See also S. Gupta, 'The gathering storm', in M. Bouton and P. Oldenberg, *India Briefing*, 1990, Boulder, 1991, pp. 25–50.

5 C. Thomas, 'New directions in thinking about security in the Third World', in Ken Booth (ed.), *New Thinking About Strategy and International Security*, London, 1991, pp. 267–86 and see P. S. Jayaramu, *India's National Security and Foreign Policy*, New Delhi, 1987.

6 B. Buzan, 'States, people, fear', in Edward E. Azar and Chung In- Moon (eds.), *National Security in the Third World*, London, 1988, pp. 14–43 and see the second edition of B. Buzan's book entitled *States, People, Fear*, London. 1991. This contains an extension of the security complex idea.

7 See, for example, Robert Jervis, *Perception and Misperception in International Relations*, Princeton, 1976. See earlier works on cognitive adaptation and conditioning such as K. Boulder, *The Image*, Chicago, 1956.

8 S. Subrahmanyam (ed.), *Our National Security*, New Delhi, 1972, cited in Jayaramu, *India's National Security* (emphasis added).

9 The classic text on this is in many senses Ernest Gellner, *Thought and Change*, London, 1964. See the chapter entitled 'Living on the upward slope'.

10 See for example Lloyde Rudolph, *The Modernity of Tradition: Political Development in India*, Chicago, 1967.

11 Similar themes have been discussed in connection with the African state and the so-called problems of 'tribalism'. See B. Freund, *History of Tropical Africa*, London. 1986 and *The African Worker*, London, 1988.

12 See Sumit Ganguly, *The Origins of War Within South Asia*, Boulder, 1987.

13 A. Dawisha, *Islam in Foreign Policy*, Cambridge, 1983, p. 4.

14 J. L. Episoto (ed.), *Islam in Asia*, Oxford, 1986.

15 J. P. Piscatori, *Islam and the Nation-State*, Cambridge, 1986.

16 Cited in Rajmohan Gandhi, *Understanding the Muslim Mind*, Harmondsworth, 1987.

17 For a further discussion of the ideas of this Islamic community and an explicit Islamic political discourse, see the very interesting Farzana Shaikh, *Community and Consensus in Islam: Muslim Representation in Colonial India*, Cambridge, 1988.

18 M. Waseem, *Politics and the State in Pakistan*, Lahore, 1989. The 'great tradition' is essentially urban, the 'little tradition' is basically agricultural and rural – but Waseem is an excellent and bold introduction to many contemporary debates within Pakistan.

19 See Tariq Ali, *Can Pakistan Survive?*, Harmondsworth, 1983.

20 See L. Hayes, *Politics in Pakistan: The Struggle for Legitimacy*, Boulder, 1984, and Omar Noman, *An Economic and Political History of Pakistan*, London, 1990.

21 Ayub Khan's policy has been quite rightly compared to colonial strategies of 'indirect rule' in terms of political representation. And it suffered from the same drawbacks: the construction of 'tame' political forces which lacked credibility because they were seen as being lackies of a particular regime. See S. Burki, *Pakistan Under Bhutto*, London, 1989. and the first part of Noman, *History of Pakistan*.

22 See 'The Pakistan economy since independence', *Cambridge Economic History of India*, Cambrige, 1983, vol, 2.

23 *Cambridge Economic History*, p. 1022.

24 *Cambridge Economic History*, p. 1023.

25 Noman, *History of Pakistan*, p. 46.

26 One of the main points in the Awami League's programme was the commitment to federalism and provincial power. See L. Rose and R. Sisson, *War and Secession: India, Pakistan and the Creation of Bangladesh*, Princeton, 1990.

27 One of the last meetings between Rehman and Bhutto took place in the Governor's Residence in Dhaka, where to the irritation of Bhutto, the Awami League banner was flying in place of the Pakistan flag. Sisson and Rose report that the final conversations took part in a bathroom, because Mujib feared that the main negotiating room had been bugged.

28 See J. L. Episoto (ed.), *Islam in Asia*, Oxford, 1987, p. 20.

29 Noman, *History of Pakistan*, p. 60.

30 See Burki, *Pakistan Under Bhutto*, p. 146 and Chapter 7 generally.

31 See Haynes, *Politics in Pakistan*.

32 The evidence for this is far from categorical. Rigging elections in South Asia is much more difficult – even for a competent and elitist bureaucracy – than is often assumed. Even in defeat, Bhutto never lost the loyalty of a signifiant number of Pakistan's working class. Although small, organised labour initially presented a serious threat to the conservative regime of Zia.

33 For an excellent historical analysis of this use of Islamic symbolism by political parties, see D. Gilmartin, *Empire and Islam: Punjab and the Making of Pakistan*, Princeton, 1988.

34 See G. W. Choudhury, *Pakistan: Transition from a Military to a Civilian Government*, London, 1989.

35 Ziauddin Ahmed, *Money and Banking in Islam*, Islamabad, 1983, p. 5.

36 As yet no so-called 'surgical' amputations for theft have taken place. In a recent case in Baluchistan, four men were whipped for rape, but since the woman could not produce a witness, she too was whipped for committing adultery.

37 Kemal Faruki, 'Pakistan' in Episoto, *Islam in Asia*, p. 75.

38 Noman, *History of Pakistan*, p. 223.

39 See L. Lifschutz, *Bangladesh: The Unfinished Revolution*, London, 1979 and C. P. O'Donnell, *Bangla Desh: Biography of a Muslim Nation*, Boulder, 1984.

40 See the important article by H. Alavi, 'The state in post-colonial societies: Pakistan and Bangladesh' in K. Gough and H. P. Sharma, *Imperialism and Revolution in*

South Asia, London, 1973, pp. 145–73.

41 See Nizam Ahmed, 'Experiments in local government reform in Bangladesh', *Asian Survey*, 28, 1988, pp 813–29.

42 Zillur R. Khan, 'Islam and Bengali nationalism', *Asian Survey*, 25, 1985, pp. 852–82.

43 This permanence is somewhat misleading since the Constitution is easily amended, and was subjected to massive omnibus reforms in 1975 and in 1979. Nonetheless in terms of 'core values' the Constitution has remained at all times politically relevant.

44 For details of electoral turnout see D. Butler *et al.*, *India Decides: Elections 1952–1989*, New Delhi, 1989. See also V. Hewitt, 'The Congress system is dead: long live party politics and the democratic system', *Journal of Commonwealth and Comparative Politics*, 27, 1989, pp. 157–70.

45 Paul Brass has discussed how religious demands could be dressed up as a language issue, as with the Sikh demands for the redivision of bilingual Punjab in 1966. Yet Sikh demands for a Punjabi-speaking state also led to the incorporation of Punjabi-speaking Hindus. See the important book by P. Brass entitled *Language, Religion and Politics in North India*, Cambridge, 1974, and his recent contribution to the New Cambridge History of India *Politics of India Since Independence*, Cambridge, 1990.

46 This is especially true of India's first-past-the-post electoral system. See D. Butler, *et al.*, *Compendium of Indian Elections*, New Delhi, 1986.

47 It is not my intention to wade into the massive literature that has grown up about Indian federalism; for a useful introduction see L. Rudolph and S. Rudolph, *In Pursuit of Lakshmi: State–Society Relations in India*, Chicago, 1987 and Rajni Kothari, *Politics in India*, New Delhi, 1970.

48 See C. Baxter (ed.), *Government and Politics in South Asia*, Boulder, 1987, and John Wood (ed.) *Contemporary State Politics in India*, Boulder, 1987. The most recent analysis can be found in M. Bouton and P. Oldenburg (eds.), *India Briefing*, Boulder, 1990.

49 For a review of this debate see Rudolph and Rudolph. *In Pursuit of Lakshmi*. See also the reviews in *Journal of Commonwealth and Comparative Politics*, June 1989.

50 This is particularly true of southern India, where sudra castes are much more frequent. See R. Kothari, *Caste in Indian Politics*, New Delhi, 1976.

51 Bal Thackeray, leader of the Bombay Shiv Sena, quoted in Y. Malik and D. K. Vaypeyi, 'The rise of Hindu militancy', *Asian Survey*, 29, 1989, pp. 311–343.

52 Salman Khurshid, *At Home in India: A Restatement of Indian Muslims*, New Delhi, 1986, p. vii. The Muslim Marriage Act was passed in 1986.

53 See a special report in *India Today*, 15 January 1991, 'Anatomy of carnage', pp. 26–9. See also the highly rhetorical M. J. Akbar, *Riot After Riot*, Harmondsworth, 1989.

54 See the excellent *Sikhs of the Punjab* by J. S. Grewal, Volume II.3 of the *New Cambridge History of India*, Cambridge, 1991.

55 It is interesting to note in passing that this is the exact reverse of the economic argument used within East Pakistan to justify the publication of the six-point programme.

56 *The Economist*, January 1991.

57 This argument has been put forward by Rajni Kothari in a recent article in the *Illustrated Weekly of India*, 7–13 December 1986. See also B. D. Graham, *Hindu*

Nationalism and Indian Politics: The Origins and Development of the BJP, Oxford, 1990.

58 See Syed Shahabuddin and Theodore Paul Wright, 'India: Muslim minority politics and society' in Episoto, *Islam in Asia*, p. 155.

59 Sanjib Baruah, 'Immigration, ethnic conflict and political turmoil', *Asian Survey*, 26, 1986, pp. 1186–231

60 Cited in Y. K. Malik and K. Vajpeyi, 'The rise of Hindu militancy', *Asian Survey*, 29, 1989, pp. 308–340.

61 See A. J. Wilson, *The Break-Up of Sri Lanka*, London, 1988. See also J. Manor, 'Sri Lanka: explaining the disaster' in *World Today*, November 1983, and David Brown, 'Ethnic revival: perspectives on state and society', *Third World Quarterly*, October-December 1989, pp. 1–17.

62 The PQLI index does not measure economic growth. The index, developed by Dudley Seers, measures social welfare and the degree of redistributive social policy. See D. Seers *et al.*, *Integration and Unequal Development*, London, 1980.

63 James Bjorkman, 'Health policy and politics in Sri Lanka: the development of the South Asian welfare state', *Asian Survey*, 25, 1985, pp. 537–52.

64 See Craig Baxter *et al.*, *Government and Politics in South Asia*, Westview Press, 1987, p. 305. Sri Lankan Moors are sometimes listed as Tamil speakers, although they often speak several languages.

65 Figures taken from A. J. Wilson, *Politics in Sri Lanka, 1947–1979*, London, 1980, p. 8.

66 Wilson, *The Break-Up*, p. 39.

67 Wilson, *The Break-Up*, p. 72. *The Betrayl of Buddhism* was written as a formal report by the All Ceylonese Buddhist Congress in 1954 and was reissued as a paperback entitled *The Revolt in the Temple*.

68 See B. Mathew, 'Sri Lanka's development councils' in *Asian Survey*, 22, 1982, pp. 1117–35.

69 Burke and Ziring, *Pakistan's Foreign Policy*, p. 467.

4

South Asia and the world economy: transition and the imperatives of reform

The political and institutional problems of nation formation confront all the states of South Asia, and these problems are engendered by social change generated by economic growth. To all intents and purposes, and regardless of rhetorical asides to the contrary, India, Pakistan and Sri Lanka set out at independence to transform what were rural agrarian societies into urban industrial ones. The social and political effects of economic backwardness compelled Nepal and Bhutan to end their isolation and, under Indian guidance, to undertake policies to industrialise. Following her independence from Pakistan, Bangladesh faced the urgent task of developing her economy after years of neglect and waste and of feeding a rapidly growing population crowded into an environmentally vulnerable area of the sub-continent.

At the beginning of the 1990s, however, the entire region is still predominantly agricultural with a majority of the population living in the countryside. Even in India, one image of which is that of an emerging industrial giant, agriculture employs on average of 60 per cent of the labour force and makes up over 30 per cent of her gross domestic product. In Pakistan the figures are slightly lower. In Nepal, 95 per cent of the population live in the rural areas and agriculture makes up over 80 per cent of GDP.[1] Have the previous policies failed? And if so, what are the likely policies for the future?

As has been noted above, all the states of South Asia have remained committed to what can been referred to as the paradigm of 'modernisation', the belief that the transformation of their societies, along lines first seen in the West, is vital to their long-term legitimacy and stability. All of South Asia's political elite refer to the need to eliminate poverty, to provide for the basic needs of their citizens, and to create industrialised, trading societies exporting a wide range of manufactured and capital goods.

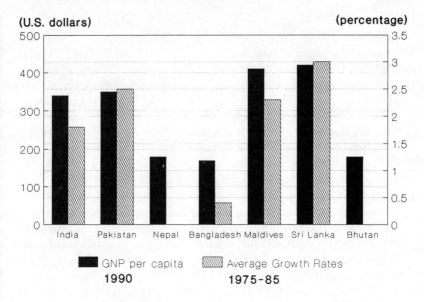

Figure 3 Economic indicators
Source: World Bank Report, 1990

Even for societies like Pakistan, which have witnessed a growing sense of political and cultural estrangement from the West, the material basis of modernisation remains a primary goal. While Chapter 3 explored the effects that economic change has had upon the sociocultural identities within the states of South Asia, it is my intention in this chapter to focus more narrowly upon the economic problems associated with growth. This is not, of course, to imply that these matters can be separated from the issues and dilemmas addressed in the previous discussion.

The politics of planning

In order to industrialise, the states of South Asia at one time or another have followed particular economic strategies of import substitution in an effort to develop a capital goods sector, and have attempted to commercialise and transform their agricultural sectors. Significantly, each state has tried to implement particular economic and social packages by recourse to economic planning. Such plans have aimed to

mobilise domestic resources and target priority areas through bureaucratic controls to ensure investments in key areas of the economy:
usually capital goods, and industrial manufacturing. Significantly, in
all cases – even India – planning has involved inputs of foreign aid.

In each country the institutions of planning have been based upon
differing balances between public and private investment. In India,
planning has created a large state sector that has sought to control and
contain foreign investment even though it has actively co-operated
with private Indian capital.[2] From the outset Indian planning 'included
a number of programmes designed to increase directly or indirectly,
the welfare of the poorer, underprivileged segments of society . . . all
(the) programmes involved substantial subsidies to the beneficiaries'.[3]

In Pakistan, planning has generally been applied in the interests of
private and foreign capital, and did not involve widespread nationalisation until the early 1970s and Bhutto's 'Islamic socialism'. In fact
after independence, and particularly during the Ayub Khan period,
Pakistan was committed to a particularly virulent neo-classical view of
development that stressed the overall importance of growth, but with
little direct reference to distribution. Pakistan's approach to development explicitly warned against the possible consequences of
premature redistribution of resources to those sections of society with
a low propensity to save and invest.[4] Bhutto did preside over the
creation of a large public sector, but this was in part dismantled by Zia.
In India much consideration and attention has gone into avoiding the
political costs of the increasing social differentials caused by changes in
income and wealth.

Sri Lanka has tended to move between these two extremes of
planning, depending on which political party is in power. The SLFP
have favoured a large state sector, while the UNP have favoured
privatisation and have actively encouraged foreign investment.
Bangladesh began at the Indian end of the planning spectrum, but after
1975 has moved increasingly towards the Pakistan variant.

The trend towards liberalisation

Since the mid 1980s the entire region has been characterised by a trend
away from the state sector towards private and foreign capital. While
this process has obviously gone furthest in Pakistan and Bangladesh, it
has also been visible within India, where attempts have been made to
roll back state involvement in the economy and to restructure planning
to encourage foreign collaboration. These reforms are not without

risks, both internally and externally. The presence of a state sector within all of the South Asian economies has provided much of the material basis for an urban-based middle class. Such a sector lies at the heart of the complex matrix of political patronage that binds political parties to the state and to important sections of society.

In India, state-led industrialisation has provided a nexus of interests that has supported private industrial development and sheltered it from undue competition through subsidies, price support policies, and tariffs. It is thus that the policies of liberalisation have been bedevilled by political and sectional pressures. Those who fear the effects of liberalisation are small-scale producers and small business enterprises that have been offered various types of protection under specific reservations. In 1980, 353 items were reserved for production by small businesses alone.[5] Added to this are around 200 public sector corporations that are run by the civil service and which are generally characterised by low productivity and inefficiency.

Both these sections would suffer from any systematic deregulation and were vocal in their protests against the Gandhi government's policy throughout 1985–6. Opposed to these, however, are a high (and increasing) number of large private firms (the classic examples being the Birla and the Tata groups), and a number of joint-stock companies in industry and manufacturing that are currently working within India. While these too share a close nexus with the senior civil servants and the politicians (through what Kochanek has referred to as 'briefcase politics'),[6] larger institutions would in some cases stand to gain from an easing up of foreign exchange controls, import licenses and the need for the government currently to license increases in production. It remains questionable to what extent these corporations could compete themselves within developed markets without access to western technology.

Pressures from the business community do not act passively on the state; state actors (politicians and civil servants) have also made gains from encouraging corruption. Yet the state itself may resist the move towards economic liberalisation. From 1986 onwards, the Rajiv Gandhi government faced a whole series of allegations over financial 'kick-backs' involving foreign companies and arms contracts.[7] Under the Indira Gandhi governments of 1970–77 and 1980–84, large business houses made enormous financial contributions to the Congress's electoral funds on the understanding that this would facilitate understandings with the government on license applications through the bureaucracy. While extreme in the case

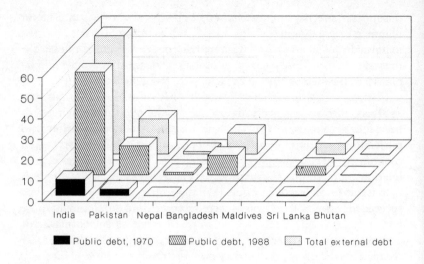

Figure 4 Total external debt (in billions of US dollars)
Source: World Bank Report, 1990.

of India, similar problems can be found in Pakistan and to an extent in
Sri Lanka.

While planning has had a profound impact upon the economic
development of South Asia and has been largely successful in
fundamentally reorientating and restructuring *colonial* economies,
there is growing evidence that the bureaucratic and regulatory
functions of state management may now have outlived their use-
fulness.[8] It must not be assumed, however, that the policies of the last
thirty to forty years have therefore been wrong. Myron Weiner has
referred to the long-standing view, held within the World Bank and the
IMF, that 'western assistance has made it possible for the Indian
government to adopt economically unsuccessful policies' and to pass
anti-western economic policies. But there are many arguments that still
favour a planning exercise.

The legacies of planning may well have 'resulted in a widening gap
between (domestic) efficiency levels and technological capabilities, and
the rapidly expanding international frontiers of global technology'[9]
but it has nonetheless provided the states of South Asia with the basics
of an industrial economy. The planning *vs* anti-planning argument,
which has contributed more than its fair share to US–Indian

misunderstandings, cannot be so easily resolved since it is not about planning *per se*, but about specific types of plans and the role allotted to government employment. It is often one of the conditions of the IMF that states seeking financial help and 'restructuring' submit economic plans for consideration, plans which are encouraged to contain policies to liberalise their economies. While it is necessary for economists to approach the arguments against planning with an open mind, it is also necessary to remember that these arguments are essentially political, especially since the mid 1980s. The scope and nature of Indian economic planning now stands at the centre of India's problematic relationship with the West, and in particular the USA.

It is more realistic to argue that the apparatus of planning has succeeded to the point at which further growth and development must now rely upon an external reorientation towards increasing both export earnings and foreign capital investments. Virtually all the South Asian economies face a growing shortfall between domestically available resources and development outlays. These shortfalls must be made up either through commercial or concessional loans, or through direct foreign investment. Since excessive bureaucratic planning discourages such loans, as well as foreign investment by multinational corporations, South Asian states are trying to 'open up' their economies.

They have also to comply with many of the conditions that are attached to IMF loans and standby agreements such as calls for reductions in domestic subsidies, lower exchange rates, wage freezes and tariff reductions. Since 1986, India, Pakistan and Sri Lanka have dangerously increased their commercial borrowings from private western banks at a time of high interest and volatile import earnings from traditional commodities such as tea, coffee, cotton and rubber. All these economies are facing difficulties.

Do these problems in themselves call for the abolition of planning? In 1990 the World Bank noted: 'Perhaps the abandonment of central planning and increased reliance on the market in eastern Europe will powerfully affect basic approaches to economic development in the coming decades in both Africa and Asia.'[10] Even if this conclusion is the right one, it is still not necessary to accept the entirety of the World Bank's argument for the wholesale dismantling of the state sector, if only because the economic rationale behind planning in India was not solely confined to the argument of economic efficiency: the rationale referred also to job-creation, the need to increase the overall purchasing power of the internal market, and to ensure political stability. While the economic imperatives for reform are greatest in India, they are present throughout the entire South Asia region. In all cases they present the states with serious domestic and international difficulties.

Internal constraints

Despite the urgency of reform, there are powerful reasons why sections of Indian, Pakistani and Sri Lankan society will try to resist the rationalisation of bureaucratic control and the liberalisation of economic structures. Significant sections of India's political elite is linked into the infamous 'permit raj' of political corruption and black money and would suffer from increased competition *vis-à-vis* the world economy. Even in circumstances where increased global competition could benefit sections of India's political elite – or sections of Pakistan's western-orientated Muslims – the results could be politically destabilising in that the benefits derived from such policies would fall unevenly across the sub-continent and within each society. The existence of a state sector is also seen by many left-wing groups and political parties as part of a real obligation to socialism, and a significant political commitment to the poor and the abolition of poverty. Socialism remains an important word within the political lexicon of South Asia. In 1985, when addressing the bicentennary of the Indian National Congress in Bombay, Rajiv Gandhi omitted to mention the word socialism in his final statement. There followed an extraordinary outcry from the opposition and from within the Congress itself, and the statement was reissued with the key word firmly in place.

While these counter-claims are more important within the Indian context (where planning and socialism have long been combined in opposition to foreign capital and an intellectual dislike of unfettered capitalism), they can also be found within Pakistan and within Sri Lanka. Because of their shared colonial heritage, much of South Asia's elite remain ambivalent in their attitudes towards international capital, if only because of its association with the West and, more distantly, the images of western dominance. The fact that none of these states have any real access to global financial institutions such as the IMF and the World Bank reinforces this sense of falling under foreign dominion.

In Bangladesh the radical left's opposition to capitalism that surfaced after the civil war has been effectively neutralised, but the present government of Begum Zia contains several political groups who oppose external interference within the economy, or are opposed to a further role for the World Bank in the restructuring of Bangladesh's economy.

In Pakistan the possible anti-capitalist, anti-commercial tendencies of an Islamic political system (apparently so vital to the internal legitimacy of the regime) could cause problems for western investment, especially concerning the payment of interest on capital funds. Since 1989 the predominantly anti-US attitudes of the government could well affect future US investment as well. Even under the UNP, Sri Lanka has been criticised by international financial agencies because of a failure to cut back on 'non-developmental' expenditure – a curious euphemism for welfare policies and food subsidies. In Sri Lanka the problem is still one of ensuring some form of communal settlement that will reassure foreign investors but also commit significant resources to food subsidies and welfare policies, as well as job creation schemes within the public sector.

International constraints

Domestic problems are by themselves difficult enough: but even if the states of South Asia are able to undertake the transition from an inward- to an outward-orientated strategy, the next question that must be asked is whether enough external resources in the form of loans can be found, or whether sufficient external markets exist to support a sustained manufacturing export drive by the South Asian economies.

All the states of South Asia are increasingly dependent upon access to concessional and 'soft' loans, either through the international financial institutions associated with the Bretton Woods Agreement, or through other agencies such as the Asian Development Bank, the Islamic Development Bank, and the Colombo Plan, founded in 1951.[11]

While India has been one of the largest regional contributors to the Colombo Plan, she has nonetheless also had free access to the fund, since the main donors are Japan and the USA. Pakistan's contributions to the fund have been quite negligible, given her overall rate of economic growth, while Sri Lanka, at the same time as contributing resources has drawn increasingly on the fund from the beginning of the 1980s. South Asian states have also borrowed heavily from the Asian Development Bank. For the first time since its inception in the mid 1960s, India was forced to borrow from the Asian Development Bank in 1986 because of initial difficulties in securing an IMF loan. In the same year China joined the ADB and also applied for a large number of loans.

Compared to the IMF and International Bank for Reconstruction and Development (IBRD) the regional financial institutions draw upon much less collateral; it is within the IMF, and the IBRD that South Asian demands have come increasingly into competition for concessional and developmental aid with the other priority areas such as the 'new' states of Eastern Europe, North Africa and Latin America. As the development crisis within Africa continues to evolve, it is clear that that region will claim more and more aid from both western and Japanese sources.

The *Far Eastern Economic Review* noted in 1990 that IMF and World Bank support to Asia and particularly the smaller states such as Sri Lanka, Bangladesh and Nepal has fallen relative to that given to Latin America and Africa. The prospects of the Soviet Union entering the market for concessional loans (or, as one commentator put it, of 'joining the Third World') would also have serious repercussions on the world financial markets, as well as India's access to the use of non-conditional, soft loans and significant amounts of military aid.

Access to further concessional loans within the Bretton Woods system also highlights the importance of America. In the mid 1980s the United States raised objections to further IMF financial assistance to India on the grounds that she no longer required 'concessional loans' and that conditions for future loans were not strict enough.[12] In 1982, in protest to a growing 'anti-US' sentiment in parts of the Third World, the United States scaled down its funding to the IDA, which affected both India and Sri Lanka.

Current negotiations between India and the IMF for another massive loan (almost US $3 billion) are leading to disagreements over the degree of further economic liberalisation within the economy. In 1989 the US Trade Department invoked the 'super 301' clause of the Omnibus Trade Act against Brazil, Japan and India for 'unfair' trade practices and a failure to reciprocate trade liberalisations, especially within her insurance markets.

Like US complaints against Japan, accusations of protectionism are often aimed at so-called informal practices and distribution outlets, and the use of non-tariff barriers that violate the spirit of GATT.[13] America has complained about India's patent protection acts, which offer limited protection to the 'intellectual property' of US multi-nationals. Furthermore, Washington has pressurised India bilaterally, as well as within the international forums of the World Bank and the

IMF, to open up her economy to foreign investment.[14] Significantly the United States remains India's largest source of direct foreign investment, one of the few Asian countries in which she has not been replaced by the Japanese. Indian attempts to encourage further US investments were a clear part of India's overall foreign policy towards the US in the late 1980s, especially under the Rajiv Gandhi administration. India's response to the '301' incident was remarkably constrained, and quite different from previous incidents, such as the rupee devaluation in 1966 which, widely believed to have been as a result of American pressure, embarrassed the government and soured Indo-US relations for some time. Yet pressures to reform domestic trade and industrial policies within South Asia are also coming from Japan and from the EC. New Delhi's recent attempts to encourage Japanese investment led to criticisms about Indian business management procedures, low levels of productivity and problems of quality control.[15]

While Japan is involved in development projects in the Maldives, Bhutan and Sri Lanka, it has not found the various incentives to invest very encouraging. Japan has co-operated with India's indigenous car manufacturer Maruti, but the Suzuki Corporation has complained about Indian government restrictions and internal bottlenecks affecting what is potentially a large middle-class market. India has in turn complained about the transfer of designs and royalty payments, and the repatriation of profits to Japan and to the East Asian NICs. In recent years, and in spite of communal unrest, Sri Lanka has benefited from the relocation of textile and manufacturing industries from South Korea and Taiwan, who have been attracted by her skilled work force.

With a decline in concessional loans, commercial banks are unwilling to lend further to states already in debt. In early 1991 several US banks downgraded India's credit-worthiness after assessing both political and economic factors.[16] Yet even if India could satisfy her creditors that she is an Asian economy with a future, there is some doubt that the international economy as a whole would be conducive to supporting export-led growth strategies.

Towards the end of the 1980s the obstacles confronting the liberal international trading regime seemed almost as great as the internal ones confronting the states of South Asia. An increased need to find foreign markets for South Asian manufactured and processed goods comes at a time when western markets (particularly in the US) are succumbing to domestic pressure to protect their own industries, especially in areas most important for South Asia: textiles and intermediate goods. Even if India could get access to advanced technology to modernise her industrial and manufacturing base, there is no guarantee that she would have access to foreign markets in which she could sell back non-primary goods.

Trade tensions between the United States and Japan have highlighted the sensitivity of industrialised countries to allowing technological co-operation which undermines their own industrial production. The possibility of extensive Third World manufactured goods penetrating the developed market economies is a state of affairs that the US and many OECD countries would find difficult to tolerate. Not only would it lead to calls for further protectionism within the industrialised countries; it would also further demands that Third World states should reduce their tariff barriers.[17] Since 1988 the US has been particularly active in retaliating against states who appear reluctant to open up their markets to American and western competition, even when such states can claim to be poor and developing.

Protectionism and tariff barriers

Non-tariff barriers (NTBs) have been proliferating throughout the international economy since the late 1970s. It has been calculated that by 1987 NTBs in automobiles, textile production and the steel and iron industries constitute a *de facto* external tariff of approximately 25 per cent of all imports to the OECD countries.[18] The fear of established regional trading blocs amid a general trend towards global protectionism feeds a general South Asian anxiety that, as a region, it will remain marginal to the world economy and in particular US economic interests. This will in turn have obvious consequences for India's profile within American strategic thinking.

This is not just India's concern. Even after thirty years of the 'special relationship' between Washington and Islamabad, the percentage of US direct investment in Pakistan is a very small proportion of US global investment. Despite encouragement from both Zia and Benazir Bhutto, US corporations remain unwilling to invest in industrial production rather than investing in the growing service sector. In spite of the efforts made by Zia, Pakistan has not been very successful in persuading the Japanese to undertake industrial joint ventures in the telecommunications and tourist industries: two noticeable growth areas in India, for example.

It is clearly not in South Asia's interests that the world economy retreats into rival trading blocs for the simple reason that, along with so much of the Third World, South Asia does not automatically belong to the US, the European, or the Japanese–Pacific areas. It follows that if such bloc rivalries are established, South Asia would find it difficult to attract and compete with foreign capital investors anxious to locate themselves within the much more lucrative markets of the US and the EEC.

European amalgamation, for example, will create one of the largest markets in the world, combining the states of Western Europe into a single economic unit of 320 million people with a combined GDP of US $6 trillion. Even if South Asia could successfully combine itself into a regional common market, consisting of one-fifth of the entire planetary population, it is still likely that it would not command a significant economic profile. In 1977 the regional GDP was US $120 billion. In 1989 it was estimated at just over US $341 billion. India has long expressed concern that one of the possible consequences of European integration will be to further regional trade between and within the developed world at the expense of Third World economic prosperity.

The World Bank has itself noted that the problems of so-called trade diversion, caused by the integration of compatible economies, may well overcome any general benefits to the developing world if the current GATT talks (known as the Uruguay Round) cannot agree on the scope and nature of future tariff reforms. World Bank estimates suggest that 1992 could well stimulate primary commodity imports to the value of US $4 billion, but it is not necessarily in these markets that South Asian economies wish to compete. The possibility of the Australians forming an Asian–Pacific trading block has also caused some concerns in India.

While the eventual form that European tariffs will take is still unknown, it is very likely that they will further discriminate against South Asian goods. The probable extension of special trading preferences to eastern European states may well fill import quotas currently at the disposal of Third World states. Pressure from GATT to remove barriers on manufactured imports could well have a damaging effect upon European manufacturing industries, taking up to 10 or 15 per cent of the domestic market.[19]

During 1988/9 world trade grew in value by 14 per cent to stand at US $2,880 billion, with a dramatic growth in manufactured goods, but South Asia's share remained largely stagnant. The current Uruguayan Round has foundered on the liberation of world farm trade and subsidies, textile sales, and the protection of technological patents and designs. Attempts will be made to resume talks in early 1991. The possibility of the United States and Europe turning their backs upon a global economy committed to non-tariff and liberalising trade relations is a serious possibility. The collective benefits of a liberal world trading system seem obvious: 'Trade will count for more in the 1990s than it has for many years. Eastern Europe cannot embrace capitalism successfully without unimpeded access to western markets. Debt burdened developing countries cannot grow their way back to credit worthiness without trade, and Europe will reap the benefits of 1992 only if its producers face global competition.'[20] As domestic pressure to retain living standards grows within the OECD countries, and mitigates against policies aimed to improve the international competitiveness of their industries, protectionism makes short-term, electoral sense in many of the western market economies.[21]

The Multi-Fibre Agreement

Bangladesh has already suffered adversely from an increase in non-tariff quota restrictions such as those embodied in the Multi-Fibre Agreement (MFA). The agreement came into force in 1974. Wolf has remarked that the object of the agreement was 'to expand trade through the progressive liberalisation of the world trade in textile products, ensuring the orderly and equitable development and avoiding (its) disruptive effects in both the importing and the exporting countries'.[22] Such a statement reads as a rather long euphemism for protectionism when and if market penetration disrupts domestic textile production. Even worse, there has been a tendency since its inception to extend the scope of the original agreement. India, Pakistan, Sri Lanka and Bangladesh have all protested that the MFA is against the spirit of GATT, and that it should be progressively phased out. For its part, the World Bank agrees, and has long criticised the misuse of the agreement.

In response to World Bank pressure to increase and diversify exports, Bangladesh attracted foreign investment from South Korean joint ventures and set up several small-scale manufacturing units. By the mid 1980s, the export of textiles to Canada, the United States, the United Kingdom and France produced US $100 million of much-needed hard currency, with the United States making up about 80 per cent of the market. Yet by 1987 the US had invoked the MFA and issued thirteen separate quotas that restricted Bangladeshi imports, despite the fact that they constituted a merely 0.5 per cent of America's total textile imports.

It is often assumed that the correct response to quota restrictions is for countries to diversify their markets, but for countries like Bangladesh and Nepal (and even, arguably, India) the lack of information and marketing skills serious inhibits the flexibility of the exporting sectors. Any demands to dismantle the MFA run into serious domestic pressure within OECD countries. Yet as long as it remains, the MFA will increasingly constrain the export strategies of developing countries.[23]

The formation of SAARC: is regionalism the answer?

Somewhat unusually, South Asia lacked any regional organisation within which the separate states could come together to discuss or act upon common problems until 1985. The reasons for this absence is related to the depth of animosity between India and Pakistan and their differences of opinion on regional and extra-regional matters. Yet throughout the late 1970s it was argued that South Asia ought to draw together as a region if only to kept abreast of what appeared to be the general trend in Europe, Latin America and East Asia, and to pool individual expertise and resources to solve common economic and social problems. If such a South Asian 'common market' could be formed, would it be helpful in dealing with matters of economic integration?

The initiative leading to the formation of the South Asian Association for Regional Co-operation (SAARC) came from the Ziaur-Rehman regime in Bangladesh, and it received enthusiastic support from Nepal, Bhutan and Sri Lanka. India and Pakistan found such a move 'useful but not essential' to the wider interests of the region and both were sceptical about its economic and political viability. The curious point about SAARC is that it is still neither an economic nor a political organisation in the sense of organisations like the EC or ASEAN, and more importantly it lacks any common security perceptions that act as an incentive for collective action. Disagreements between India and Pakistan over Soviet, Chinese and American policies (and throughout the late 1980s, arguments between India and Sri Lanka) impinge upon the degree of co-operation that was possible even in matters such as trade and technical co-operation. Sri Lanka complained in 1989 at the SAARC foreign ministers, meeting in Islamabad about India's refusal to withdraw the IPKF. Nepalese sympathy for Sri Lanka's position, surfacing at the same session, became part of the general deterioration in Indo-Nepalese relations.

Although it has outlined several areas for discussion, the actual aims of the organisation remain deliberately out of focus.

Between 1977 and 1980 President Ziaur-Rehman undertook various attempts to initiate a summit of the seven South Asian states, and in 1980 he issued a working paper on the likely form and scope of a regional organisation.[24] Anxious to encourage Indian participation, the paper stressed economic and cultural factors over political and bilateral issues. Indian coolness to the proposal, based upon a traditional fear of being isolated within the region by a Pakistan-led coalition, was tempered by a wish to avoid being accused of wrecking the initiative altogether. In August 1983, the proposal for SAARC was drawn up, and then ratified at New Delhi in 1985.[25]

Between these two dates, a series of meetings took place at foreign minister and secretary of state level to establish the principles of the organisation. It was agreed that the association would be established on the principle of the 'equality' of each member, a significant concession from India, appearing to contradict her earlier stress upon Indian primacy. It was further agreed that a Common Action Programme (CAP), first discussed in 1983, would prioritise specific areas and delegate them to specific countries. The CAP established separate committees on agriculture, rural development, telecommunications, meteorological forecasting, and on health and population control. Yet both India and Pakistan reiterated their belief at the outset that SAARC would not discuss *political* issues, and would not supersede bilateral discussions on trade.

SAARC has evolved the practice of rotating the presidency of the organisation between the member states, a practical application of the principle of the equality of each state. Such a move ensures that states such as Nepal and the Maldives attain a significant profile within the region that will be of immediate benefit to them. In 1986 a permanent headquarters was set up to house the organisation in Dhaka. In 1990 SAARC also set up a post of secretary-general to help with the overall co-ordination of policies. The institutionalisation of SAARC has been uneven, however, with a failure to agree on a common fund or to act with any decisiveness on any issues listed in the Common Action Programme. In 1987 it was agreed that special topics of concern within the region were narcotics trafficking, the role of women in development, and terrorism. Significantly – given the level of irredentism within South Asia – the 1987 meeting failed to come to any agreed definition over terrorism, or to issue any strongly-worded condemnation of terrorism throughout the region.

The frequency of meetings at various levels of government have tended to exaggerate the importance of the organisation, but it has so far provided a useful forum for important 'informal' bilateral discussions within the region. In 1990 for example, the November Summit held at Male, capital of the Maldives, allowed Chandhra Senkhar and Naswar Sharif to meet for the first time.

The potential for SAARC becoming a collective security arrangement is remote, but it is not impossible and the suggestion has already been made. In 1989 Pakistan suggested that, like ASEAN, SAARC should take on issues of regional security, while India cautioned against 'premature moves' and also warned that SAARC had no jurisdiction to represent the region in any external body such as the United Nations, the Commonwealth or the Non-Aligned Movement. Yet it is possible that SAARC could provide the region with a framework in which to establish confidence, building measures between New Delhi and Islamabad.

For the present, the benefits of a genuinely regional approach to South Asia's problems are thus elusive. If SAARC could present itself as a framework for greater economic co-operation, it would firstly have to work hard to improve intra-regional trade links. Trade within South Asia is very small, about 2 per cent of South Asia's US $40 billion trade total in 1986, and bilateral trade relations between the states shows a serious imbalance in favour of India. Attempts to use SAARC as a platform on which to launch joint industrial or manufacturing ventures threaten the smaller states with further integration into India, while India remains reluctant to allow access to what is still an essentially protected domestic market. Pakistan has continued to restrict Indian trade, especially that involving investments by private Indian firms, because of strategic considerations.

The economies of the South Asian states are not immediately compatible. SAARC does open the way for various commodity agreements (such as on tea and coffee) and in some cases combined overseas marketing. Yet with the exceptions of Nepal and Bhutan, the remaining states are all attempting to diversify their trade away from primary commodity goods. While regional integration may be complementary to wider trade liberalisation, it is not an alternative to wider links with the global economy, since it will not automatically provide the required economies of scale for the types of goods that these economies, especially India, now wish to trade in.

Any comprehensive trade agreement worthy of the name 'common market' would benefit India disproportionately. Even if successful, economic strength would gradually impinge upon political and strategic considerations – issues that lie at the heart of the Indo-Pakistan divide – and would probably be resisted. A political dialogue within SAARC would also automatically involve discussions on Kashmir. If the momentum of the EC is a model of the successful regional organisation, the road of regional co-operation in South Asia is blocked until the Indo-Pakistan crisis is settled.

In a symposium on SAARC held in 1985, Mohammed Ayoob noted that 'we therefore have a situation in South Asia that is conducive neither to regional co-operation nor regional polarisation'. Again, while it could be argued that the end of the cold war will now ease up these tensions, regional differences will remain.

Nepal

Nepal, Bhutan and Bangladesh are amongst the poorest countries in the world. Nepal's per capita income is just US $170. All three states are characterised by a low domestic savings ratio, poor educational and health facilities, and a high degree of rural unemployment and landlessness.

In terms of trade, Nepal is dominated by India. In 1987 her trade deficit with India was US $144·06 million. Trading relations with Pakistan are minimal, and while contributions from Bangladesh and China (both suppliers of material and markets) have grown throughout the 1980s, India remains paramount. To some critics this is the deliberate outcome of a long period of Indian influence: the economic side of the defence agreement. In many respects, however, it is the inevitable outcome of Nepal's geopolitical location.

Under Indian influence Nepal adopted formal planning in the 1950s, and in the 1956–75 period launched five separate five-year plans. The planning strategy initially aimed at developing basic infrastructure, increasing agricultural output and improving educational facilities. Recently, under the terms of an internationally supported 'adjustment programme' announced in 1985, a more direct basic needs approach has been adopted, aimed at eradicating rural poverty through a rural works programme and a mass literacy drive.[26]

The success of planning in Nepal has been mixed, partly because of the degree of extreme backwardness prior to 1951, and partly as a failure of the economic priorities within the plans themselves. The first two plans were not decisive enough in tackling agricultural production and were too 'urban biased' in their outlays. Overly influenced by

Indian thinking on industrial self-reliance, the plans sought to stimulate agricultural output and transfer resources towards industrial development. Although Indian experts correctly conceptualised Nepal as suffering from a classic low income equilibrium trap, where investments were low because of the low level of domestic resources, they over-estimated the general health of the agricultural sector to stand up to a sustained squeeze on resources, or to respond to so-called market incentives to produce more.

The reasons for the poor state of Nepalese agriculture are not hard to find: it had long suffered from a period of neglect in the precolonial period, characterised by a largely illiterate peasantry producing food close to the margin of subsistence. Cultivation practices varied from district to district, as did tenurial rights and agreements. Legal complications affected the efficiency of modern cultivation, while attempts at land reforms ran into serious political opposition and were difficult to reinforce. The problems of undertaking land reforms were part of the political crisis that overcame Nepal's first multi-party constitution in the early 1960s, and which led to the abolition of party politics.

The physical environment of Nepal was hostile to any aim of increasing food production by increasing the area under cultivation. Apart from the flat fertile Terai area that makes up 17 per cent of Nepal's landmass, food crops are grown in hill areas that are vulnerable to rapid soil erosion. This is one of the reasons why, along with a failure to disseminate modern technologies and increase irrigation, yields actually decreased between 1966 and 1973. As productivity fell behind the annual population growth rate, export earnings declined as food was used for internal consumption. Between 1974/5 and 1984/5 Nepal moved from being a net exporter of food to a main importer.[27] At the beginning of the 1980s, there were many accusations of wasted resources and corruption.

Since Nepal's entire development strategy was based upon increased per capita income through agriculture, the failure to increase agricultural output meant that foreign sources quickly came to dominate plan outlays, initially from India. Yet even concessional loans and grants have failed to jolt the economy into a pattern of steady growth. By 1987 there appeared little return from an investment of about Rs30,378 million since 1951. Some engineering projects have been a success in that they have started to utilise Nepal's energy potential: by 1989 US $29·2 million had been invested in two small hydroelectric generators. Yet such capital projects must be part of a

comprehensive strategy to deal with industrial and urban development, which in turn must address the issues of political decentralisation and participation within the development process.

Popular demands for a greater say have long been at the root of both
Nepali and Butanese political unrest, and especially in the late 1980s.
Following the decision in 1990 to move towards a multi-party system,
there is now a possibility that greater public participation will improve
the scope and effectiveness of the plan outlines, yet the most urgent
matters to tackle remain rural poverty, agricultural productivity, and a
programme of population control to avoid further pressure on scarce
resources.

Between 1951 and 1956 there were four changes in the government
interspersed with two periods of direct control from the monarchy.
The 1960 royal coup led to a series of institutional reforms that over-
centralised economic policy formulation. The entire basis of the
panchayat schema within Nepal was to neutralise a national opposition, and although it sanctioned the setting-up of a national
assembly, the powers of patronage and appointment remained firmly
in the hands of the king and his advisers. Unlike the Indian versions of
local and district councils, they had no development functions at all
and were not involved in the drawing-up of growth targets. Nepal's
leading economist, Dr Devendra Pandey, called upon international
donors to withhold all future sources of funding until Nepal was
committed to democracy, on the grounds that previous funds had been
wasted.[28]

Attempts to diversify economic activity away from agriculture
towards the encouragement of small-scale industrial projects had
largely failed because of high rates of illiteracy, inefficient government
support for local and district initiatives, and low levels of domestic
demand. At the end of the fifth plan (1975–80) the Nepalese
government noted that: 'if the nation fails to make concrete improvements in the existing economic conditions during the course of
the next five to ten years, the social and economic consequences for
Nepal could well be serious'.[29] It has recently been noted that if current
population growth rates continue, and Nepal's economy fails to pick
up, Nepal will remain one of the poorest states in the region well into
the next century.[30]

The matter of planning is pressing since the fulfilment of basic needs
is just one part of any long-term strategy aimed to transform the
economy. Eventually, Nepalese industry can only develop in the
context of internal demand, and wider access to markets through

India. Even a regional approach that opens up trade and transit through Bangladesh (and Pakistan) would require Indian participation and encouragement.

Bhutan

Sharing similar environmental conditions with Nepal, Bhutan seems to offer little prospect for agricultural development through extensive cropping.[31] Only about 5 per cent of the landscape is suitable for cultivation. Increased production can only come through the rationalisation of small peasant holdings and improved irrigation and water control. As a remote kingdom, Bhutan had no infrastructure at all prior to her first five-year plan in 1961. Until 1974 the economy was not even fully monetised, with taxes often being collected in kind, and with the Indian rupee circulating alongside the official currency.

Yet Bhutan has several advantages over Nepal: a low, relatively static population, a resource-rich environment, especially in timber and minerals, and a high percentage of concessional loans that have, since 1971, made a significant impact upon economic performance. Bhutan has, until very recently, had little scope for private and foreign trade and investment. Virtually all trade is carried on through the public sector, such as the Bhutanese Food Corporation, set up by Indian public finance. Planning in Bhutan has moved away from developing essential infrastructure towards developing various resource-based projects such as logging and pulp production. The Mitsui Corporation of Japan have recently completed a telecommunications centre, and have installed direct dialling facilities (ISD) to India.

Recent schemes have also involved joint ventures being set up with Indian private companies, especially in chemical processing. In 1989 the Bhutanese Development Financial Corporation (BDFC) decided to try and encourage a dramatic increase in private and foreign investment. Following similar developments in the Maldives, it has recently been recognised that tourism could well provide sound economic prospects for the future, but there are still sources of domestic opposition. It is still feared that any foreign development – be it in the form of investment or tourism – could prove destabilising to so-called traditional values, especially if it involves further migration from India and Nepal. There are also serious drawbacks to excessive reliance upon tourism as a source of foreign revenues, especially in a region that is generally characterised by domestic instability.[32] Attempts to encourage industrialisation must also try to ensure sound environmental management in order to avoid the sort of environmental damage witnessed in Nepal (and parts of India's north-west states, such as Himachal Pradesh and the infamous Sanjay Gandhi hydroelectric project on the Sutlej river). Some attempts are already being made. Private fellings and loggings are banned, and extractive industries are carefully licensed through the state.

Bhutanese planning is, like Nepal's, an offshoot of India's own development experience. Since the early 1970s Bhutan has gradually taken control of her economic institutions of planning. In 1971 Bhutan created its own Planning Commission after joining the United Nations, while in 1988 the government regrouped the pre-exisiting Butanese zonal councils (the so-called *Dzongkhags*) to facilitate decentralisation to and to stimulate growth. As with Nepal, this was partly in response to demands for greater participation by a monarchical regime facing greater social unrest. 1990 saw the formation of the Bhutanese Civil Service, although a large number of entrants are educated within India through various sponsored Indian placements. India still provides a large part of Bhutan's plan outlays – over 52 per cent between 1983 and 1987.

The rest of Bhutan's much-needed foreign resources come from the UN and the work of the specialist agencies. The FAO have helped to finance a project aimed at developing food buffer stocks. In terms of trade agreements, Bhutan signed a bilateral treaty with Bangladesh in 1989, while attempting to encourage some expansion in trade and assistance from China. The recently-opened 336-MW Chukha hydroelectric power station was constructed by Indian expertise, and was funded by a mixture of Indian grants and loans. The station will export 85 per cent of its power to India. Indian technical expertise also helped construct a radio station at Thimphu.

The achievements of Bhutan have still to be judged, but they appear to be more successful than Nepal. The example of Chukha project, although relatively small, holds out an example for Indian policy towards Nepal and to the Himalayan region as a whole, while less grandiose schemes such as increasing primary education and basic health care must also be pursued. The pace of economic change must be dramatically increased, while at the same time both Bhutan and Nepal must evolve the political institutions through which to manage such change.

Bangladesh

In 1987 Bangladesh's per capita income was US $160. 30 per cent of the

Bangladeshi population is classified as landless labourers, and she has consistently failed to achieve planning targets for rural employment programmes. Bangladesh has a serious problem of indebtedness despite a high level of concessional loans. In 1988 Bangladesh received grants of US $214 million for food aid, US $580 million for commodities, and US $1·2 million on project aid. Despite some successes in increasing paddy production throughout the 1980s, food output has yet to recover from the terrible flooding of 1988.

In common with the two Himalayan kingdoms, the Bangladeshi economy has since independence laboured under a large external debt and has been characterised by a low domestic savings ratio. Since 1975 Bangladesh has been relatively successful in attracting foreign funds and support from a whole source of international agencies and countries, especially the Middle East. Like Pakistan, the trends in favour of privatisation have been much greater, if only because the traditions of an established public sector are so much weaker. Even under the Awami League government, planning institutions were weak and generally advisory,[33] and the mismanagement of public enterprises led to the inefficient allocation of resources and wasted valuable funds.

The commitment to public sector planning in Bangladesh ended in 1975 with the assassination of Mujib Rehman. After the ending of India's influence, Bangladesh's planning apparatus has attempted to encourage foreign and private investment along lines similar to Pakistan under Zia, but Bangladesh's requirements are excessive. In the late 1980s, what Kissinger allegedly named the 'international basket case' has also suffered from an increase in non-development expenditure in the form of relief programmes and government health schemes. Vast amounts of money have been required to deal with the profound consequences of environmental disasters.

As with Nepal and Bhutan, the staple food crop of Bangladesh is paddy, yet the conditions of production could not be more different. The delta lands of Bangladesh, regularly inundated with silt, are amongst the most fertile in the world. Yet continual population pressure has led to a form of agricultural involution in which, given constraints on increasing the area of production, each plot of land has been more and more intensively worked. An added problem is that, under Muslim property law, the redivision of land amongst the sons leads to the continual fragmentation of landholdings, despite government attempts to consolidate ownership. As with Nepal, mistrust of district politics, combined with a certain degree of institutional neglect, has discouraged local initiatives and encouraged an inefficient reliance upon the central government. Population pressure has continued to force people to live in close proximity to the Ganges flood delta and on many of the low-lying islands and spits that are constantly emerging – and submerging – in the mouth of the Ganges.

As Bangladesh enters the 1990s it will continue to require a vast amount of financial aid to assist in agricultural development, in attempts to improve schooling and to improve the general health of the population, and to develop its manufacturing base. Ensuring continued support will be difficult, especially because levels of efficiency within Bangladesh are often criticised by international aid agencies, and because the amount of aid to Bangladesh is conditioned by demands from other areas such as the Middle East and Africa.

The Asian Development Bank has on occasion criticised Bangladesh's commercial banks for poor recovery rates of loans from development projects. As Just Faaland and J. R. Parkinson have noted, 'it is not easy to see how donor countries can be persuaded to maintain an effort on the scale needed (to ensure development). Bangladesh is not a country of strategic importance to any but her immediate neighbours.'[34] This is especially so if aid and investment is directed at illegitimate regimes supported by the military. These circumstances have changed since November 1990, but the typhoon and floods of May 1991 merely emphasised how reliant Bangladesh is on the so-called international community, regardless of the types of political regime.

The fourth five-year plan (1990–95), disrupted as it has been by the restoration of a civilian regime, was premised on the need to provide further tax incentives to attract further foreign investments. Like Nepal, a fundamental lack of a skilled labour force is one of the greatest obstacles to foreign investment, as are such obstacles as the Multi-Fibre Agreement discussed above. Moreover, incremental aid aimed at solving short-term appeals for assistance have not made an appreciable impact upon the Bangladeshi economy, especially since one of the main problems remains that of population growth. In 1987/8, Bangladesh's export earnings paid for a mere 40 per cent of the import bill. In the same year, she had taken US $10 billion from multilateral aid sources, 52 per cent of her GDP.[35] The entire agenda of Bangladesh' foreign policy must address her need for foreign assistance. One Bangladeshi scholar recently noted: 'the door must be kept open to all possible sources of economic aid, as a development strategy, the policy of non-alignment is quite a powerful weapon because it draws the best from both blocks'.[36] Bangladesh has yet to reassess the implications of 1989 for such a strategy.

The Sri Lankan economy

Throughout the 1950s and early 1960s Sri Lanka's economy seemed as promising as her democratic record.[37] Since the 1970s Sri Lanka has failed to maintain its outstanding position amongst LDCs, and has still to make the transition from a predominantly agrarian economy to an industrial one. As with all the other states of South Asia (with the exception of Nepal and the Maldives), the service sector makes up the largest share of non-agricultural products, with industry making up on average 28 per cent of her GDP. Until 1972 much of Sri Lanka's plantation economy remained under foreign ownership, while most of her exports remained essentially 'traditional' primary products. Coexisting alongside this enclave economy was a peasant-based system of cultivation, growing and marketing some cash crops, such as rubber and coffee.

Under the Bandaranaike SLFP–left wing coalition governments, and under the First Republican Constitution (1972–8), Sri Lanka extended its public sector through nationalisation and set up a rigid planning framework as part of a general left-wing orientation and as part of an attempt to speed up socialist industrialisation. In an attempt to absorb growing unemployment amongst a well-educated work force, public sector employment soared during the mid 1970s. In 1976 the state was the largest employer in the country. As part of its socialist programme, the government also extended food subsidies and general welfare policies that increased government spending at a time when revenues from traditional exports were falling rapidly. The result was an extended balance of payments crisis and high levels of domestic inflation. The change in government and constitution in 1977 took place against a growing budget deficit, diminishing foreign investment and increasing long-term indebtedness.

The World Bank has been critical of Sri Lanka's welfare expenditure, which in 1989 was calculated to consist of 5–6 per cent of Sri Lanka's GDP. Such programmes, including the infamous free rice scheme, dates back to the 1950s and is unique within the South Asian region. While recognising that a specifically targeted scheme would bring great benefits to the poorest sections of society, the Bank believe that the Sri Lankan scheme is too inclusive and wastes important scarce financial assets.

Under the SLFP, World Bank criticisms of Sri Lanka consisted of the standard complaint that extensive state involvement tended to encourage inefficiencies and adversely affect productivity. In response to such criticisms, and in line with their own ideological proclivities, the UNP has turned since 1978 further towards international institutions such as the IMF, the World Bank and the Asian Development Bank for both short- and long-term economic assistance. Unlike the SLFP, the UNP was willing to act upon the World Bank's critique of a large public sector and a high degree of subsidies, and open the way for a significant degree of privatisation. The Jayewardene government started to deregulate the economy soon after coming to power, limiting the role of the state and encouraging private enterprise. The new industrial strategy was an attempt to encourage Sri Lankan exports and further her participation within the global economy, not just in traditional exports, but also in manufactured goods, and in some finished machine parts.

Certainly by the mid 1980s these policies appeared to be working; the unemployment rate was dropping while a strong growth rate of 4–5 per cent ensured a healthy balance of payments. Yet the growing effects of the civil war, along with a failure to diversify and promote exports meant that the momentum could not be maintained. Since 1987 Sri Lanka has witnessed increasing inflation and a return to rising unemployment, with an increasing resource gap between revenues and expenditure.

A larger share of Sri Lanka's goods go to the developed world market than India: 62 per cent in 1989, compared to India's 43·8 per cent, and there is a much greater amount of foreign investment within the Sri Lankan economy as a percentage share of GDP than the case of India.[38] Since the late 1970s Sri Lanka has also attempted to encourage foreign investment from Japan and the East Asian NICs, especially her manufacturing and capital goods industry. While Sri Lanka has shown some interest in joining ASEAN, this is primarily for security reasons aimed at avoiding Indian regional dominance.

As with the other South Asian economies, the role of the international financial agencies can be affected by domestic political infighting. The present SLFP opposition has accused the UNP government of 'imprudently' borrowing from private commercial sources to meet current spending requirements, or of 'selling the island to the West'. Like Bangladesh, Sri Lanka must increasingly compete for significant concessional loans against East European states, and must seek to fulfil the requirements of efficiency and performance laid down by donor countries. In both countries such conditionality can – and has – fuelled resentment. Given the curious combination of ideological and *racial* identities, it is not unlikely that an anti-western government could well come to power, and that much of the Jaywardene period could be undone through excessive renationalisation.

As with planning in India, to highlight ostensibly economic criticisms of Sri Lanka's welfare policies is to miss their *political* rationality. As with the provision of government jobs, many economic policies are aimed at dealing with a deeply politicised society. They are part of an attempt to 'buy back' sections of the population into mainstream politics. For Sri Lanka the consequences of high unemployment is not simply an idle workforce; it is a radicalised workforce that could (and has) fallen prey to the many political factions currently engaged in domestic violence. Since 1990, unemployment has been rising in Sri Lanka, especially amongst urban youth.

High budget deficits have led to soaring domestic interest rates and have discouraged investment because local firms and businesses are unable to borrow the large sums of money needed to start new projects. Moreover, the failure of the UNP government to bring peace to the island has also had an effect upon the economy. Multi-National Corporations (MNCs) are unlikely to invest in areas where conditions are bordering upon civil war, although it is often argued that since terrorism is confined to the North and the North-East, its effects upon the economy are marginal.

Calculating the effects of the civil war on Sri Lanka's economy is notoriously difficult, since it is hard to attribute trends within the economy to one or two variables, especially in an economy that is as open as Sri Lanka's.[39] The number of dead since 1987 is calculated to be somewhere in the region of 60,000.[40] Since 1989/90, the level of violence in and around the Jaffna peninsula has been considerable, with heavy fighting reported throughout August 1990 as the Sri Lankan security forces attempted to relieve troops cut off in Jaffna fort. In early 1991 the National Security Minister was assassinated in Colombo.

The level and intensity of ethnic violence since 1983 has set an atmosphere of doubt and suspicion over the government's ability and willingness to deal with the situation.[41] The number of joint ventures declined rapidly between 1983 and 1985, from fifty-six a year to fewer than thirty. The effects of violence on tourism has also been serious, with the Sri Lankan tourist board reporting losses of Rs2,285 billion for 1985 alone. It has been calculated that civil disturbances since 1983 cut as much as 1 per cent off the annual growth rate in both 1984 and 1985.[42]

Many Tamil organisations have threatened multinational corporations with violence unless they withdraw. In 1987 there was a threat by EROS to poison exports of Sri Lankan tea to US and British markets. One effect of indiscriminate public terror by both Tamil and Sinhalese groups has been to increase public transport costs and the times of journeys. Rose and Samaranayake note that a six-hour train journey from Colombo to Jaffna now takes about thirty-six hours. There is also little confidence in public bus companies since these have often been the targets of attack.

The effects of terrorism are not just confined to Sri Lanka; they are also found throughout the states of South Asia. The level of political terrorism in the Punjab has had an incalculable effect upon the prosperity of one of India's wealthiest regions. Civil unrest throughout metropolitan Pakistan in the 1989–90 period, especially in and around Karachi, undermined confidence in the economy as a whole. Since the mid 1980s a great many businesses have moved away from Karachi to safer but significantly less developed areas, in the North-West – but the sheer level of violence in Sri Lanka, and the scale of the government's response, is unfortunately unique in South Asia.

Sri Lanka requires a continual aid commitment over the next decade in order to manage her economy and pursue her industrial development plans. In the mid 1980s the Jayewardene government set up a series of commissions to increase the efficiency of the remaining state-run industries and to continue to encourage foreign investment through the setting-up of special export zones, exempt from income and local taxes and other trading restrictions. While India too has increased her bilateral contributions – US $80 million in credits were offered under the auspices of the Indo-Sri Lankan Accord – political factors rule out any closer economic co-operation for the time being. While the government under Premadasa is committed to targeting donor aid towards industrial projects, it does so in a context of growing social division. Recent evidence shows that income inequalities have worsened within rural areas and between rural and urban areas.[43]

It is worth attempting to calculate the likely economic costs of partition for Sri Lanka, and what the prospects would be for a sovereign state of Eelam. The territorial dimensions of the state would make it smaller than Bhutan, just slightly larger than of Wales. The terrain is low-lying, relatively dry land with some irrigation facilities but little immediate prospect of economic growth. It has been suggested that the prime exports of a 'Tamil' state would consist of onions and dried fish.

Such a state would make little sense, either in terms of the national and social consensus it could construct, or with regard to its degree of economic independence. Given the divisions within the Tamil groups fighting for a state of Eelam, it would be subject to massive sociopolitical instability. Because of internal divisions within the Tamil majority, the prospect of it falling under Southern Indian control is extremely likely, even if it was against the better political judgements of a federal government in New Delhi.

The Indian economy: crisis of transition?

India's commitment to planning was much more intellectually consistent and sustained than any of her neighbours, and much more systematically executed. From the time of the Industrial Policy Resolution (1948) onwards,[44] India has adopted a highly bureaucratic approach to economic management that has emphasised the internal resources of the country and down-played the importance of external trade links with the world market. Unlike Pakistan, and covered under the general rubric of socialism, India did not follow an export-led growth strategy nor encouraged foreign investment within her economy. In this respect India has had an unusually small profile within the world economy since 1947, and her share of world trade actually declined throughout the 1970s.

In 1973/4, India's share of world exports was little more than ·5 per cent[45] In 1973 India imported a mere 9·5 per cent of all manufactured goods, while her ratio of imports to GNP was 6 per cent – one of the lowest figures in the world.[46] Her imports were likewise skewed away from manufactured goods: in 1989 only 9·1 per cent of India's world imports consisted of manufactured goods, compared to 51·1 per cent for Pakistan, 48·3 per cent for Sri Lanka and 76·5 per cent for Bangladesh.[47]

Bhagwati and Desai remarked that India's policies on trade and production 'could be summed up cynically but realistically: that India should produce whatever it can, and that India should export whatever it produces'. While India could export some of her manufactured goods to the communist bloc states and parts of the Third World, she did not actively promote exports. Since the 1989 transformations in Eastern Europe, India has lost an important market for her technological production, as the 'new' states of Europe turn to the US or to Western Europe.

Strict anti-monopoly laws and an emphasis upon equity shares have discouraged multinational operations and joint ventures between Indian capital and foreign companies. Somewhat paradoxically, however, India has always needed foreign aid to fund her plan outlays. By the end of 1964, India was receiving bilateral foreign aid from twenty-one countries, and through three multilateral agreements. In fact until 1966, the United States remained India's largest single aid giver. In the second and third five-year plans, foreign assistance contributed between 18 and 25 per cent of plan outlays.[48] The legacies of planning have been impressive. John Mellor noted as long ago as 1979 that: 'The building of post-colonial India has moved on three inter-related fronts: the political system has been broadened, and the administrative structure and the industrial base have been extended.'[49] Yet compared to Pakistan, India's overall growth rates have tended to be disappointing: 4·5 per cent as opposed to 3·5 per cent on average throughout the 1970s. Yet the record for Indian agricultural development, following the application of the Green Revolution technology from the mid 1960s on, has led to dramatic breakthroughs in food production. Between 1960 and 1980, Indian agriculture grew on average 30 per cent faster than China's, and 23 per cent faster than Pakistan's.

In a recent book on India, one commentator noted that the late 1980s were characterised as a period of high growth, based upon dramatic increases in agricultural production, buoyant industrial output and increasing exports.[50] Rising exports have involved India in both western and eastern markets, and much of the Third World. A wide range of economic co-operation is offered through the various technical assistance programmes and the setting-up of numerous joint ventures formed between Indian companies and foreign industry situated in Africa, the Middle East and East Asia. Between 1978 and 1988 India was offering assistance to, among others, Algeria, Colombo, Madagascar, Mexico, Indonesia and Vietnam under the ITEC and the Technological Co-operation Among Developing Countries scheme (TCDC).[51] Since the mid 1980s, India has shown interest in aggressively pursuing export markets, and her exports grew rapidly between 1988 and 1990, as a result of more aggressive marketing and a policy of gradual devaluation of the rupee. Yet whether this trend can be maintained is open to doubt.

Recent optimism about the overall dynamics of the Indian economy have recently been qualified by two areas of concern: the persistence of poverty, and a growing amount of international indebtedness. Since the late 1970s, the degree of political commitment within India towards a planned economy has been fundamentally eroded, but it has not been replaced by any broad agreement as to the extent and direction of economic reform. Since the Indira Gandhi government of 1980–84, the management of the Indian economy has been characterised by a whole series of stop–go policies.

Calculations over levels of poverty are difficult and controversial, but evidence points to persistent areas of poverty within India, especially within the countryside. It has been calculated that in the mid 1980s, there were over 320 million Indians living below the poverty line.[52] The definition of what constitutes the poverty line is a profoundly political concept, as indeed are attempts to calculate how many individuals fall below the poverty line. The Indian Planning Commission defines it as those people living on Rs20 per month at 1961 prices. The belief that India's poor are worse off now that at any time since independence, and that they have missed out entirely because of the particular bias of Indian planning, is not borne out by the evidence. Between 1970 and 1988, 'the percentage of persons living in poverty has decreased in all periods and the total number living in ultra-poverty has also decreased'.[53] Yet since the mid 1970s the poor in India have become increasingly concentrated in specific areas and thus require specific, district- or provincial-based anti-poverty programmes. Raising average annual growth rates is only one condition for the elimination of poverty; the key issues are still distribution and gainful employment, especially in the countryside. The poor remain a powerful and increasingly vocal section of India's political system. No government can choose to ignore them, or to give them the impression that its policies are not attempting to improve their condition.

In February 1991 the Indian economy was in a state of free fall, with the budget estimates for 1991/2 being suspended for a period of four months following the fall of the Chandra Senkhar government.[54] In a startling turn around since the early 1980s, India is now the fourth largest debtor nation in the world. In part this has been caused by a move away from planning, and the cautious macro-economic policies that planning encouraged. The crisis has also, in part, been created by a move away from concessional borrowing towards private and commercial loans on the world financial markets.

Both the Seventh Plan and the draft Eighth Plan (1990–95) have been premised on the need to press ahead with further deregulation and to offer more incentives for an export drive. Between 1985 and 1990 deregulation appeared sufficiently permanent to encourage a number of US–Indian joint ventures to increase, but India showed a reluctance to reform anti-monopolies legislation to facilitate private corporate expansion, or indeed to reform legal requirements that compelled equity shares in any foreign collaboration. Yet India was willing in 1989 to announce de-investment plans within the more lucrative sections of the public sector, and to sell shares to private companies.

The crisis of half-hearted reforms

Subject to conflicting domestic pressures, the Rajiv Gandhi government was too liberal for the socialists, and too socialist for the liberals. Between 1985 and 1987, income differentials increased, especially between the urban and the rural sector, which gave rise to the view that the Congress was for the urban and wealthy.[55] To many external commentators, the momentum towards liberalisation appeared to falter in the wake of V. P. Singh's resignation from the government, after which Rajiv Gandhi appeared to proceed more cautiously.

Detailed analysis of the Indian economy over the 1980s shows an increasing shortfall between government revenue and government expenditure, on both the current and the capital accounts. Whether or not such an impasse has been reached as a result of liberalisation, or through the final constrictions of a planned economy, is open to serious dispute.[56] There are several key causes for this increasing gap in resources. One is a large and antiquated tax structure that is inefficient and unrealistic in its demands. High direct taxation has usually encouraged widespread evasion, while indirect surcharges have often shifted the burden of taxes on to the poor. During V. P. Singh's period as finance minister, a much-needed reform of the tax system took place, but the government was reluctant to allow the ministry to raid business premises to ensure that revenues were collected. Disagreements between V. P. Singh and Prime Minister Rajiv Gandhi led to Singh's move to Defence, and then his eventual dismissal from the government in 1986.

By 1986 it was noted that domestic revenue merely balanced current spending, while borrowed money was used to finance planned development.[57] Even with a domestic savings rate of 23 per cent (the highest within South Asia), India has consistently failed to utilise the required level of funds to fill her growing development expenditures. From 1975 to 1985 the amount of current government spending has increased dramatically. One significant area has been that of defence, especially the increase in FY 1989/90. Other costs have been an increase in government subsidies to various pressure groups within India such as the rural poor, and support to farmers to ensure cheap fertiliser and diesel. In 1985 the budget estimates for an anti-poverty programme (outside of the plan outlay) was in the region of Rs18·5 billion. Attempts to cut back on these programmes would – and has – led to widespread political resistance.

By the late 1980s increased borrowings had depleted Indian reserves and led to a series of emergency meetings with the IMF to gain access to credit. From 1986 onwards the government took recourse to inflationary deficit financing. In 1989 India's public and private debt was over US $44 billion dollars. On 21 February 1991 India had just US $42·5 million in her foreign currency reserves, the equivalent of about two weeks of imports.[58] With this growing dependency on foreign loans, India falls further under international pressure to reform and liberalise her economy: current negotiations over the IMF standby agreement of US $2 billion has a whole series of conditions, all referring to the imperatives of further increases in exports and export performance, cutting back subsidies, and further devaluation in the rupee. These negotiations have taken place at a time when India has been without effective government.

It has already been noted that the amount of demands made upon the Indian state (and the financial resources the state commands) dramatically increased throughout the 1980s. The political difficulties of squaring short-term obligations and long-term commitments has already resulted in the cancellation of the FY 1991/2 budget estimates for the fear that, in a potential election year, necessary cuts – part of IMF conditionality – will create political unpopularity. The decision to suspend the budget (bitterly opposed by the finance ministry) will affect India's ability to comply with IMF conditions to ensure further access to loans.

The nature of the current dilemma increases the arguments against further reform. Part of the anti-liberalisation argument is that an open Indian economy will lead to the destruction of those benefits that have derived from a planned economy, and they point to the current crisis over the deficit as a consequence of what lies ahead in the future if the Indian state deviates from the Nehruvian policies of the 1950s. As the medium-term forecasts for India stress macro-economic instability and poor growth prospects, it is possible that the current political instability within India could produce a government that may attempt to return her to a more isolationist policy. Several parties are committed to this, including the BJP, because they fear that further economic integration with the world economy will endanger the very real benefits that India has made since independence. Such a reaction was already apparent in some of the policies of the V. P. Singh government, who sought to stress the agricultural and anti-poverty aspects of their economic programmes in contrast to those of the Congress. John Adams recently noted: 'In many ways the National Front (was) more attuned to the continuities of Indian economic policy than was Rajiv's Congress . . . in that it was more in keeping with the talk of self-reliance and socialism than were the free marketeers associated with the Congress.'[59] Following the assassination of Mr Gandhi on 22nd May, 1991, it is quite possible that the Congress-I could move away from endorsing any further liberalisation of the economy.

The economic prospects for Pakistan

At times, like India, Pakistan has favoured import substitution as during the first five-year plan announced in 1955. Economic policy has nonetheless been sporadic and tied up with the fate and interests of particular regimes. Moreover, even under Zulfika Bhutto economic regulation has never reached the elephantine excesses of New Delhi's bureaucracy and has usually been confined to the public sector only. In this respect Pakistan's economic history is in many ways the exact opposite of India's. Her growth rates have been generally higher and she has had a higher share in world trade. Between 1950 and 1980 income per capita more than doubled, and between 1977 and 1988 per capita incomes grew on average at 3·8 per cent per annum. The World Bank, susceptible to high aggregate figures, is believed to be considering whether to promote Pakistan from the 'low-income' to the 'middle-income' bracket, which would put it in the company of countries like Turkey, Brazil and Mexico.

The Ayub Khan period was without doubt the heyday of the 'liberal' economy, as much as it was they heyday of Pakistan–US co-operation. Pakistan benefited from export promotion and diversification, and laid the foundations for later industrial gains in such sectors as steel, petrochemicals and services. The momentum failed during the political crisis that overtook Pakistan in the late 1960s, in which Pakistan lost access to the (declining) foreign revenues of the East wing, and fell victim to the inflationary effects of the war and the US embargo.

Z. Bhutto moved economic policy and management towards a specific version of India, with a large socialist sector and active state management. The commanding heights of the economy were brought into the hands of the state bureaucracy at the very time that this was being de-professionalised and opened up to less qualified entrants.[60]

These policies, as much out of favour with the IMF as the socialist policies of the SLFP in Sri Lanka, were reversed by Zia. As with his fellow officer Ayub Khan, Pakistan under the military appeared more inclined to fulfil the requirements of IMF conditionality than a civilian regime. Nonetheless the economic successes of Pakistan were very real, even if the distributional aspects have left something to be desired, and have often been part of the political dialogue between the military and the civilian regimes. In a classic study of Pakistan, Griffin and Khan noted that 'experience shows that faster growth does not inevitably lead to greater prosperity. In some cases it can actually lead to a decline in the standard of living for the rural and urban poor'.[61] During the 1960s it was frequently alleged that most of Pakistan's industrial and financial wealth was owned by a mere twenty-one families.[62] It has already been noted that the economic disparities between East and West Pakistan contributed significantly to the political alienation of the Bengalis. Despite the reversal of Z. Bhutto's nationalisation, many of Pakistan's remaining public sector corporations are run bureaucratically, and with an eye to internal political gains. Unlike India, there have not been any moves as yet to deinvest public sector undertakings through private flotations.[63] Yet interestingly enough, Pakistan's record on poverty is as good as, if not slightly better than, India's.

Much has been written about the apparent increase in income inequality in Pakistan during the 1960s. The economic polarisation between the two wings was the main contributory factor to the cause of the civil war in 1971. Recent findings, however, indicate that the levels of absolute poverty are lower in Pakistan than in India, especially in the cities.[64]

As with India, future development plans must rely increasingly on foreign resources. Pakistan has a low domestic savings ratio, and her record of mobilising domestic funds through tax and revenue have consequently been poor. Growth rates in agriculture have generally lagged behind those of India, especially in the Punjab. While India favoured a decentralised scheme of spreading and supporting 'green revolution' technology, Pakistan favoured a highly mechanical approach based upon extending irrigation works through a centralised bureaucratic system. Evidence suggests that agricultural investment and productivity also suffered from large-scale imports of cheap grains from the US from the late 1960s onwards.[65] India's agricultural growth has generally been more sustained than Pakistan's.

Until the recent crisis in India, Pakistan's indebtedness was amongst the worst – about 25 per cent of GDP – of the South Asian economies. High domestic interest rates have created conditions unfavourable for sustained domestic investment, and have led to an increased search for loans and grants from abroad. While Pakistan has continued to receive a regular inflow of remittances from the Gulf states, these have been declining in recent years. It has been estimated that between 1979 and 1987 Pakistan's total aid commitment from all sources totalled US $10 billion, an average of US $1·45 billion per annum.[66] One of the growing difficulties for Pakistan, and indeed for other South Asian economies, has been the growth of a large 'informal' or black economy whose resources technically elude the state. In Pakistan, the growth in the black economy is linked to the heroin trade. Exact measurements are hard to come by, but following the Soviet invasion of Afghanistan, the 'parallel' economy has expanded in border states such as Baluchistan and North West Frontier Province.

Given the openness of the economy throughout the 1980s, and given the economic dimensions of Pakistan's security relationship with the United States, she has a much higher percentage of foreign investment within her economy than India. Since the late 1970s she has received a much larger amount in grants and concessional loans than India has. In 1986 alone, Pakistan received US $2·6 billion from the aid consortium along with another US $3·2 billion loan from America. The decision by the United States to suspend aid will thus have a serious effect upon Pakistan's balance of payments.

Since 1989 Pakistan's trade deficit has increased, and her indebtedness has grown dramatically. Since 1988, the two civilian governments of Benazir Bhutto and Naswar Sharif have remained committed to an open economy while stressing a 'basic needs' strategy to eliminate rural poverty. In 1989 the Bhutto government announced a medium-term adjustment programme in which public spending would be targeted at basic education and public hygiene. Yet, as with India (and Sri Lanka), such increases in welfare spending and 'anti-poverty' programmes, while generally favoured by the World Bank, will be increasingly scrutinised to ensure that they do not violate existing agreements on conditionality and structural readjustment.

Finally, it is necessary to note that all of the South Asian economies remain vulnerable to increasing energy costs. Following Iraq's invasion of Kuwait, oil prices doubled between August 1990 and January 1991, even those these price rises were not as severe as were feared. The increases had serious economic repercussions for the states of South Asia. While India, Pakistan and Bangladesh all have limited access to some domestic fossil fuel reserves (coal oil and gas), they remain dependent upon Middle Eastern supplies. The war dramatically curtailed workers in the Gulf states from sending back remittances. Bangladesh has over 100,000 people working in Kuwait and Iraq, and throughout the 1980s they have provided the Bangladeshi economy with an average of US $100 million per annum. This is also the case with Pakistan.

India has over 200,000 people working in the Gulf states, and these are drawn disproportionately from the states of Kerala and Gujarat. Given India's federal system, these two provinces faced serious revenue losses in excess of 1 per cent gross state product.[67] Sri Lanka has been seriously affected by the price increases and in February 1991 sought US $450 million to deal with a foreign exchange crisis caused by increased oil bills. While the individual Gulf states, along with Japan, the EC and the US have created a common fund to help developing countries, only Bangladesh and Pakistan have been mentioned in the South Asia region. Significantly, both of these states committed troops to the services of the United States-led Coalition.

Summary

An overview of the economic developments throughout the 1980s reveals that the economies of South Asia are divided into two distinct sets: those of India, Pakistan and Sri Lanka that contain a manu-facturing/services sector and witnessed periods of sustained growth and relative macro-economic stability compared to Latin America and some of the more prosperous African countries, and the states of Nepal, Bhutan, and Bangladesh which still face significant difficulties in terms of infrastructural development and economic diversification.

The Maldives fall between the two: as a micro-state it has a relatively environmentally limited economy which is dependent upon tourism, and some fish food processing aimed primarily at the Japanese market. As yet it lacks a significant industrial and manu-facturing base, and much of the social or territorial prerequisites needed to support them. Like Bangladesh, the Maldives remain vulnerable to environmental change and escalating costs of ensuring adequate protection against rises in sea level, the land being on average a mere 10 metres above sea level. In 1978, the Maldives joined the Asian Development Bank, the World Bank, and the IMF in order to gain access to international aid so as to begin the construction of expensive sea defences.

It is often asked why, in comparison to other Asian countries (especially the so-called NICs of Singapore, South Korea, Hong Kong and Taiwan), India's and Pakistan's development have been disappointing to many. The comparison is obviously unfavourable, given the regional dimensions of India and Pakistan compared to what are in a majority of cases 'enclave' economies. Yet the comparison is often made in the developmental literature to support a counter-factual argument against planning and 'inward-orientated' growth.[68]

Certainly both India and Pakistan are facing the social and political difficulties of opening up their economies, and they suffer from the additional anxiety of doing so at a time when a global liberal trade regime is itself under question. In stark contrast to the military notions of strength discussed earlier, the economic problems of South Asia – cause and consequence of the enormous social strains discussed in Chapter 3 – make it marginal to the world economy and to the perceptions of other states outside the region. This is particularly true of India.

In contrast to her military profile, India's economic profile is minute and reveals dramatic weaknesses in her ability to influence and determine events around her. India imports about 1% from the region, while regional exports make up a mere 28 per cent.[69] Of all the states of South Asia, India can only be said really to dominate Nepal and Bhutan in an economic sense, and she has done that in such a way as to cause resentment and misunderstanding. The Maldives, for example, is dominated by Far Eastern trade, and bilateral aid from Japan. Srikant Dutt has noted how many of India's foreign joint ventures with other developing countries were either moribund or sustained for purely political reasons. At the beginning of the 1990s, for an economy of her size and territorial dimensions, the size of her trade is remarkably undeveloped. What effects do these economic weaknesses have on India's political and military claims throughout the region, and indeed throughout the world?

The implications are – and they are discussed in the final chapter – that they substantially diminish the nature of her claims. The importance of economics was well understood by Nehru, and it gave Indian foreign policy under Nehru an essential consistency. In a recent seminar on India's military deployment, a Soviet academic asked the telling question whether or not India's military and strategic plans outstripped the country's economic strength to sustain them. What use is a blue-water navy, deployed to extend some non-existent or underutilised 'extended economic zone' across the Indian ocean when the costs of maintaining it constitute a serious economic liability? For an economy with little or no external trade, what is there to defend apart from the immediate land borders to the east and the west? It is because of her lack of economic strength that Indian claims to 'great power' status strike many commentators as absurd.

Notes

1 *World Development Report*, World Bank, Washington, 1990 and *Economic Trends in the Developing Economies*, World Bank, Washington, 1989.

2 This is a complex affair. In 1950 Indian government expenditure accounted for barely 8 per cent of aggregate national expenditure, and by 1967 this had more than doubled. Yet private capital had also grown dramatically. See S. Clarkson, *The Soviet Theory of Development: India and the Third World in Marxist–Leninist Scholarship*, London, 1978.

3 *The Cambridge Economic History of India*, Volume Two, Cambridge, 1982,p. 958.

4 A good overview of the thinking behind Pakistan's first two decades of 'development economics' can be gleened from reading W. W. Rostow, *The Stages of Economic Growth*, Chicago, 1971.

5 Stanely Kockanek, 'Brief case politics in India', *Asian Survey*, 27, 1987, pp. 1278–1301.

6 S. Kockanek cites an IMF report that 'implied' [*sic*] that there was as much as US $1·8 billion invested in Swiss bank accounts by private Indian companies.

7 For an excellent discussion on Rajiv Gandhi's government and the corruption scandals over Bofors, see Nick Nugent, *Rajiv Gandhi: Son of a Dynasty*, London. 1990.

8 There is of course a massively involved debate as to whether planning was ever useful. J. N. Bhagwati and S. Desai, *Planning For Industrialisation: Industrialisation and Trade Policy since 1951*, London, 1971. See also I. Little *et al.*, *Industry and Trade in Some Developing Countries*, London, 1970 and Ian Little, *Project Appraisal and Planning for Developing Countries*, London, 1974.

9 *Economic Trends*, p. 210.

10 *World Bank Report*, Washington, 1990, p. 24.

11 The Colombo Plan – an abbreviation for Co-operative Economic Development in South and South-East Asia – was founded in 1951. Arising from a Commonwealth initiative it was finally extended to involve six non-regional states, including the US and Japan. It is made up of twenty-six countries.

12 Sarbjit Johal, 'India's search for capital abroad', *Asian Survey*, 29, 1989, pp. 971–1002.

13 See Raju Thomas, 'US transfers of dual use technologies to India', *Asian Survey*, 30, 1989, pp. 560–631.

14 Despite Indian complaints over 'super 301', the issue was resolved with remarkable speed and with remarkable Indian sensitivity to American concerns, an indication of the need for India to ensure access to technology, although in a sense American objections were patently ludicrous. See J. Adams 'Breaking away: India's economy vaults into the 1990s' in M. Bouton and P. Oldenburg, *India Briefing 1990*, Boulder, 1990, pp. 77–100.

15 *The Economist*, London, 20 October 1990, p. 91.

16 Under the present GATT regime, Third World states states are allowed to set up tariffs for 'developmental' purposes to protect infant industries, etc. Once these industries have been established the tariff barriers are to be gradually withdrawn.

17 *World Development Report*, Washington, 1990.

18 All figures here are taken from the *World Bank Report*, 1990.

19 Editorial, *The Economist*, 1–7 December 1990, p. 2.

20 This is one of the arguments that has been put forward by Robert Gilpin. See *The Political Economy of International Relations*, Princeton, 1987.

21 M. Wolf, *Indian Exports*, World Bank, Washington, 1982.

22 The paradox is even greater when it is appreciated that US support within the AID Bangladesh consortium supports policies aimed at trying to diversify her traditional exports and to integrate her into the world economy. Both the UK and France also imposed quotas and quality controls against Bangadeshi, Indian and Pakistani textile production.

23 See E. Ahamed (ed.), *The Foreign Policy of Bangladesh: A Small State Imperative*, Dhaka, 1984, and M. G. Kabir and S. Hassan, *Issues and Challenges Facing Bangladesh Foreign Policy*, Dhaka, 1984.

24 See Craig Baxter, *Government and Politics in South Asia*, Boulder, 1987, p. 305.

25 See P. Blakie *et al.*, *The Struggle for Basic Needs in Nepal*, Oxford, 1980, and L. Rose and J. Scholz, *Nepal: Profile of a Himalayan Kingdom*, Boulder, 1980. See also L. S. Baral, *Political Development in Nepal*, New Delhi, 1983.

26 Narayn Khadka, 'Nepal's 7th Five Year Plan', *Asian Survey*, 28, 1988, pp. 555–68. See also A. Schloss, 'Making planning relevant: the Nepal experience 1968–1976', *Asian Survey*, 20, 1980, pp. 1008–20.

27 *Far Eastern Economic Review*, November 1989, p. 32.

28 Shanker Sharma, 'Nepal's economy: growth and development', *Asian Survey*, 26, pp. 897–905.

29 Sukhdev Shah, 'Nepal's economic development problems', *Asian Survey*, 28, 1988, pp. 945–962.

30 See Leo Rose, *The Politics of Bhutan*, London, 1977, and the excellent Imaeda Yoshira and Imaeda Pommeret, *Bhutan: A Kingdom of the Eastern Himalayas*, London, 1984.

31 For a general economic and political assessment of the impact of tourism within South Asia see Linda K. Richter, *The Politics of Tourism in Asia*, Honolulu, 1989.

32 See N. Islam, *Development Planning in Bangladesh: A Study in Political Economy*, London, 1977.

33 Just Faaland and J. R. Parkinson, *Bangladesh: The Test Case of Development*, London, 1976.

34 *Economic Trends*.

35 Cited in E. Ahamed (ed.), *The Foreign Policy of Bangladesh: A Small State Imperative*, Dhaka, p. 24.

36 D. R. Snodgrass, *Ceylon: An Export Led Economy in Transition*, Illinois, 1966. See

also J. A. Wilson, *The Politics of Sri Lanka 1947–1979*. London, 1980.

37 *Direction of Trade Statistics*, IMF, Washington, 1990.

38 Sri Lanka's growth rate has been on average 4 per cent between 1965 and 1980, and 4.9 per cent between 1980 and 1986. She has been above India's but below Pakistan's, which averaged nearly 7 per cent between 1980 and 1986. *World Development Report*, 1988. This slowed in 1989–90.

39 European Parliamentary Report, cited in *Keesings Contemporary Archive*, 1990.

40 The unwillingness of the government to deal with district administration is one of the themes in A. J. Wilson's book, *The Break-Up of Sri Lanka*, London, 1989. See also M. R. Singer, 'New realities of Sri Lankan power' *Asian Survey*, 30, 1990, pp. 409–28.

41 Leo Ross and Tilak Samaranayake, 'Economic impact of the recent disturbances', *Asian Survey*, 26, 1986, pp. 1240–85.

42 *Economic Trends*.

43 See V. N. Balasubramanyam, *The Indian Economy*, London, 1984, and S. K. Ray, *The Indian Economy*, New Delhi, 1987.

44 M. Weiner, 'Assessing the political impact of foreign assistance', Ch.3 in J. Mellor (ed.), *India: A Rising Middle Power?*, New York, 1979.

45 Only the Soviet Union was below India. See Martin Wolf, *India's Exports*, New York, 1982.

46 *Far Eastern Economic Review Year Book*, Hong Kong, 1990.

47 S. Clarkson, *The Soviet Theory of Development*, London, 1978.

48 Mellor, *India: A Rising Middle Power?*, p. 6.

49 Adams, 'Breaking away: India's economy vaults into the 1990s', p. 76.

50 For an interesting but rather polemical discussion on this see S. Dutt, *India and the Third World: Altruism or Hegemony?*, London, 1984.

51 See Alan Heston, 'Poverty in India: some recent policies' in Bouton and Oldenberg, *India Profile 1990*, p. 103. For a general discussion on this see Iqbal Khan, *Fresh Perspectives on India and Pakistan*, Oxford, 1985.

52 Heston, 'Poverty in India', p. 107.

53 *Financial Times*, 11 February 1991.

54 See Adams, 'Breaking away: India's economy vaults into the 1990s'.

55 Some have no such doubts, however. See *The Economist* 'A survey of India', London, 4 May 1991.

56 Cited in A. Benard, 'A maturation crisis in India', *Asian Survey*, 27, 1987, pp. 408–18.

57 *The Financial Times*, 21 February 1991.

58 Adams, 'Breaking away: India's economy vaults into the 1990s', p. 97.

59 See S. J. Burki, *Pakistan Under Bhutto: 1971–1977*, London, 1985. The result was to increase corruption and the misuse of state funds.

60 Keith Griffin and Azizur Rahman Khan, *Growth and Inequality in Pakistan*, London, 1971.

61 See Tariq Ali, *Can Pakistan Survive?*, Harmondsworth, 1973.

62 See R. LaPorte and M. B. Ahmed, *Public Enterprises in Pakistan: The Hidden Crisis in Economic Development*, Boulder, 1989 and S. J. Burki and R. LaPorte, *Pakistan's Development Priorities*, Boulder, 1984.

63 *Economic Trends*. See also the 1990 *World Development Report* that deals in some depth with the measurement of poverty and assesses how policies have tried to eliminate it.

64　Holy Sims, 'The state and agricultural productivity', *Asian Survey*, 26, 1986, pp. 483–500.
65　LaPorte and Ahmed, *Public Enterprises*.
66　See ODI Briefing Paper, *The Impact of the Gulf Crisis on Developing Countries*, London, March 1991.
67　See for example the excellent Keith Griffin, *Alternative Strategies for Economic Development*, London, 1989.
68　Far Eastern Economic Review, *Asian Yearbook*, Hong Kong, 1990.

Future prospects for regional stability and disarmament in South Asia

Having fleshed out the region's domestic and international linkages in some detail, it is necessary to return to Indo-Pakistan relations. Much reference has been made to Indian claims to regional pre-eminence, and always, the hint of global ambition. This has often been presented by India's political elite as a claim to either 'great power' or 'regional power' status. Yet what do these terms mean? And how are Indian claims linked to the difference between her military and her economic potential, noted in the previous chapter? P. N. Haksar's statements are typical of the nature of India's claims: 'The events of 1971 in our sub-continent sent a message across the chanceries [sic] of the world – that Indira Gandhi's India, with its triumph over Bangladesh, was emerging as a power in its own right.'[1] Such essentially Edwardian language is common to many official and elite statements about India's capabilities after the Bangladesh war. India has certainly seen her international reference points as being, not Pakistan or Sri Lanka, but China, the Soviet Union and to a lesser extent the USA. In a famous broadcast to the nation Nehru once referred to India's manifest destiny to become the 'third or fourth' most powerful nation in the world.

Nowhere is the word 'power' quantified or discussed. One may forgive politicians and elder statesman a degree of rhetorical excess, but even in India's large (and growing) security/foreign policy literature, the terms of 'great' and 'regional' are used without precision as if they are interchangeable.[2] More often than not the term power is equated in India with a particular martial logic and military success without any resulting economic dimensions.[3]

Great powers and middle powers: global *vs* regional capabilities

Berridge and Young have argued that a great power is a state with hegemonic powers working in defence of 'special interests' involving the management of the world system.[4]

This global managerial function is a crucial aspect of the definition: it denotes a state at or near the top of an international hierarchy of states, capable of setting the international agenda and maintaining systemic order either alone, or through collective action with other great powers. Although the term 'great power' has subsequently become confused by the expression 'superpower'[5], great powers must have a capacity to act globally.

Global reach cannot be defined in terms that simply limit it to military capability, or to military 'power projection'. Even in its particular nineteenth-century usage, 'great powers' were invariably states with global economic and commerical interests. Military strength alone is not enough to ensure 'great power status'. As we have seen in the case of the Soviet Union, an attempt to sustain a global military reach without a dynamic and growing economy can lead to political collapse and global disengagement.[6] If this definition is accepted then the term 'great power' makes clear analytical sense, even if attempts to prove a particular country's status still remains empirically difficult and highly subjective.

What then of non-great powers? Within an international system as a whole, great powers act upon lesser powers as subjects. Baldur Nayar has referred to subject powers as the mere objects of great power policy, without leverage to influence the shape of the international system.[7] Yet it follows that if the international state system consists of a hierarchy, not all the subject states are themselves equal, but further differentiated in terms of power and their overall ability to resist and influence great powers. It is at this juncture that the term 'middle power' is introduced into the literature.

A middle power is essentially a regional power, unable to sustain a global role, but dominant within a particular regional context. Nayar defines a middle power as a state that has enough capability 'to foreign policy autonomy within a specific region, an ability to lay claim to regional primacy', and 'the right to police and uphold a particular regional order which may at times significantly diverge from great power interests'. To some commentators the term 'region' has presented some difficulties: does it, for example, refer to a geographical, cultural or a political subsystem? Nayar, following Wight[8], defines a region as being a 'geographically restricted area culturally united but often politically divided', a term that is closely related to the Buzan and Rizvi concept of 'security complex'.

India as a middle power?

Thus defined, India appears to have good grounds to claim middle power status but not yet great power capability, i.e. her position of regional supremacy is not yet matched by real global influence in terms of military reach or economic importance. She may well aspire to global influence, but has yet to claim it. Much of the literature on middle powers (such as Brazil, for example) stresses that such states may seek to graduate further up the hierarchy of states. At the end of the 1970s, Mellor noted that 'middle powers' referred to a series of 'rising political, economic and military' states whose 'large aggregate size' indicated that they 'will eventually play a global role'. To do so, states must augment their power capabilities[9] and must (a) accept the basic principles and values that underpin the current world system and (b) be tacitly accepted as bona fide great powers by those states currently enjoying great power status. Bull has referred to the dangers of adjustment that follow from the 'promotion' of states to great power status – leading to possible resistance: 'the security dilemma within the international system is such that [existing] great powers may well resist the emergence of others'.

If this terminology is used to address the concrete examples of South Asia, we appear to be on familiar ground. Yet there are still practical difficulties in allotting the term 'middle power' automatically and uncritically to explain India's regional policy since 1971. The definition of a middle power is still a multidimensional one, which combines economic and political strength with military capability. It follows from the discussions on India's political and economic difficulties that, on close examination, even her claims to regional supremacy can be summed up as being one-dimensional: based upon military projection alone. Moreover, military commitments (modelled on Bangladesh, and badly applied to Sri Lanka in 1987) are not so much part of an attempt positively to restructure external relations, but generally reactive and poorly thought through. Invariably India has been compelled to act through domestic weakness, and as an extension of domestic concerns. The only exception to this was indeed the 1971 Bangladesh war, wherein Indian skilfully acted on Pakistan's weakness.

Within India's elite there is a marked divergence between the rhetoric of power and the realities of that power. Rajiv Gandhi initiated the Indo-Sri Lankan accord with the remarks that 'the agreement is a major landmark in the four decades of India's freedom. It is an agreement that does not have a parallel anywhere in the world.' Yet just four months into the accord it became clear that India's real abilities were very limited.

The Indo-Sri Lankan fiasco is indicative of one major drawback to India's regional policy. In *The Anarchical Society*, Bull argued that great power states relied upon the acceptance of that status by other great powers, and by lesser states subject to great power management. It is possible to extend this caveat to the term 'middle power': a middle power must be recognised by other states within the region as a paramount power, otherwise the claim is based upon coercion and diplomatic intimidation. Throughout the previous chapters it has been shown that India's 'large aggregate size' has not automatically advanced her claims to regional pre-eminence, and that many of the smaller states have submitted to India's claims with great reluctance, and often with the accusation that they have been bullied.

Given Pakistan's size and history, her attitude to India is not in itself surprising. Of all the states of South Asia, it has been Pakistan's consistent refusal to succumb to India's dominance that has most irritated New Delhi, and has cast Pakistan in the capacity of 'spoiler'. Pakistan has refused to concede to New Delhi on the grounds of national security, alleging that India has never yet reconciled herself to the creation of a Pakistani state.

The entire basis of the Indo-Sri Lankan accord was that of implied threat and unattainable objectives. Although the Maldives turned to India to ask for help in November 1988, they had first turned towards the Sri Lankan government for help.[10] As soon as the Indians had dispatched over 1,000 paratroopers, the Gayoom government was reported to be 'grateful but alarmed' and urged them to be returned as soon as possible. In 1989 following the trial of the coup leaders, Gayoom called for a 'collective security' doctrine based upon the United Nations and the Security Council, despite clear Indian offers to come to a comprehensive security arrangement. These sentiments are found elsewhere within the region, even within sections of the Bhutanese court. The net effect of such regional mistrust make the prospects for a collective security arrangement centred upon Indian primacy impossible, and yet India will not accept anything else.

If India's claims to middle power status are questionable in terms of their regional legitimacy and sustainability, it follows that India's claims to nascent great power status must also be re-examined. Nayar noted in 1978 that 'India is a middle power with great power ambition since given her size, population, strategic location and historical past, India cannot *but* aspire to great power status'.[11]

Yet such ambitions fall foul of India's ambivalent position within the world, with one face staring forward into the future where her potential will have been realised, the other looking back into domestic poverty and regional instability. It is only at this point that the full dilemma of India's position in the closing years of the twentieth century becomes clear. With the ending of the cold war, and with the transformation of US–USSR global relations, and the rise of a multi-polar world, much of India's previous policies are redundant. Yet attempts to derive a new consensus over both domestic, regional and foreign policy issues occur when India is at her weakest since independence, when the elite consensus over core nationalist values has almost disintegrated, and when the institutional processes of government are clogged by regional deals and the strain of mediating exclusive ethnic identities. The growth of Hindu militancy within India is having direct repercussions on regional politics, and it is not even necessary for a Hindu fundamentalist party to come to power to ensure that certain aspects of their programme are taken up by weak coalition governments.

More seriously, the opening up of the wider international system may well *downgrade* South Asia's regional significance compared to other regions, such as the Middle East, the so-called Pacific Basin, or even Europe. And even more ironically, this marginality is the result of India's success in keeping South Asia out of the cold war equation throughout the 1950s and 1960s.

Indo-Pakistan nuclear ambitions and nuclear strategy

The tendency to equate power with military capability alone has profound consequences for the future stability of the region, especially given Pakistan's refusal to concede Indian primacy. India and Pakistan stand at the centre of a conventional arms race that, since 1974, has threatened to go nuclear with the deployment of a nuclear device followed by the continual proliferation of more and more nuclear weapon systems. Between 1980 and 1990, Indian defence expenditure has increased by 250 per cent. In 1987 India was one of the largest importers of weapons in the world. Yet as a proportion of her GNP, and in terms of her per capita spending, Pakistan has the highest defence budget in the region.

Throughout most of her history, Pakistan's level of expenditure has been supported by a combination of military (or military-backed) governments, and concessional aid and 'soft loans' from the US. Given the uncertainties over the future of US–Pakistan relations, the fear that India will move into a position of overwhelming conventional superiority has suggested to some strategists that what Pakistan needs – and needs urgently – is an atomic bomb.

Since the early 1970s sections of the Pakistani military have stressed both the counter-value and the counter-force utility of nuclear weapons: that is, as weapons of fear against large and vulnerable civilian targets in India, and for battlefield use against a conventionally superior foe. Moreover, Stephen Cohen has argued that the Pakistani doctrine of 'offensive defence' – seen in the context of conventional wars with India – could easily accommodate a strategic doctrine of first or pre-emptive nuclear strikes against Indian nuclear facilities or rather large massings of mechanised Indian infantry.[12]

There are also clear signs that sections of India's military (and their political masters) want to acquire atomic weapons, and in anticipation of deployment, have already developed aspects of a pre-emptive nuclear strategy. This desire is in spite of having the conventional edge on Pakistan. It should not be surprising that in both India and Pakistan strategic planners assume that the opponent would use a nuclear weapon to underscore a sudden forward attack on either Kashmir or Azad Kashmir.[13] The discussion of actual nuclear doctrine has been remarkably absent within both India and Pakistan. Apart from the official options school (discussed below) the Indian debate reveals two other clearly-identified camps: the 'great power minimum deterrence' group and the 'war fighting group'. It seems reasonable to assume that such groups also exist within Pakistan.

The first camp believe that there would be little relationship between nuclear deterrence in South Asia and western literature on vertical proliferation. That is, it would not be necessary for India to become involved in increasingly complex and sophisticated systems such as assured second strike capabilities, hardened silos and increasingly expensive C^3 (Command, Control and Communication) equipment. Recently one commentator has pointed out that 'the strategic doctrines of nuclear war that are applicable to the developed world are not quite relevant here [in India]. Concepts like massive retaliation, assured second strike, graduated response do not apply to third world scenarios.'[14] It is believed that a few deployments – either on a strategic wing of the airforce or on an adapted liquid fuel missile – will be enough to underscore India's defence commitments without risks of further escalation.[15] The logic of the minimum deterrence school is that the use of a bomb lies as much in its political symbolism as its actual credibility to be used. Following actual deployment, there is very little need to work out any particular strategy, since deployment is premised on the belief that the weapons will never be used.

The war fighting school believe that India should deploy immediately (and should have deployed after 1974), and moreover, that once deployment has taken place, India must accept the logic of deterrence and press on to add expensive additions to her stockpiles, and continually update the strategies of when and how nuclear force will be used. The minimum deterrence school are criticised for failing to appreciate the link between deployment, strategic doctrine and credibility. Moreover it is argued that given India's security environment *vis-à-vis* Pakistan and China it is extremely unlikely that a relatively small weapons system would suffice.

It is argued that the sophistication of conventional weapons means that the minimum deterrence school makes assumptions that are far too naive. The complexities of Indian and Pakistani air defences would make a nuclear airstrike difficult, while simple missile technology would have to be carefully placed to ensure maximum deterrence; this would raise issues for both countries. For India to cover both Pakistan and China would mean deploying IRBM in some of her most politically unstable areas (the North-East), while because of Pakistan's territorial depth, the only locations that would be safe from an Indian attack would put missile sites up against the Afghan–Iranian border.

Even before the 1974 PNE, the Indo-Pakistan nuclear game of 'yes we have, no we don't' was curiously asymmetrical, despite common security doctrines. Pakistan desired an atomic device in order finally to contain the Indians military modernisation programme. Sections of India's political elite wanted the bomb, not necessarily to intimidate Pakistan (although this would have been an added bonus), but to point at China, and – more crucially – to underscore her aspirations to be a great power. Since 1974, this asymmetry has remained. Obviously if Pakistan was to deploy first, India would react immediately, but Pakistan's nuclear ambitions are only part of the complex motive that propels India's nuclear ambitions. One clear motive is the belief that great powers are also nuclear powers, and that nuclear powers, enthroned in the Security Council of the United Nations, have 'special interests' in the management of global affairs. Such sentiments are expressed by many self-proclaimed Third World writers. Ali Mazuri believes that to insist that non-nuclear states should renounce access to nuclear weapons is to deny these states access to the essential symbols of apparent modernity.[16]

Based upon the dubious authenticity of Nixon's remark about China, some Indian policy-makers believe that although the US can ignore over 800 million Indians at the onset of the New World Order, it would be difficult to ignore over 800 million Indians with nuclear weapons. Are nuclear weapons a short cut to global influence? If so, has India the technological capability to develop and deploy them? What would it cost, economically and diplomatically, to possess them? Would a nuclear weapons programme detract further from the wider priorities of industrial and economic development? And what would be the effects of a nuclear India on China and Pakistan, and the wider international community?

The response of the smaller South Asian states to a nuclear arms race within the region would be to increase their support for calls for a nuclear free zone, and to articulate their opposition within the international forums of the UN, NAM and the Commonwealth. Nepal has tried since the mid 1970s to sell its idea of a 'peace zone' and would strongly resist the deployment of nuclear weapons, as would Bhutan. Sri Lanka would be particularly concerned about an Indian bomb, because of the consequences of her own minority problem, and because of its implications for the Indian Ocean. Bangladesh would have no immediate benefit from any mutual defence agreements with India: a nuclear India would increase all of her fears and would probably involve general appeals to the wider international community for security guarantees. The wider political reverberations would be endless because of the Nuclear Non-Proliferation Treaty. (NPT) In 1983 Sen Gupta concluded that: 'In sum a nuclear India will have to face at least for some time, a hostile West, a frigid USSR, a perturbed China, an angry Pakistan, and a cluster of fearful smaller states.'[17]

Pakistan: the weak link?

Some Indian strategists believe in the political status of the bomb, and since 1974 India has generally pursued a diplomatic strategy of preserving her options; hence it could be argued that India poses the most immediate threat to the non-nuclear status of South Asia. Yet paradoxically the key weakness in the chain of nuclear proliferation for South Asia is Pakistan, because of the severity of her insecurity complex against India's conventional military profile. The only way out of this conundrum is either for Pakistan to receive a watertight nuclear guarantee from a nuclear power (the US, or possibly China), or for her to persuade India to mutually forgo the nuclear option altogether as well as to open the way for conventional arms limitation talks. Evidence for such arguments comes from India's responses to the numerous Pakistani proposals which have aimed to open up regional nuclear installations for inspection, to outlaw pre-emptive strikes against each other's nuclear installations, to forgo the use of a nuclear first strike strategy, and ultimately to declare the entire zone of South Asia as a nuclear free zone. This continual stream of offers, often with the enthusiastic support of the smaller states, is a cause of constant embarrassment for India since her consistent refusals imply that she will not trust Pakistan on matters of verification, and that her nuclear ambitions are cast further afield than parity with Pakistan. India, alone of the states of South Asia, appears to disbelieve that the region will be better off without nuclear weapons at all.

New Delhi's official doctrine under the Rajiv Gandhi and V. P. Singh governments was to reserve the option to deploy nuclear weapons conditional on Pakistan moves, but not to forgo the nuclear option just to satisfy Islamabad. In terms of her security environment, Pakistan falls between the devil and the deep blue sea: she cannot receive the guarantees she requires from the US to her satisfaction, and she cannot get New Delhi categorically to reject the bomb. Following the Soviet invasion of Afghanistan, Stephen Cohen mused that: 'it is an open question whether the new mutual dependencies that will be created between the United States and Pakistan will in the long run enhance or weaken Pakistan's security'.[18] The answer, that has been emerging since the signing of the Geneva Accords, is that it has weakened her security, because US support was premised upon a special set of circumstances that went against the trend of a declining US–Pakistan relationship throughout the 1970s.

South Asia and the nuclear Non-Proliferation Treaty

The key to eliminating nuclear weapons from the South Asian equation is a security regime that satisfies both India and Pakistan. This would seem, to all intents and purposes, impossible. From the onset of the nuclear age, there existed a general consensus amongst the nuclear powers (with the exception of China after 1964) that the horizontal proliferation of weapons into the hands of more and more states would greatly add to global instability.[19] Thus the United States, Britain, France and the Soviet Union agreed to draw up an international treaty aimed at preventing the testing and developing of nuclear weapons by non-nuclear powers. The treaty, adopted by the UN General Assembly in 1968, sanctioned the use of nuclear technology for civilian purposes under the international supervision of the International Atomic Energy Association (IAEA). Yet the agreement outlawed attempts by non-nuclear states to 'divert' nuclear materials and information towards a weapon programme. A non-nuclear state was defined as a state that had not 'manufactured and exploded' a nuclear device prior to January 1967.

India objected to the treaty because it 'froze in' the permanent nuclear powers and restricted the sovereign rights of other states to defend their national security. The treaty of 1968 made no specified provision for collective security against non-nuclear states threatened by states already in possession of nuclear weapons. In this respect India was once again conscious of China's nuclear explosion in 1964 and the threats that a nuclear China posed. To assume that, in the event of another border clash with China, the international community would come to the rescue of India would be highly irresponsible, and contradicted India's fundamental principles of foreign policy.

India also objected to the NPT on the grounds that it did not differentiate between horizontal proliferation – the graduation of more and more states to nuclear weapons – and vertical proliferation – the acquisition by the already existing nuclear powers of more and more nuclear weapons systems. This difference is a critical one given the perception of India's foreign policy elite that the NPT was not just an arms control agreement, but an arms reduction agreement.[20] Yet the finished document nowhere compelled the nuclear powers into making arms reductions at all.

Prior to the NPT, India had supported and initiated various calls within the Non-Aligned Movement to limit and remove nuclear weapons.[21] India's policy approach, outlined at the Eighteenth National Disarmament Conference in 1962–3, was that any treaty that dealt with nuclear weapons must do so comprehensively, it must eliminate them within a specified time subject to satisfactory guarantees, and must not merely reflect the strategic concerns of the great powers. Sen Gupta has summarised India's refusal to sign the treaty on three grounds: 'the imbalance of obligations between nuclear and non-nuclear powers, inadequate security guarantees [for the non-nuclear powers] and discrimination for the use of peaceful nuclear explosions (PNE)'.[22] India's policy towards the NPT not only ensured that Pakistan would not sign, but led to international speculation that there was some ulterior motive: the desire to join the 'nuclear club' of the five permanent members.

India's decision to conduct a PNE in 1974 – the first nuclear test by a previously non-nuclear state since China – reinforced this speculation and led to international condemnation. India's insistence that it was a 'peaceful' device was seen as being particularly duplicitous since it did not jeopardise any extant agreements India had signed with foreign countries to assist her with her civilian nuclear power programme.[23]

Like so much of India's posturing on global issues, it would be absurd to pretend that an ideological objection to nuclear weapons was not also part of a realistic policy aimed at reserving India's option to deploy such weapons. In 1986, K. Subrahmanyam argued that: 'nations that are not signatories of the NPT have reserved their options . . . and have as much ethical, legal and strategic justification to have nuclear weapons as [the] signatories . . . Proliferating nations preaching non-proliferation create distrust as to their intentions in practising coercive diplomacy and dominance over the rest of the world.'[24]

India's position on the NPT implies she is in favour of other states advancing similar arguments. Does this mean that India, like China in the 1960s, supports nuclear proliferation? Many commentators believe that this is not the case. The late Hedely Bull noted with reference to France, China and India that 'while they have sometimes justified proliferation with arguments that apply to others as well as themselves, they have at no time argued in favour of general and complete nuclear proliferation. [They] have been principally concerned to remove the obstacles to their own inclusion into the nuclear weapons club.'[25] India's objections to the NPT are based simply upon power: her desire to be a nuclear state.

It is possible that, if granted the status of a nuclear power India could be brought into the 'fire break' and co-opted into preventing further violations of the NPT regime. This would amount to becoming a *de facto* great power. This, with various other conditions, would be the price that New Delhi would try and exact for forgoing the deployment of nuclear weapons. In 1974 George H. Quester noted that 'if we [the US] concede that India has made it safely into the ranks of the nuclear explosives nations [*sic*] New Delhi may still not wish to allow many other nations into these ranks'.[26] Like all the other great powers, India may well begin to resist the dilution of her influence through having to share it with other states. Yet Pakistan, technically a threshold state, although it has never acknowledged a nuclear test, would not tolerate the sanctioning of an Indian bomb, however theoretical it was, regardless of the security arrangements offered by the US[27] Her response would be to move rapidly to develop and deploy her own device, which would force India to respond in kind regardless of any previous understandings with the wider international community.

The costs of the nuclear option

Even if it is assumed that the international community would sanction some form of selective proliferation within South Asia, could India and Pakistan afford it, and what effect would this have upon their current developmental policies? The 'guns vs. grains' argument about defence expenditure is inconclusive, and often uncritically assumes that the relationship between defence expenditure and development is automatically inverse.[28] The World Bank noted with obvious displeasure that 'military expenditure has increased more than twice as fast as per capita incomes in the developing world since 1960': but is such expenditure non-productive?

That military spending has distorted economic growth and re-directed scarce resources away from productive investment appears superficially to be truer for Pakistan than for India, especially for the first decade after independence, yet even then the evidence is speculative and counter-factual. Indian defence expenditure may well have grown, but recent figures suggest that government spending on defence has declined as a proportion of total government expenditure from 31 per cent in 1964 to an average of 20 per cent throughout the 1970s. In 1988 it stood at 19·3 per cent. This compares favourably to the Pakistan figures of 39·9 per cent (1972) and 29·5 per cent (1988), and Sri Lanka's figures of 9·6 per cent in 1988.[29]

These resources might well have been invested into export-based industries and have resulted in real gains in foreign exchange, or subsequent foreign exchange used to purchase expensive western arms might well have been freed for capital goods imports, but it could just as likely have ended up in the public sector being invested in underutilised and inefficient stock. Moreover, while a considerable literature has grown up that identifies military expenditure as inflationary, there is little correlation within India whose domestic inflation has been traditionally quite low.

Increased defence spending can have potentially beneficial connotations for an economy, providing jobs within the public sector and providing backward and forward linkages with other public companies. In India, Hindustan Aeronautics has benefited substantially from defence contracts. And India seems set to begin an arms export drive to help fund the increasing costs of her defence requirements.[30]

That poor states cannot and should not commit themselves to sophisticated military establishments, including ones that subscribe to the manufacture and deployment of nuclear weapons, is hotly debated. K. Subrahmanyam has dismissed the entire debate as a 'foreign fabrication, a piece of neo-colonial brainwashing'[31] since in the past India's economic growth has been capable of supporting 'necessary increases'.

Certainly defence spending throughout South Asia has not been excessively out of line with overall economic performance (as has been the case, say, in the Soviet Union or indeed in Israel), but it is also equally misleading to see the contributions of arms expenditure to development in the same way as increases in primary health care or basic schooling. Moreover, there is growing evidence that current military expenditure, coinciding with a period of general economic transition and increased regional insecurity, could well provide growing pressures on scarce investment resources and have distorting effects on overall economic growth. There can be no doubt that the extent and degree of Soviet aid towards India's modernisation significantly disguised the real cost of her rearmament and that in current circumstances she may well face increased costs. Likewise, India's desire to move away from Soviet procurement will further undermine her foreign currency reserves.[32] There can be little doubt that arms deals for Jaguar and Mirage fighter bombers helped contribute to the seriousness of India's balance of payments by the late 1980s.

The same can be said for the degree of concessional US aid to Pakistan, especially during the 1970s. With the present US–Pakistan disengagement over Pakistan's nuclear weapons programme, costs will increase and Pakistan will find her access to American technology severely limited. Both India and Pakistan are now under strict IMF conditionality as to the type and scale of government expenditure. Since India's defence industry still relies upon expensive imports of foreign technology, restrictions on imports and the encouragement of currency devaluations will seriously restrict planned modernisation in the absence of a sustained drive to sell Indian weapons abroad in which profits are ploughed back into weapons production and research.

Amit Gupta has noted that while India has proved largely incapable of competing in advanced technologies like aircrafts and tanks, she has developed an almost entirely indigenous missile programme. The success of the Prithva (SRBM) and the Agni (IRBM) tests at the end of the 1980s are therefore of immediate significance in circumstances where India's dependence on complex foreign conventional technology is increasing. The belief exists that nuclear weapons might actually be cheaper. The declining cost of the bomb relative to 'smart' technologies will further tempt both states to deploy it. Quester has noted in a recent article on threshold states that 'for decades the general worry about global nuclear proliferation has not been that nuclear weapons would prove to be too expensive, but rather that they would be too cheap.'[33] It has been calculated that a modest weapons programme for India could be funded for around US $700 million, which is not out of line with conventional spending, and would probably prove less over time.[34] In the early 1980s Sen Gupta calculated that the costs of developing a fairly sophisticated nuclear weapons system would add an additional 5 per cent of GNP to defence expenditure (increasing to about 9 per cent of GNP).[35] Given Pakistan's lower defence costs in absolute terms, the price estimates for Pakistan would be slightly higher, which might increase defence expenditure towards 10–12 per cent of GNP.

Even if we accept this assumption, there are great difficulties in arriving at a cost-benefit analysis of a nuclear weapons programme for either India or Pakistan, since the debate is largely hypothetical and based upon comparisons with conventional expenditure. There is sufficient evidence to support the argument that, in the short term, the option is cheaper. Yet this calculation is premised on the assumption that nuclear deployment in South Asia would be a relatively simple affair, and that it would not involve an arms race driven by a rapid and sustained vertical proliferation of more accurate and precise weaponry – an assumption made by the minimum deterrence school. This assumption is highly dubious, since the experience of the conventional arms race shows that a balance of power on the basis of mutual security can be elusive. The notion of a stable nuclear balance (and hence the assumptions of cheapness) must be examined further: 'Fundamental asymmetry pushes India and Pakistan to define their national security in fundamentally different ways and makes the tasks of establishing common security needs particularly difficult.'[36]

While there are obvious differences between conventional and nuclear weapons, and care must be taken in extrapolating the dynamics of conventional strategy into the nuclear domain, the assumption of continued nuclear stability following actual deployment is highy unlikely. It is much more likely that the two states will be locked into a nuclear arms race. At every stage of Pakistan's rearmament after 1979 India protested that the types of weapon being supplied were far in excess of her requirements. India has attempted tirelessly to match specific weapons systems and to fill in perceived conventional weaknesses. India's search for a deep strike aircraft, which led to the expensive western arms deals with Britain and France, was based upon the fears of Pakistan's American-supplied F-16s. A nuclear arms race in South Asia would then, on the face of it, involve vertical proliferation and would dramatically destabilise the region, having knock-on effects on China and the Middle East, if the states were themselves able to sustain it.

Nuclear deployment and international sanctions

In the absence of any collective security arrangement between India and Pakistan, is there anything the wider international community can do to prevent a sustained nuclear arms race within the sub-continent? The intriguing factor about South Asia is that although the psychological and military conditions are now favourable to supporting the deployment of nuclear weapons, there is still some doubt whether India and Pakistan could sustain a nuclear arms race in the face of international sanctions authorised by the NPT, and supported by both Soviet and American foreign policy. The Achilles' heel for both states would be that sustained vertical proliferation would involve access to sophisticated western technology that would not be forthcoming unless both states guaranteed their non-nuclear status.

The commitment of the United States and the Soviet Union to the NPT has hardened appreciably since the mid 1980s, especially with regard to 'threshold' states. China has also been attending the various review conferences on the treaty as an observer since 1985. At both the 1985 and the 1990 conferences, it was noted that 'a great number of countries throughout the world genuinely welcome a barrier to further nuclear proliferation' even in circumstances in which horizontal proliferation is not linked to the controversy of vertical proliferation.

There is an essential irony to the current Pakistani position over the nuclear dilemma that escapes most commentators: Pakistan's determined resolve to get the bomb has led to the current US arms embargoes, which has in turn exacerbated Pakistan's sense of insecurity. By undermining Pakistan's external supply of weapons and aid, the current US sanctions policy has merely furthered the determination of previous regimes to get hold of an atomic device. The most obvious move for any US administration would be to resume sufficient arms sales to assure, as in 1954, that she is committed to Pakistan's territorial integrity. Unlike 1954, she will have to do so with sufficient conviction for Pakistan to believe it.

Such a policy would lead to further outrage and consternation from New Delhi. The initial US response to the PNE in 1974 was remarkably tame, much less than the British reaction. While India has been the subject of US technical embargoes, these have often had less to do with the threat of their 'deflection' from industrial to military use, than with the fear that they would find their way into the hands of the Soviets. Pakistan's nuclear industry has proved much more vulnerable to sanctions than India's. In 1971 India had signed a trilateral agreement between the US and the IAEA to safeguard her civilian programmes, but a significant part of her programme established by Dr. Bhabha and the Atomic Energy Commission, involving co-operation with the Canadians, was unsafeguarded and provided the plutonium used for the 1974 test. Thus even if the US was capable of buying Pakistan's support, India would attempt to exact a much higher price. New Delhi would probably demand not just US weapons at rates identical to Pakistan, but also greater access to industrial technology, and even probably some higher profile within the UN. Yet until the root of the insecurity between India and Pakistan is removed, such policies will only further the conventional arms race (even if with sufficient alacrity to prevent the desire for nuclear weapons), and more seriously, there remains the possibility of either state acquiring some device behind the back of any US administration, or the powers of the UN

The effectiveness of safeguards

The problems about how reliable safeguards are in preventing states going nuclear were discussed at the time of the NPT. Most IAEA safeguards apply to nuclear fuel reprocessing and not enrichment, since it is extremely difficult to 'divert' plutonium from spent fuel rods into a weapons programme, while enrichment presents profound technological difficulties[37] Despite continual allegations that plutonium has been removed from the KANUPP plant in Pakistan, there is little concrete evidence to prove this.[38] In 1980 it was reported that 'Pakistan was still unable to design and build her own nuclear power plants, although she has demonstrated her ability to restart, fuel and operate KANUPP'.[39] Indigenous production of heavy water and fuel rods have all been voluntarily placed under IAEA safeguards.

Earlier, under the regime of Benazir's father, the Americans were successful in pressurising the French to withdraw from a deal to construct a nuclear reprocessing plant signed in 1973, the CHASMA plant near Karachi. The French withdrew in 1979, but not until after most of the blueprints had been delivered to the Pakistani scientists. It is alleged that CHASMA has a small-scale 'experimental' enrichment process that could provide material for a fusion bomb. Pakistan has an operational reprocessing plant and CANDU power station (KANUPP) near Karachi. The station burns 'natural' uranium (U 235) and the fuel is safeguarded. Pakistan also has further research facilities at PINSTECH, near Nilore, which are now believed to be capable of fuel enrichment.

Various scare stories about damaged cameras and poor monitoring equipment at KANUPP significantly underestimate the stringency of IAEA procedures. What safeguards cannot automatically prevent (at least as they were conceived within the NPT) is the determined efforts of a regime to assemble expertise and equipment from a variety of foreign sources to provide the basis for an indigenous bomb programme. While the 'London Club' organisation was formed in 1976 to ensure that nuclear suppliers could monitor the sales of nuclear-related technologies to non-nuclear states, this is not as clear-cut a process as is often suggested, since much of the technology involved is so-called 'dual-use'.

Pakistani ingenuity appears to have laid hold of some very sophisticated technology – mainly through industrial espionage or simple theft – such as gas centrifugal capabilities.[40] As recently as 1990 a Pakistani national was arrested in the US for attempting to purchase high-temperature furnaces from the US company Consarc. Corp. New Jersey.[41] This followed an announcement in 1988 by the infamous Dr Khan that Pakistan now has the technology to enrich natural uranium to about 90 per cent of weapons grade material.

The recent US embargo against Pakistan was carried out because of apparent evidence that Pakistan was clandestinely acquiring nuclear technology in spite of American support (i.e. from about 1973 onwards, before the actual Indian test), and for consistently refusing to open up her nuclear research facilities to international inspection. Even following the waiver of the Symington Amendment, the Americans continued to call on Pakistan to renounce its ambitions. Although such statements were dismissed by the Indians as a careful ploy to disguise actual US–Pakistan co-operation, there is no evidence to prove that Pakistan was a special candidate for 'selective' proliferation, or that the Americans were themselves insincere about their policies.

Official denials by the recently-removed Bhutto government before a joint sitting of Congress that 'Pakistan did not have a bomb and had no intention of building one'[42], were ignored by the Bush presidency. The Benazir Bhutto government sought to assure the US that Pakistan's nuclear programme was entirely civilian, aimed at coping with her increasing energy demands and her developmental needs. Yet in early 1989 a report prepared by the US Foreign Affairs and National Defence Division noted that: 'Under President Zia, Pakistan has moved apparently to the brink of a capability to build nuclear weapons, or possibly even to deploy a small number of nuclear weapons. The nuclear weapons option enjoys broad support within policy making circles and among the public at large.'[43]

India's argument about the difference between a 'peaceful' nuclear explosion and a weapons test (a distinction that India was responsible for developing) was in part a political necessity to prevent being penalised under IAEA safeguards. Nonetheless the Canadians withdrew their support from India's civilian programme at protest at the 1974 test. To a large extent, India's decision to forgo further tests may well have been the result of sanctions.

Of the two routes that a state can take towards acquiring nuclear weapons – reprocessing and enrichment – Pakistan is believed to have taken the latter one, a process that India has apparently yet to master.[44] It is believed that international sanctions led by the US, have proved crucial for directing Pakistan's research efforts in favour of enrichment, and hence towards clandestine methods of procurement.

Certainly Z. Bhutto was determined to undermine the NPT by utilising western technological support and Middle Eastern finance, and by co-opting skills from China. Ashok Kapor speculates that after Bhutto's death in 1979, General Zia merely continued the project, and decided to pursue the scheme without an actual test. Sen Gupta has argued that without a series of testings it is almost impossible effectively to weaponise a system. Up to fifty tests may be carried out to conclude the designs for one warhead. Other specialists argue that there is no need to test a weapons system before its actual use. George

Quester notes that the bomb that was dropped on Hiroshima had not been previously tested. While it is possible that the Pakistanis have asked the Chinese (or, as some Indians suggest, the Americans) to test a device, it remains unlikely.

Much of the work on the Pakistani bomb is pure speculation, and the assumption that it exists (or worse, that it is already being stockpiled) is greatly exaggerated. She is widely believed to have a 'bomb in the basement', wherein she has: 'produced but not detonated nuclear weapons and has made a practice of keeping the warheads disassembled. . . perhaps requiring only a few turns of the screwdriver to complete assembly.'[45] However, there is little chance that such speculation can be verified. Much the same can be said about the Indian bomb as well. While there is no doubt about a Pakistani weapons programme (both under Z. Bhutto and General Zia), no concrete evidence exists to support the high level of speculation. There are several strands to this speculation: one assumption is that apparent Pakistani needs for civilian nuclear technology is an out-and-out lie. This is often the opinion of the many Indian commentators on the Pakistani bomb.[46]

Energy imports make up 60 per cent of Pakistan's energy needs and, as discussed in Chapter 4, shortages in Pakistan's energy facilities are responsible for a bottleneck in her future industrial expansion. That she is in need of plentiful sources of electricity is self-evident to anyone who visits metropolitan Pakistan (and the same argument can be extended to India). Much of Pakistani policy towards the Middle East is based upon ensuring her security of oil supply. Many other assumptions – about the inherent warlike nature of – military (or even Islamic) regimes have been considerably weakened since the events of 1988. There is virtually no evidence to support the widely-held belief that Pakistan is stockpiling weapons.

If 'many of the hypothetical senarios concerning the development of an Islamic bomb are totally misleading and unrealistic in their conceptualisation, their basic arguments, and in their conclusion'[47], the same argument can be used about Pakistani speculation over the Indian bomb, in spite of the 1974 PNE. The Sarabhai Profile[48] of 1970–80 was a ten-year integrated programme for developing civilian nuclear, research and remote sensing/satellite technologies for India, the key element of which was a 'peaceful' explosion. While this was successful, and was to many analysts a 'disguised weapons programme'[49] it cannot be automatically assumed that India has been able to press on with the development of a nuclear weapons arsenal –

although it often is. To many commentators since[50], the test was premature, since India suffered under international embargoes on sophisticated technological equipment which postponed further tests and created constraints within her civilian programmes as well.

India's nuclear expertise is more broad based than Pakistan's and has led to the domestic construction of several plutonium reactors (the R-5 stations), and an experimental fast breeder programme. Much of her nuclear power programme is suffering from slippage and delays in the completion and commissioning of plants. India has one un-safeguarded output of Pu-239 from the CIRUS reactor.[51] India is supplied with enriched uranium for the CIRUS reactor from the US, but has continually complained about delays in delivery. A recent agreement with France has replaced US supplies, but these remain safeguarded. Since 1988 India's heavy water projects have also fallen behind schedule. Currently India plans to create a civilian power capacity of 1200 MW by the beginning of the next century, yet of the five nuclear power stations announced in 1985, only three have been commissioned and are reporting to be functioning well under capacity.

These technical bottlenecks will have created some difficulty in the amount of production of Pu-239 to be used for fissile weapons. It has already been noted that India appears to suffer from all the difficulties of enrichment associated with developing a fusion bomb (U-235). While associated technology such as delivery and guidance systems in both India and Pakistan had reached high levels of sophistication, the availability of nuclear materials for warhead development, and the designs and the development of the warheads themselves, are a major constraint on an actual weapons deployment programme, especially one in which the pressure would be to undertake rapid vertical proliferation. There is, then, some evidence that international sanctions have had some effect in slowing down Indian and Pakistani research on fissile, and in particular, fusion weapons.

Towards a collective security framework for South Asia?

Could US (and international) sanctions, combined with adequate security guarantees, secure a non-nuclear South Asia? Only if the states of South Asia themselves accept the legitimacy of such an arrangement, and complement it with their own policies of confidence-building measures. This, not surprisingly, is the main problem. Many of the arguments presented in this book are premised on the fact that, throughout the coming decade, South Asia will be subject to a whole series of contradictory pressures, some emanating from the inter-national environment, some from purely regional trends, and others from domestic political changes. Much has been made of how the economic interactions at these various levels will create both tensions and opportunities towards further growth and development, although the tone has been one that is predominantly cautious and even at times gloomy. Concerning specific matters of defence and security, the picture is more ambivalent.

While the domestic and regional pressures are set to reinforce Indo-Pakistan misperceptions and maintain high levels of defence ex-penditure, and while the pressures are themselves capable of main-taining an arms race, the type and scale of this race is still critically dependent upon foreign involvement and support. This is particularly true of a nuclear arms race. External support for both India and Pakistan have fuelled a conventional arms race far in excess of what these two states were capable of producing; the fact that India's reliance was on foreign collaboration in production and not on arms imports merely served to disguise India's dependence.[52] While the dynamics of regional instability would tend to lead to vertical proliferation of nuclear weapon systems, it is unlikely that either state would be able to produce and develop the technological knowhow unless it was based upon further foreign help.

What has happened since 1989 is a process of disengagement in which international cold war issues have gradually been unwound, and in which US and Soviet interests have been redefined both with respect to themselves, and to their so-called client states throughout the world. Although it is possible to exaggerate the areas of consensus in the so-called New World Order, the Gulf war has revealed the extent to which US and Soviet interests can coincide on regional security issues. It follows from this that there is a unique opportunity to address the problems of nuclear proliferation in South Asia at the international level, and to rethink and readdress some of the long-standing criticisms that have been made about the NPT by the Non-Aligned Movement, and by India in particular. This rethinking is essential for ensuring that regional attempts to foreclose the nuclear option (based upon a bilateral arrangement between India and Pakistan) can be agreed upon.

Of the many criticisms India has of the NPT, three are essential: that it did not prevent vertical proliferation among the already existing nuclear powers, that it did not open the way towards the eventual total elimination of nuclear weapons, and that – for the duration of the interim period necessary to disarm totally – the security guarantees to defend non-nuclear powers from nuclear powers were inadequate.

Even with the ending of the cold war, it seems unlikely that the second condition will ever be fulfilled. The Gorbachev era has seen successful arms reduction talks in the European and the Asian theatres, and some weapons systems have been eliminated under the 1987 INF treaty, but the commitment to some form of nuclear arsenal remains, and China remains to many (even within India) a pariah state with which it is impossible to come to any real agreement. Even if the status of nuclear weapons as a realistic, useful weapons system is now at an all-time low (reinforced by the experiences of the Gulf war), the world is a long way from actually outlawing them, or so reducing them in status that no country has the desire to obtain them.

On the other hand the ability to place *limits* on vertical proliferation is a very real one, even though the START talks have stalled over technical disagreements of how to classify and count particular weapons. If a START treaty were to be ratified in the near future it would eliminate about 30 per cent of strategic weapons and go some way to justifying further attempts to limit horizontal proliferation. Would this satisfy Indian demands?

Two problems remain in the way of India's acceptance of a reworked NPT: one is the problem of a collective security arrangement that would rest upon the use of extra-regional support – primarily a UN force, but ostensibly an American one.[53] While this would be acceptable to Pakistan (and almost every other state within the South Asia region) it remains impossible for India to concede because of her claims to middle power/great power status. It is at this point that the argument returns to the problems of 'one-dimensionality' discussed above: the symbolic significance that the atomic bomb has for India's political elite, and the importance of an independent foreign policy that is seen to be free from manipulation and pressure. In some respects this is the most intractable problem.

To renounce the bomb is, for the Indian elite, to renounce being regionally pre-eminent. To accept external mediation in times of regional crisis or conflict would be to lose claims to be the regional security manager which, again, is part of the psychological claim India has to a middle power with global aspirations. While many of these claims have been shown to be unrealistic, they are politically important to India, more so now than at any other time, and to accept a collective security doctrine, either at the level of the UN, or under a mutually supportive US defence agreement between India and Pakistan, remains unacceptable, unless it could be attached to a greater role for India within the UN. In other words, it is not that the NPT failed to guarantee the security of the non-nuclear states; it is simply that it prevented them from doing it themselves.

The greatest weakness here, like so much of India's current thinking on international relations, is to try and change India's conceptualisation of power and influence away from a military, overtly geostrategic logic, towards one of economic influence and commerce. Such attempts to do so come up against the economic difficulties that India has been facing since the mid 1970s, and the apparent failure of her economic policies within the region to date. The greatest challenge to Chinese hegemony, if such a challenge has to be made, would lie not in a nuclearised India, but in a dynamic and expansive Indian economy able to influence the economies of the Near East and the Pacific basin, and to which China would be attracted for reasons of her own modernisation programmes and her own economic development.

In an interesting paper published in 1987, C. Subrahmanyam noted that India would only ever renounce the nuclear weapon when there had been a shift in general global attitudes towards nuclear weapons themselves and their supposed influence. He argued that some form of treaty – less along the lines of the NPT and more along those of the 1925 Geneva Protocol outlawing chemical weapons – could 'strip nuclear weapons of their legitimacy, their mystique, and their use as the currency of international power'.[54] While such a transformation in attitudes towards weapons of mass destruction appears to be taking place within international opinion, it is not taking place within India or Pakistan. Both sets of elites still perceive 'arguably – that nuclear weapons enhance national security in their external and internal spheres[55]

To 'opt' for non-nuclear status would have to rest upon a domestic consensus within India and Pakistan. This of course returns the entire discussion to the internal political systems of the two main states and the changes that have been taking place within India and Pakistan since the mid 1980s. The 'one-dimensionality' of Indian claims to regional and global influence – an influence based upon military capability and power – are a curious inversion of the Nehruvian view inherited at independence, that influence was to be conveyed through diplomacy and high morals. This change reflects the sad fact that the imagery and symbolism of Nehruvian foreign policy have almost gone. In a much-welcomed contribution to the literature on India's foreign policy since 1971, Bradnock noted that: 'throughout the 40 years of Independence,

India's foreign policy has retained a fundamental consistency of strategic outline which has survived both changes in personal leadership and changes in government – Nehru's Panscheel – are still held up today as the basis of New Delhi's foreign policy today.[56] Yet undue emphasis upon this continuity draws attention away from the very profound changes that have taken place in India's outlook on the world. Until this alters, no level of international reassurance can guarantee the security requirements of both India and Pakistan.

Conclusions

The middle class and the ideology that supported Nehru's commitment to internationalism have been in decline since the mid 1970s. While there remains an ideological affinity to the aspirations of the United Nations, there is little belief that as an organisation the UN is capable of accommodating India's needs. Since the 1971 war, these needs have become increasingly defined in terms of military power and special Indian security interests. Present international changes may revive some sort of Nehruvian language of co-operation and mutual respect, but this language has little value within India, let alone within the emerging discourse of India's political elite.

The terrible truth is that the unravelling of India's political system might not only involve the collapse of an internal order based upon secularism, parliamentarianism and redistributive economic policies; it could also diminish India's ability to share in what Hedley Bull referred to as international society, a series of commonly-held cultural values which – if incorporated into a state system – could provide added cohesion, unity and security. State systems rarely rest upon shared values other than those of threat or coercion. The expansion of international society[57] was ostensibly western in origin, based upon a legal and diplomatic definition of state behaviour, which was in turn seen as being part of the language of being 'modern'. Bull puts it much more elegantly: 'If contemporary international society does have any cultural basis, this is not any genuinely global culture, but it is rather the culture of so-called modernity . . . if we ask what is modernity in culture it is not clear how we can answer this except by saying that it is the culture of the dominant Western powers.'[58] There can be no doubt that Nehru and his generation (as much as Jinnah and Senanayake) were committed to the material benefits of so-called modernity, even to the point of encouraging cultural reforms and changes. This generation have passed on, and although they have been replaced in part by a western-educated middle class, they have also been replaced by something else, something more stridently 'indigenous' and obscure, something akin to a form of pseudo-traditionalism, the symbolism of which consists of a categorical rejection of the West.

It should not be surprising that in Pakistan, fundamentalist religious parties reject not just a capitalist, urban-based economy, but the 'core values' of individualism and consumerism that sustain it. To conceptualise such obscurantism as a new medievalism may seem deeply offensive (or even uninformed), but it seems to many adequately to describe what is happening within some Islamic thinking. How long such thinking will remain from power remains a moot point.

A Hindu India would suffer from many of the problems and drawbacks encountered by an Islamic Pakistan – a state exclusiveness that affects economic integration by affecting policies, an obscurantism that affects the use and development of scientific knowledge and research, and which fuels the sort of endemic provincial violence that has done so much to undermine the very real gains India and Pakistan have made since independence. It has often been noted that the images and themes of India are to do with 'peace' and inner harmony, in which the country has become – to the western mind at least – a sort of massive ashram. Such an image disguises one of the most violent societies in the world. As early as 1951 the noted historian and diplomat P. N. Panikkar remarked: 'our vision [of Indian interests] has been obscured by an un-indian wave of pacifism . . . Apart from the Buddhist and Jain heresies which the good sense of the Hindus rejected long ago, it is not known what religious basis there is in Hinduism for the form of pacificism which has come . . . to be associated with the Hindu.'[59]

This is not to dismiss indigenous regional Hinduism as violent, or inferior, but to question the institutional forms in which culture is used by politicians, and how the language and symbols of such a culture can be adapted to deal with India's developmental needs. The tragedy of Pakistan is not that it is Islamic, but that Islam has become the cover for the political fudges and compromises of discredited and illegitimate elites – in which Qur'anic erudition has replaced critical reasoning. An explicit and chauvinistic Hinduism will limit the social and intellectual interchange that has taken place between South Asia and the western world to the mutual benefit of each, and to the gradual development of international society. It will also further the crisis of nation formation and the overwhelming economic rationality and interdependence that must sustain it.

The disintegration of India has been a favourite prediction from many academics and journalists over the years. Such pessimism has usually overlooked the extraordinary dynamism and resilience within India, the strength of her political elite, and the success of her development programmes. As the 1990s unfold, these predictions will be reissued to deal with the rise of ethno-linguistic exclusiveness. The real threat for India is not that the state will disintegrate and 'Balkanise', but that the ability of the state to interfere in and organise civil society will falter. As it does so, the various ethnic and linguistic minorities (especially the Muslims) will become subject to competing loyalties as the secular state becomes increasingly incapable of maintaining and defending their interest and the interests of a composite 'Indian' nationalism.

The result of all this would be further to marginalise South Asia as a region within the world economy, and further to weaken any of the claims made by India to be a middle power with great-power pretensions. The prospects for Pakistan are even bleaker and could well precipitate a crisis. In the wake of the Gulf war and extended talks about the New World Order, the issues are whether the states of South Asia can reform themselves enough to get the attention, the funding, and the future that they deserve.

Notes

1 P. N. Haksar, *India's Foreign Policies and its Problems*, New Delhi, 1989, p. 53.
2 See P. Singh, *India and the Future of Asia*, New Delhi, 1966; J. N. Chaudhuri, *India's Problems of National Security in the 1970s*, New Delhi, 1973, and D. Kennedy, *The Security of Southern Asia*, London, 1965. See also the interesting Yu T. George, *Intra-Asian International Relations*, Boulder, 1989.
3 In a recent conference paper submitted to the ECPR conference in 1990, a student from the University of Oslo referred to 'great regional powers' – evidence of the sort of confusing terminology that is rife within this particular area of study.
4 G. Berridge and J. Young, 'What is a great power?', *Political Studies*, 36, June, 1988, pp. 224–34.
5 This term was first used by W. R. T. Fox in his book, *The Superpowers*, London, 1944.
6 Japan is an interesting example of a state that has increasing managerial responsibilities within the world economy, but as yet no military apparatus (or even global foreign policy) through which to undertake those responsibilites. See Kazuo Chiba, 'Japan and the New World Order', *Pacific Review*, 4, 1991, pp. 1–4.
7 See B. R. Nayar, 'A world role: the dialectics of purpose and power' in J. W. Mellor (ed.), *India: A Rising Middle Power?*, Colorado, 1979.
8 M. Wight, *Power Politics*, Leicester, 1978.

9 J. S. Nye and R. O. Keohane, *Transnational Relations and World Politics*, Cambridge, 1971.
10 Far Eastern Economic Review, *Asian–Year Book*, Hong Kong, 1989.
11 Nayar, 'A world role', p. 122 (emphasis added).
12 S. Cohen, *The Pakistan Army*, California, 1987.
13 Rather like the two Berlins after World War II, Kashmir provides the setting for much of Pakistani and Indian war gaming. See A. Banerjee, *The Indian Defence Review*, New Delhi, 1989.
14 Banerjee, *The Indian Defence Review*.
15 See R. Ram, 'India's nuclear defence policy', *Indian Defence and Strategic Analysis Journal (IDSA)*, 14, 1982.
16 Noted in Caroline Thomas, *In Search of Security*, Brighton, 1987. Thomas refers to Ali Mazuri's belief that all states should have the right to acquire nuclear weapons as symbols of 'statehood'. See Mazuri's essay entitled 'Africa entrapped: between the protestant ethic and the legacy of Westphalia' in H. Bull and A. Watson, *The Expansion of International Society*, London, 1987, pp. 289–308.
17 B. Sen Gupta, *Nuclear Options for India*, New Delhi, 1983, p. 23.
18 Cohen, *The Pakistan Army*, p. 152.
19 See B. Buzan (ed.), *The International Politics of Nuclear Deterrence*, London, 1987.
20 Thomas, *In Search of Security*, Brighton, 1987.
21 See A. K. Chopra, *India's Policy on Disarmament*, New Delhi, 1984.
22 Sen Gupta, *Nuclear Options for India*, p. 2.
23 Interestingly enough, America's initial reaction was quite lame. The State Department redrafted the offical US response after vigorous British protests and then under pressure from the non-proliferation lobby. See J. S. Nye, 'Non-proliferation: a long term strategy', *Foreign Affairs*, 56, 1978, pp. 601–23.
24 Cited in B. Buzan (ed.), *International Politics of Nuclear Deterrence*, p. 100.
25 H. Bull, *The Anarchical Society*, London, 1977, p. 243.
26 George Quester, 'Can proliferation be stopped?', *Foreign Affairs*, 53, 1974, pp. 77–97.
27 It is possible that a Pakistani device has been tested in China under the protocol of an agreement signed in 1986.
28 See P. Terhal, 'Guns vs. grains: macro-economic costs of Indian defence 1960–70', *Economic and Political Weekly*, 16, 49, (5 December 1981), pp. 1998–2014. More generally see E. Benoit *Defence and Economic Growth in Less Developed Countries*, Lexington, 1973.
29 *World Bank Report 1990*. Table 11: 'Central Government Expenditure'. See also Raju Thomas, *India's Security Policy*, Princeton, 1986. J. Benard has argued that India has reclassified various aspects of its defence budget under different headings (especially pensions and salaries) to disguise the increase in defence spending. See A. Benard, 'A maturation crisis', *Asian Survey*, 27, pp. 408–18.
30 *Keesings Contemporary Archives*, 10, 35, p. 37006.
31 K. Subrahmanyam, 'Indian nuclear forces in the 1980s' in *Indian Defence and Strategic Analysis Journal (IDSA)*, Vol. 5, No. 4, 1972.
32 One of the interesting consequences of the just-concluded Gulf war was the poor performance of much Soviet hardware and equipment. The supremacy of western air power has increased Indian anxiety about her air weakness vis-à-vis Pakistan's air force, which consists mainly of US supplied F–16s.
33 G. H. Quester, 'Conceptions of nuclear threshold status' in Regina C. Karp (ed.),

Security With Nuclear Weapons? Different Perspectives on National Security, Oxford, 1991, p. 214.

34 See M. V. Bratersky and S. I. Lunyov, 'The costs of India's nuclear weapons programme' *Asian Survey,* 30, 1990, pp. 927–42.

35 Sen Gupta, *Nuclear Options for India.*

36 Praful Bidwai and Achin Vanaik, 'India and Pakistan' in Karp, *Security With Nuclear Weapons,* p. 269.

37 Sen Gupta notes that the basis of IAEA safeguards is to place the burden of proof on the directors of specific nuclear installations to establish that fissile material *has not* been diverted into a weapons programme.

38 Not surprisingly KANUPP has been the subject of a series of speculations. It has been alleged that the authorities have deliberately carried out 'slow burns' on fuel rods (to increase the amount of Pu 239) for subsequent extraction. This still involves a complex recovery process since Pu 240 is also produced, an isotope that is poisonous to fissile reactions and has to be removed.

39 A. Sreedhar, *Pakistan's Bomb: A Documentary Study,* New Delhi, 1986.

40 The classic case is the 'Khan Affair', wherein between 1972 and 1975 Dr A. Q. Khan is alleged to have obtained specifications for gas centrifugal equipment from a Dutch research institute essential for fuel enrichment. See Sreedhar, *Pakistan's Bomb* which reproduces the entire report from the subsequent Dutch investigation. See also Ashok Kapur, *Pakistan's Nuclear Development,* London, 1987.

41 See 'No nukes, please', *Newsweek,* November 1990, pp. 38–9.

42 Keesings *Contemporary* Archives.

43 R. P. Cronin, *Pakistan After Zia: Implications for Pakistan and US Interests,* US Foreign Affairs and National Defense Division, 1989.

44 Thorium can provide access to U–233 which can provide the trigger for a nuclear fusion device.

45 G. H. Quester. 'Nuclear threshold status', *Foreign Affairs,* 50, 1974, pp. 77–97.

46 See for example P. B. Sinha and R. R. Subramanyam, *The Pakistan Bomb,* New Delhi, 1980. It was pointed out that Z. Bhutto's announcement for a massive increase in the size of Pakistan's civil power programme was 'far in excess' of Pakistan's energy needs. Such views echo the objections raised about Pakistan's excessive 'defence needs'

47 B. Rasul, 'Pakistan's nuclear power programme', *Asian Survey,* 25, 1985. The author is particularly critical of D. K. Palit and P. K. S. Namboodri, *Pakistan's Islamic Bomb,* New Delhi, 1982 and S. Weissman and H. Krosney, *The Islamic Bomb: The Nuclear Threat to Israel and the Middle East,* New York, 1981.

48 Sen Gupta, *Nuclear Options for India.* See also Anita Bhatia, 'India's space programme: causes for concern', *Asian Survey,* 25, 1985, pp. 1013–54.

49 G. Quester, 'India and non-proliferation' in Mellor, *India: A Rising Middle Power.*

50 See for example the discussions in N. Ram, 'India's nuclear policy' and K. Kant, 'Should India go nuclear' in *Indian Defence and Strategic Analysis,* 14, 1982.

51 The Madras Atomic Power Plant produces poor weapons grade plutonium because it is contaminated with Pu–240, which is poisonous to a chain reaction.

52 See Andrew L. Ross, 'Arms acquisition and national security: the irony of military strength' in E. Azar and I. In-Moon (eds.), *National Security in the Third World,* London, 1988, pp. 152–187.

53 This is because India still sees the UN as being very much an extension of US diplomacy, either because it is manipulated by the US and her allies, or because the

organisation is incapable of standing up to Washington in circumstances where they disagree. This links up with Indian criticisms for changes to be carried out within the UN to make it more representative.

54 K. Subrahmanyam cited in B. Buzan (ed.), *Nuclear Deterrence*, London, 1987, p. 112.
55 Sinha and Subrahmanyam, *The Pakistani Bomb*, p. iv.
56 R. W. Bradnock, *India's Foreign Policy Since 1971*, London, 1991, p. 17.
57 See the excellent series of essays produced in H. Bull and A. Watson *The Expansion of International Society*, London, 1987.
58 Bull, *The Anarchical Society*, London, 1977, p. 39.
59 K. M. Panikkar, *India and the Indian Ocean*, London, 1951, p. 12.

Epilogue

The world is not what it was. Since 1989 (and since the failed Soviet coup in August 1991) we appear to inhabit quite a different political and social landscape. One can now buy maps of Germany (not West Germany or that deceptively assuring title of the German Democratic Republic). One can even struggle with the pronunciation of once obscure – but now vitally independent – provinces of the former Soviet Union. What once seemed impossible, a Lithuanian seat at the United Nations General Assembly, an IMF visit to Moscow, the *serious* talk of a federal Europe, has happened overnight and at such speed that the mind is left disorientated and numbed.

The same is true of South Asia. Since 1988 regional events appear to have been thrown into a kind of panoramic fast-forward, in which people, events, elections, riots and peace talks rush under the very eyes of scholarly interests. As soon as one event is comprehended (the assassination of President Zia, the election of V. P. Singh, the withdrawal of the IPKF), it is immediately thrown into a radically different perspective by unexpected and random events. In retrospect, it is tempting to conclude that the India and the Pakistan of the 1950s and even early 1960 were rather placid places of slow-moving events isolated from each other and from the world.

None the less recent events – most dramatically the assassination of Rajiv Gandhi and the election of India's second minority government under Congress-I Prime Minister Narasimha Rao, in June 1991 – fit into many of the patterns already identified in this book. The same can be said of Pakistan, Sri Lanka, Bangladesh and even Nepal. To be sure, the pattern is more convoluted and intricate than before: enough to expose immediate commentary to ridicule, but the patterns hold. It is not my intention here to offer an update of events since the manuscript of this book passed from disk to text, but to reinforce some of the arguments by reference to one or two developments.

Let me begin with Bangladesh. President Ershad was placed under house arrest in November 1990 and brought to trial in May 1991. Throughout this period Bangladesh attempted to return to civilian and prime-ministerial rule. The subsequent election of Begum Zia and the Bangladesh National Party to power clarified a new commitment to civilian rule but failed to clarify the framework of the country's political institutions. While leading members of the Ershad regime (in both government and the armed forces) are removed from office and in some cases put on trial, the old question of whether Bangladesh should be a prime-ministerial or a presidential system remains unsettled. This question is in essence about the power between the executive and the legislature, and about the relationship between Dhaka and the districts, particularly the Chittagong Hill tracks. It is also a question still – twenty years after the civil war – about how popular participation can assist economic and political development.

Throughout the summer months of 1991 Begum Zia initiated a process of political reform, the centrepiece of which is a bid to establish a presidential system through the holding of a national referendum, but it is not clear to what extent the Awami League (or the Islamic opposition parties) will co-operate with this project. This political restructuring takes place within a country beset by financial hardship and environmental vulnerability – underlined by the extent of the 1991 typhoon disaster – and while there are clearly positive and encouraging events taking place, such as Begum Zia's visit to China and the offering of further aid and assistance through Dhaka's links with East Asia – the fragility of the Bangladesh polity remains. It is also unclear to what extent the military are reconciled to the full democratisation of Bangladesh, especially if the process leads to increased dissent between the party leaders.

Turning now to Pakistan, differences between the civilian–military and prime-ministerial–presidential images of political order are being fought out *as part of* the unresolved relationship between Islam and the basis of Pakistani statehood. On 28 May, 1991 the Pakistani government of Naswar Sharif passed the Sharia't Bill, bringing Pakistan's civil criminal code into line with Islamic punishments. Thus a civilian coalition government continues with the logic of the Hudood ordinances passed by General Zia, and more distantly, with the setting up of an Islamic Council by Ayub Khan.

Whether the bill will assist in the construction of an Islamic Pakistani nation has yet to be seen, but the chances are slight. Benazir Bhutto – the leader of the Opposition – has denounced the move as nothing more than an attempt to construct a theocratic state along the lines favoured by the military – while several Islamic parties have criticised the government for not taking the Islamicisation process far enough. As always, party leaders and democratic parties in Pakistan are hedged in by powerful institutions which are not in themselves accessible through the democratic process. Made more vulnerable by internal factionalism, party government in Pakistan is still not assured.

These struggles, between democratic and authoritarian forces, and between secular ideologies and religious, confessional identities, are also present in Nepal, where on 26 June 1991 Nepal elected its first party-based national assembly in almost thirty years. After an intense and somewhat violent campaign, the once banned Nepali Congress party won a clear majority of seats in the national assembly and set about a fundamental reworking of Nepal's political institutions. As with Bangladesh, the aim is to ensure that increased popular participation within economic and political development will help mobilise the countries' resources towards solving widespread poverty and towards achieving growth.

Yet it is within India herself that the institutional and regional crisis of South Asia is playing itself out, like a fever or an illness. Chandhra Senkhar resigned as Prime Minister in March 1991 and opened up the possibility of Rajiv Gandhi returning to power at the head of a minority government. Eventually – despite chronic political and economic instability – the President accepted the advice of Chandra Senkhar and called for fresh elections to be held on 20, 23 and 26 May.

The central issues of the election campaign were, not surprisingly, the future of India's commitment to a secular state, the future relationship between the state and industrial and economic activity and the future of Indo-Pak relations with regard to the crisis within Kashmir and the Punjab. The assassination of Rajiv Gandhi in Tamil Nadu on 21 May – the day after the first round of national voting – was a tragedy that showed up a number of impasses into which India appeared to be heading.

Domestically it revealed the extent to which social and political violence is overwhelming the ballot box. Elections have still not been held within the Punjab, and the situation in Kashmir has now been likened by one informed scholar to that of the *Intifada*. In May 1991 an Amnesty International Report stated that up to 10,000 Sikhs were being held under preventive detention, while religious groups in Kashmir accused the Indian government of occupying mosques and places of Muslim worship and disrupting prayer meetings.

Regionally, the murder provided further evidence of the difficulties of irredentism. It is now almost certain that Rajiv Gandhi was killed by a member or supporter of the Tamil Tigers, and that he had been murdered for the signing of the Indo–Sri Lankan Accord signed in 1987. The fact that there were so many groups and political activists with a motive to kill him, not least Sikh and Kashmiri militants, underlined the extent to which domestic turmoil threatens to endanger bilateral relations and, more seriously, plunge the area into a fourth Indo-Pak war.

Kashmir remains the flashpoint. Throughout the summer months of 1991 India repeatedly accused the Pakistan government of supplying arms and training camps for Kashmiri militants. Ironically, the Indian government was duplicating Sri Lankan accusations against Delhi concerning the relationship between Tamil Nadu and the Tamil Tigers made from 1983 onwards.

In a recent talk at SOAS David Taylor commented: 'If Pakistan were to give up its irredentist claim to Kashmir then in an important respect it would lose its claim to statehood measured separately from that of India.'[1] Yet for India to concede that her political institutions have failed to keep the only Muslim majority province 'loyal' would spell the end of the Indian Union as it has emerged since independence. Such a concession would in turn weaken Indian claims to statehood and further imperil Indian secularism.

There is a third impasse as well – an international one – in which the image grows of an India that is just another banana republic of sham elections and caste killings, a place of fanatical and religious murders. The problems that beset India (and by extension the rest of South Asia) do not get a good press in the West, particularly in Britain. The death of Gandhi and the Sonia fiasco – in which the Congress-I asked Rajiv's Italian wife to lead the party – gave rise to 'in-depth' stories of dynasty and spectacle that were as informative as they were original.

Anxious to portray the scale of the crisis, people spoke of the end of democracy and the fall of the world's largest democratic state: few bothered to note that Rajiv Gandhi was not in fact the prime minister, and that he was simply the leader of the opposition. Few commentators really comprehend the complexities of the caste issues, and few appreciate that with the proper context caste can still be seen as a political attribute.

While it would be wrong to deliberately underplay the extent of India's crisis, it is wrong, even pernicious, to portray them in dramatic language. Despite the chaos of Gandhi's death and the drama surrounding the attempt to persuade Sonia Gandhi to become the leader of the Congress-I, the Indian political process completed its tenth election. The fact that the election took place at all is worthy of comment.

More interestingly, the pattern of political Balkanisation was reaffirmed at the same time as was the tenacity of India's political maturity. In opposition, the Janata Dal party of V. P. Singh disintegrated into competing factions, while the Congress divided into pro- and anti-liberalisation factions. 1991 saw the end of Congress's traditional vote banks in the Hindu states. The patterns of growing Hindu revivalism were also confirmed by the rise of the BJP from 88 seats to 119, although this was less than many people had feared.

None the less the government – once it had rallied its parliamentary support – introduced a 'place of religious worship bill' aimed at preventing a repetition of the Ayoyda crisis. It will now be impossible to state that a mosque is in fact a temple or vice versa. In the face of sustained intimidating and walk-outs by the BJP and the Shiv Sena, the defence of the secular state continues. Only when the secular political forces consolidate themselves into strong and accountable parties will the crisis be overcome. That Kashmir had entered a unique and difficult phase of political estrangement calls for active and imaginative civilian leadership: it does not call for military or executive power.

Finally the economic patterns of liberalisation and global integration have continued and strengthened. Prime Minister Rao's statement on India's economic policy opened up the way for further economic liberalisation, trade reform and foreign collaboration. India's new industrial policy announced on 23 June 1991 cut more industrial activity free of state regulation (and subsidy), while opening the way for a significant devaluation of the rupee throughout the year. In July a whole series of aid consortiums led by the IMF released money to India on the firm understanding that more liberalisation would follow. In Pakistan the move towards privatising previously held public industries continues as part of a whole series of conditions aimed at encouraging foreign aid and investment. In May 1991 the European AID Pakistan consortium pledged US $2,300 million in credits and soft loans.

Such conditionality and foreign involvement must address the domestic and institutional weakness of the South Asian states with some sensitivity. The IMF has long realised the difficulties of allowing strict conditionality to provide a basis for domestic opposition and violence to a government labouring under debt. None the less restructuring programmes for both India and Pakistan must address the issues of credit worthiness, fully aware of the links between the legitimacy of a government and the need to present immediate economic benefits to a restive and politised society.

While for the time being India has reassured her creditors that there is a competent and accountable government in control of the state, Pakistan continues to labour under active US suspicion. Naswar Sharif has attempted to assure Washington that the stories about the Pakistan bomb are not true and that mere rumours should not be enough to stand in the way of much needed aid and economic assistance. The US senate has yet to be convinced however of the sincerity of Pakistani intentions, and in an atmosphere clouded by further revelations of illegal imports of nuclear technology throughout June and July 1991, Islamabad is still frozen out of the American embrace. Whether this is an opportunity for India has yet to be seen.

The international trends of the last few years – speeded up beyond all recognition – underscore South Asia's ambivalent position within the emerging global order. India's hesitation in condemning the Soviet coup in August 1991 was evidence of her conservatism when faced with dramatic international changes. Yet following his election Prime Minister Rao's first foreign visit was to Germany, not Russia. Such new priorities are evidence of the importance of new trade links and new sources of technological imports. The final collapse of the Soviet Union – referred to by a commentator as the doom theory – presents a major challenge to both the principles of the Non-Aligned Movement and India's position within the institutions of the United Nations. Yet India has other and more pressing priorities . . . .

Vernon Hewitt
Bristol, November 1991

Notes

1 David Taylor 'The Kashmir Crisis', *Asian Affairs*, vol. 23, no. 3, October 1991, p. 305.

Bibliography

Afroz, S. 'Pakistan and the Middle East Defence Plan 1951' *Asian Affairs* 75, 1988, pp. 170–9.

Agrawal, A. N. *The Indian Economy: Problems of Development Planning*. New Delhi, 1988.

Agrawal, A. N. et al. *India: Basic Economic Information 1989–90*. New Delhi, 1989.

Ahamed, E. (ed.) *The Foreign Policy of Bangladesh*. Dhaka, 1984.

Ahluwalia, I. J. *Industrial Growth in India: Stagnation since the Mid-Sixties*. New Delhi, 1985.

Ahmad, E. *On Changes in Inequality in Pakistan*. London, 1981.

Ahmed, A. S. *Religion and Politics in Muslim Society*. Cambridge, 1983.

Ahmed, N. 'Experiments in Local Government Reform in Bangladesh' *Asian Survey* 28, 1988, pp. 813–29.

Alavi, H. and Harriss. J. (eds.) *The Sociology of Developing States: South Asia*. London, 1987.

Ali, T. *Can Pakistan Survive?* Harmondsworth, 1983.

Anderson, W. 'The Soviets in the Indian Ocean' *Asian Survey* 24, 1984, pp. 910–53.

Ayoob, M. *India and South East Asia: Indian Perceptions and Policies*. London, 1990.

Ayoob, M. *India, Pakistan and Bangladesh*. New York, 1975.

Azar, E. and In-Moon. I. (eds.) *National Security and the Third World*. London, 1988.

Bajpal, U. S. (ed.) *India's Security: The Politico-Strategic Environment*. New Delhi, 1983.

Balasubramanyam, V. N. *The Indian Economy*. London, 1984.

Ball, N. *The Military in the Development Process*. Claremont, 1981.

Baral, L. S. *Opposition Politics in Nepal*. New Delhi, 1977.

Baral, L. S. *The Politics of Balanced Interdependence: Nepal and SAARC*. New Delhi, 1988.

Barnds, W. *India, Pakistan and the Great Powers*. New York, 1972.

Barton, W. 'Pakistan's Claims to Kashmir' *Foreign Affairs* 28, 1950, pp. 299–308.

Baxter, C. et al. (eds.) *Government and Politics in South Asia*. Boulder, 1987.

Benoit, E. *Defence and Economic Growth in the LDCs*. Lexington, 1973.

Berridge, G. R. and Young, J. W. 'What is a Great Power?' *Political Studies* 26 June 1988, pp. 224–34.

Bhaduri, S. and Karim. S. *The Sri Lankan Crisis*. New Delhi, 1989.

Bhagwati, J. N. *India in the International Economy*. London, 1973.

Bhagwati, J. N. and Desai. P. *Planning For Industrialisation: Industrialisation and Trade Policy Since 1951*. London, 1971.

Bhargava, G. S. *South Asian Security After Afghanistan*. Lexington, 1983.

Bhatti, M. A. *Draft 7th Plan: Critique and Suggestions*. Islamabad, 1988.

Bhooshan, B. S. *The Development Experience of Nepal*. New Delhi, 1979.

Binder, L. *Religion and Politics in Pakistan*. California, 1961.

Bjorkman, J. 'Health Policy and Politics in Sri Lanka: Developments in the South Asian Welfare State' *Asian Survey* 25, 1985, pp. 537–52.

Blaikie, P. et al. *The Struggle for Basic Needs in Nepal*. London, 1979.

Bond, G. *The Buddhist Revival in Sri Lanka: Religious Tradition, Reinterpretation and Response*. Columbia, 1988.

Booth, K. and Baylis, J. (eds.) *Britain, NATO, and Nuclear Weapons: Alternative Defence Vs. Alliance Reform*. London, 1989.

Booth, K. (ed.) *New Thinking About Strategy and International Security*. London, 1991.

Bouton, M. and Oldenburg. P. (eds.) *India Briefing 1990*. Boulder, 1991.

Boyce, J. *Agrarian Impasse in Bengal: Institutional Constraints to Technology*. Oxford, 1987.

Bradnock, R. W. *India's Foreign Policy since 1971*. London, 1990.

Brass, P. *Language, Religion and Politics in North India*. Cambridge, 1974.

Brass, P. *The Politics of India Since Independence*. Cambridge History of India. Cambridge, 1990.

Bratersky, M. V. and Lunyov, S. I. 'India at the End of the Century: Transformation into an Asian Regional Power' *Asian Survey* 30, 1990, pp. 927–42.

Braun, D. *The Indian Ocean: Region of Conflict or 'Peace Zone'?* London, 1983.

Brecher, M. *Nehru: A Political Biography*. London, 1959.

Brown, D. 'Ethnic Revival: Perspectives on State and Society' *Third World Quarterly* October-December 1989, pp. 1–17.

Bull, H. *The Anarchical Society*, London, 1977.

Bull, H. and Watson. A. (ed.), *The Expansion of International Society*. London, 1987.

Burke, S. M. *Mainsprings of India and Pakistan's Foreign Policy*. New Delhi.

Burke, S. M. and Ziring, L. *Pakistan's Foreign Policy: An Historical Analysis*. Karachi, 1991.

Burki, J. A. *Pakistan Under Bhutto*. London, 1985.

Burki, S. J. and LaPorte, R. *Pakistan's Development Priorities*. 1984.

Butler, D. et al. *The Compendium of Indian Elections*. New Delhi, 1986.

Buzan, B. and Rizvi, G. *South Asian Insecurity and the Great Powers*. Basingstoke, 1985.

Buzan, B. *The International Politics of Deterrence*. London, 1987.

Buzan, B. *People, States and Fear*. London, 1991.

Cambridge Economic History of India. Two Volumes. Cambridge, 1983.

Chakravarty, S. *Development Planning: The Indian Experience*. New Delhi, 1987.

Chattopadhayaya, H. *Indians in Sri Lanka*. Calcutta, 1979.

Chaudhuri, J. N. *India's Problems of National Security in the 1970s*. New Delhi (1973).

Chazan, N. (ed.) *Irredentism and International Politics*. London, 1991.

Cheema, P. I. C. *Pakistan's Defence Policy 1947–1958*. London, 1990.

Chitala, V. P. *Energy Crisis in India*. New Delhi, 1975.

Chopra, A. K. *India's Policy on Disarmament*. New Delhi, 1984.

Chopra, A. P. *The Future of South Asia*. New Delhi, 1986.

Chopra, C. P. *Before and After the Indo-Soviet Treaty.* New Delhi, 1972.

Choudhury, G. W. *Pakistan: The Transition from a Military to a Civilian Government.* London, 1988.

Choudhury, G. W. *India, Pakistan and the Major Powers.* New York, 1975.

Clarkson, S. *The Soviet Theory of Development: India and the Third World in Marxist-Leninist Scholarship.* London, 1978.

Cohen, S. P. et al. *India: An Emergent Power?* 1978.

Cohen, S. P. *The Pakistan Army.* California, 1983.

Cohen, S. P. *The Security of South Asia: American and Asian Perspectives.* Illinois, 1987.

Cohen, S. *The Indian Army and its Contribution to the Development of a Nation,* California, 1971.

Crook, J. H. *Social Change in Indian Tibet,* London, 1980.

Cronin, R. P. 'Pakistan After Zia: Implications for Pakistan and US Interests' *Congressional Papers.* US Foreign Affairs and National Defence Division. 25 January 1989.

Dalton, D. and Wilson, A. J. *The States of South Asia: The Problems of National Integration.* London, 1982.

Datta Ray, S. K. *Smash and Grab: The Annexation of Sikkim.* New Delhi, 1984.

Dawisha, A. *Islam in Foreign Policy.* Cambridge, 1983.

Deepak, L. *Prices For Planning: Towards the Reform of Indian Planning.* New Delhi, 1980.

Dharamdasari. M. *Indian Diplomacy in Nepal.* Jaipur, 1976.

Donaldson, R. N. *Soviet Policy Towards India: Ideology and Strategy.* Cambridge, Mass., 1974.

Dowdy, W. L. and Trood, R. B. *The Indian Ocean: Perspectives on a Strategic Arena.* Duke, 1985.

Duncan, P. *Indo-Soviet Relations.* London, 1987.

Dutt, S. *India and the Third World: Altruism or Hegemony?* London, 1984.

Dutt, V. P. *India's Foreign Policy.* New Delhi, 1984.

Eldridge, P. J. *The Politics of Foreign Aid in India.* London, 1969.

Engineer, A. A. (ed.) *Communalism in India.* New Delhi, 1985.

Engineer, A. A. *Islam and the Muslims: A Critical Reassesment.* Jaipur, 1985.

Episoto, I. (ed.) *Islam in Asia.* Oxford, 1986.

Evans. H. 'Bangladesh: South Asia's Unknown Quantity' *Asian Affairs* 75, 1988, pp. 306-16.

Faaland, J. and Parkison, J. R. *Bangladesh: The Test Case for Development.* London, 1976.

Faaland, J. *Aid and Influence: The Case for Bangladesh.* London, 1981.

Far Eastern Economic Year Book. Hong Kong, 1988, 1989 and 1990.

Farmer, B. H. *An Introduction to South Asia.* London, 1983.

Freer, A. C. *India and the Pacific.* London, 1937.

Gandhi, I. *India and Bangladesh: Political Speeches.* New Delhi, 1973.

Gandhi, R. *Understanding the Muslim Mind.* Harmondsworth, 1987.

Gangal, S. C. *India and the Commonwealth.* New Delhi, 1970.

Ganguly, S. *War in South Asia.* Boulder, 1986.

Ganguly, S. 'Avoiding War in South Asia' *Foreign Affairs* 69, 1990–91 pp. 57–73.

Gellner, E. *Thought and Change,* London, 1967.

Gilmartin, D. *Empire and Islam: Punjab and the Making of Pakistan.* Princeton, 1988.

Gilpin, R. *The Political Economy of International Relations*. Princeton, 1987.

Goswami, B. N. *Pakistan and China: A Study of Their Relations*. Karachi, 1971.

Government of Pakistan. *Political Settlement Relating to Afghanistan*. 4 April 1988.

Graham, B. D. *The Challenge of Hindu Nationalism: The BJP in Contemporary Indian Politics*. London, 1990.

Grewal, J. S. *The Sikhs of the Punjab*. The Cambridge History of India. Cambridge, 1991.

Griffin, K. B. and Khan, A. R. *Growth and Inequality in Pakistan*. 1972.

Gupta, A. 'The Indian Arms Industry' *Asian Survey* 30, 1990, pp. 847–61.

Gupta, S. 'Great Power Relations, World Order and the Third World' in Rajan, M. and Ganguly, S. S. (eds.) *Selected Essays*. New Delhi, 1981.

Hamid, N. and Tims, W. *Agricultural Growth and Economic Development: The Case of Pakistan*. OECD Technical Papers. No 13. April 1990.

Handerson, P. D. *India: The Energy Sector*. New Delhi, 1975.

Harris, C. and Anand, S. *Food and the Standard of Living: An Analysis of the Sri Lankan Data*. Institute of Economics and Statistics. Oxford, 1989.

Harris, N. *India-China: Underdevelopment and Revolution*. London, 1974.

Harris, N. *The End of the Third World?* London, 1987.

Hasrat, B. J. *Land of the Peaceful Dragon: Bhutan*. New Delhi, 1980.

Hassan, S. and Kabir, M. G. *Issues and Challenges Facing Bangladesh Foreign Policy*. Dhaka, 1983.

Hayes, L. *Politics in Pakistan: The Struggle for Legitimacy*. Boulder, 1984.

Hewitt, V. M. 'The Congress System is Dead: Long Live Party Politics and the Democratic System' *Journal of Commonwealth and Comparative Politics* 27, 1989, pp. 157–70.

Hirway, I. *Abolition of Poverty in India With Special Reference to the Target Group Approach in Gujarat*. New Delhi, 1986.

Hobson, H. V. *The Great Divide: Great Britain, India and Pakistan*. Karachi, 1985.

Hong-Wei, W. 'Sino-Nepali Relations in the 1980s' *Asian Survey* 25, 1985, pp. 512-34.

Horn, P. *Soviet-Indian Relations: Issues and Influences*. New York, 1982.

Hussain, C. Muhammad. *Development Planning in an Islamic State*. Karachi, 1987.

Hussain, I. *The Strategic Dimensions of Pakistan's Foreign Policy*. Lahore, 1989.

Hyder, S. *Reflections of An Ambassador*. Lahore, 1988.

IMF, *Direction of Trade Statistics*. Washington, 1990.

IISA, *The Military Balance: 1989-90*. London, 1991.

Islam, K. *Development Planning in Bangladesh: A Study in Political Economy*. London, 1977.

Islam, N. *Foreign Trade and Economic Controls in Development: The Case of United Pakistan*. Yale, 1981.

Islam, S. (ed.) *Yen For Development: Japanese Foreign Aid and the Politics of Burden Sharing*. New York, 1991.

Ispanhani, M. Z. *Roads and Rivals: The Politics of Access in the Borderlands of Asia*. London, 1991.

Jackson, R. H. *Quasi-States: Sovereignty, International Relations and the Third World*. Cambridge, 1990.

Jain, G. *China in World Politics*. New Delhi, 1976.

Jalal, A. *State of Martial Rule: The Political Economy of Defence in Pakistan*. Cambridge, 1990.

Jalal, A. *The Sole Spokesman: Jinnah and the Pakistan Movement*. Cambridge, 1987.

Jeffrey, R. *What's Happening to India? Punjab, Ethnic Conflict, Mrs Gandhi's Death and the Test of Federalism*. London, 1986.

Jervis, R. *Perception and Misperception in International Politics*. Princeton, 1976.

Jha, B. K. *Indo-Nepalese Relations 1951–1972*. New Delhi, 1973.

Johal, S. 'India's Search for Capital Abroad' *Asian Survey* 29, 1989, pp. 971-82.

Kabir, M. G. and Hassan, S. *Issues and Challenges Facing Bangladeshi Foreign Policy*. Dhaka, 1984.

Kabra, K. N. *The Black Economy in India: Problems and Policies*. New Delhi, 1982.

Kamal, K. L. *Democratic Politics in India*. New Delhi, 1984.

Kant, K. 'Should India Go Nuclear' *Indian Defence and Strategic Analysis Journal*, 14, 1982, pp.

Kapur, A. *International Nuclear Proliferation, Multi-National Diplomacy and Regional Aspects* New Delhi, 1979.

Kapur, A. 'India's Foreign Policy Perspectives and Present Predicaments' *Round Table*, 295, 1985, pp. 230-9.

Kapur, A. *Pakistan's Nuclear Development*. London, 1987.

Karp, E. C. (ed.) *Security With Nuclear Weapons? Different Perspectives on National Security*. London, 1991.

Kavic, L. *India's Quest For Security 1947–1965*, Berkeley, 1967.

Kennedy, C. H. *The Bureaucracy of Pakistan*. Oxford, 1987.

Kennedy, D. *The Security of Southern Asia*. London, 1965.

Keesings Contemporary Archives. London. (Published monthly.)

Khadka, N. 'Nepal's 7th Five Year Plan' *Asian Survey* 28, 1988, pp. 555–72.

Khalizad, Z. *Security in South West Asia*. Aldershot, 1984.

Khan, A. *Friends, Not Masters: A Political Autobiography*. London, 1967.

Khan, M. A. *Islam, Politics and the State*. Karachi, 1985.

Khan, A. R. *The Economy of Bangladesh*. London. 1972.

Khan, M. H. *The Economics of the Green Revolution in Pakistan*. New York, 1975.

Khan, R. *The Indo-Pak Strategic Equation in the Context of Regional Security*. New Delhi, 1985.

Khan, Z. A. *Pakistan's Security: The Challenge and the Response*.

Khan, Z. R. 'Islam and Bengali Nationalism' *Asian Survey* 25, 1985, pp. 852–82.

Kurshid, S. *At Home in India: A Restatement of Indian Muslims*. New Delhi, 1986.

Kidron, M. *Pakistan's Trade with the Eastern Bloc Countries*. London, 1972.

Kochanek, S. 'Brief Case Politics in India' *Asian Survey* 27, 1987, pp. 1278–1301.

Kodikara, S. *The Foreign Policy of Sri Lanka*. New Delhi, 1982.

Kohli, S. N. *Sea Power and the Indian Ocean*. New Delhi, 1978.

Kothari, R. *Politics in India*. New Delhi, 1970.

Kothari, R. *Caste in Indian Politics*. New Delhi, 1976.

Kreisberg, P. H. 'India After Indira' *Foreign Affairs* 63, 1985, pp. 871-91.

Krueger, A. O. *Benefits of Import Substitution for India*. London, 1975.

Kumar, S. *Documents on India's Foreign Policy, 1972–74* New Delhi, 1975.

Kumar, L. *India and Sri Lanka: The Sirimavo–Shastri Pact*. New Delhi, 1977.

Labh, K. *India and Bhutan*. New Delhi, 1974.

Lamb, A. *Asian Frontiers: Studies in a Continuing Problem*. London, 1968.

Lamb, A. *The McMahon Line: A Study in the Relations Between India, China and Tibet*. London, 1966.

Lamb, H. *British and Chinese Central Asia*. London, 1964.

LaPorte, R. and Ahmed. M. B. *Public Enterprises in Pakistan: The Hidden Crisis in*

Economic Development. Boulder, 1989.

Lateef, K. *Economic Growth in China and India: 1950–80*. Brighton, 1976.

Lewis, J. P. *Quiet Crisis in India: Economic Development and American Policy*, Washington, 1962.

Lifschutz, L. *Bangladesh: The Unfinished Revolution*. London, 1979.

Lipton, M. and Toye. J. F. J. *Does Aid to India Work?* London, 1990.

Lipton, M. *The Erosion of a Relationship: India and Britain since 1960*. 1975.

Little, I. et al. *Industry and Trade in Some Developing Countries*. London, 1970.

Little, I. *Project Appraisal and Planning for Developing Countries*. London, 1974.

Luard, E. *A History of the United Nations: Volume Two, 1955-65*. London, 1989.

Malik, H. *Soviet-American Relations with Pakistan, Iran and Afghanistan*. Basingstoke, 1987.

Malik, Y. and Vaypeyi, D. K. 'The Rise of Hindu Militancy' *Asian Survey* 29, 1989, pp. 311-25.

Marwah, O. and Pollack, J. *Asia's Major Powers*. Boulder, 1978.

Mason, E. S. *Economic Development for India and Pakistan*. Cambridge, 1966.

Mathew, B. 'Sri Lanka's Development Councils' *Asian Survey* 22, 1982, pp. 1117–35.

Maududi, M. *The Islamic Law and the Constitution*. Lahore, 1976.

Maxwell, N. *India's China War*. Harmondsworth, 1971.

Mellor, J. W. (ed.) *India: A Rising Middle Power?* New York, 1979.

Misra, G. *Indo-Pak Relations: From Tashkent to Simla*. New Delhi, 1987.

Misra, K. P. and Chopra, V. D. *South Asia – Pacific Region: Emerging Trends*. Bombay, 1988.

Moinduddin, H. *The Charter of the Islamic Conference*. Oxford, 1987.

Moore, B. *The Social Origins of Dictatorship and Democracy*. Harmonsdworth, 1966.

Moore, R. J. *Making the New Commonwealth*. Oxford, 1987.

Mukerjee, D. 'US weaponry for India' *Asian Survey* 27, 1987, pp. 595-614.

Mumtaz, K. and Shaheed, F. *Women of Pakistan: Two Steps Forward, One Step Back*. London, 1987.

Namboodri, P. K. and Palit, D. K. *Pakistan's Islamic Bomb*. New Delhi, 1982.

Nayar, K. *Distant Neighbours*. New Delhi, 1970.

Nehru, J. *Letters to the Chief Ministers*. Five Volumes. New Delhi, 1988, 1989.

Nissanka, H. S. S. *Sri Lanka's Foreign Policy*. New Delhi, 1984.

Noman, O. *Pakistan: A Political and Economic History Since 1947*. London, 1990.

Northedge. F. S. *The Foreign Policy of the Powers*. New York, 1968.

Nugent, N. *Rajiv Gandhi*. London, 1990.

Nye, J. S. and Keohane, R. O. *Transnational Relations and World Politics*. Cambridge, 1971.

Nye, J. S. 'Non-Proliferation: A Long Term Strategy' *Foreign Affairs* 56, 1978, pp. 601-23.

O'Donnell, C. P. *Bangladesh: Biography of a Muslim Nation*. Boulder, 1984.

ODI. *Briefing Paper*. 'The Impact of the Gulf Crisis on Developing Countries'. London, March 1991.

OECD. *Economic Policies and Agricultural Performance in Sri Lanka 1960–1984* Washington, 1990.

Olschak, B. C. *The Dragon Kingdom: Images of Bhutan*. Boston, 1988.

Olson, L. *The Japanese in India Today: Japan's Role in India's Economic Development*. New Delhi, 1980.

Panikkar, K. M. *India and the Indian Ocean: An Essay On The Influences of Sea Power on Indian History*. London, 1951.

Pemble, J. *The Invasion of Nepal: John Company at War*. Oxford, 1971.

Piscatori, J. P. *Islam and the Nation State*. Cambridge, 1986.

Prasad, B. *India's Foreign Policy*. New Delhi, 1979.

Premachandra, A. *Export Instability and Growth in Sri Lanka*. New Delhi, 1987.

Quester, G. 'Can Proliferation Be Stopped?' *Foreign Affairs* 53, 1974, pp. 77–97.

Quester, G. (ed.) *Nuclear Proliferation: Breaking the Chains*. Madison, 1981.

Qureshi, A. *Anglo-Pakistan Relations 1947–1976*. New Delhi, 1978.

Rajan, M. S. *Great Power Relations, World Order and the Third World*. New Delhi, 1981.

Rajan, M. and Ganguly, S. S. *India and the International System*. New Delhi, 1981.

Ramakant, A. *Nepal – China – Indian Relations*. New Delhi, 1976.

Rana, A. P. 'Non-Alignment and the Expansion of International Society: A Grotian Perspective on India's Foreign Policy' *BISA/ISA Paper* 28 March 1989.

Rao, R. *Sikkim: The Story of Its Integration with India*. New Delhi, 1978.

Rao, V. K. R. V. *Food, Nutrition and Poverty in India*. Brighton, 1982.

Rao, V.K.R.V. *India's National Income 1950-1980: An Analysis of Economic Growth and Change*. New Delhi, 1983.

Ray, S. K. *The Indian Economy*, New Delhi, 1987.

Rengger, N. J. (ed.) *Treaties and Alliances of the World*. London, 1990.

Richards, P. *Basic Needs, Poverty and Government: The Policies of Sri Lanka*. Geneva, 1981.

Richter, L. *The Politics of Tourism in Asia*. Honolulu, 1989.

Robinson, F. et al. (eds.) *The Cambridge Encyclopedia of India, Pakistan, Bangladesh, Nepal, Bhutan, Sri Lanka and the Maldives*. Cambridge, 1989.

Romberg, A. 'New Stirrings in Asia' *Foreign Affairs* 64, 1985, pp. 515-38.

Rose, L. and Scholz, J. *Nepal: Profile of a Himalayan Kingdom*. Boulder, 1980.

Rose, L. *The Politics of Bhutan*. Boulder, 1977.

Rose, L. *United States–Pakistan Relations*. Cornell, 1985.

Ross, L. and Samaranayake. T. 'Economic Impact of the Recent Disturbances in Sri Lanka' *Asian Survey* 26, 1986 pp. 1240–58

Rostow, W. W. *The Stages of Economic Growth: A Non-Marxist Manifesto*. Chicago, 1971.

Roy, S. *Pricing, Planning and Politics: A Study of Economic Distortions in India*. London, 1984.

Rudolph, L. *The Modernity of Tradition: Political Development in India*. Chicago, 1986.

Rudolph, L. and Rudolph, S. *In Pursuit of Lakshmi: State-Society Relations in India*. Chicago. 1987.

Sajjad, H. *Foreign Policy of Pakistan: Reflections of an Ambassador*. Lahore 1987.

Saravanamuttu, P. and Thomas. C. *Conflict and Crisis in North-South Security*. London, 1989.

Schloss, A. 'Making Planning Relevant' *Asian Survey* 20, 1980, pp. 1008-20.

Schwarz, W. *The Tamils of Sri Lanka*. London, 1988.

Seers, D. et al. *Integration and Unequal Development*. London, 1980.

Segal, G. (ed) *Arms Control in Asia*. Basingstoke, 1987.

Sen Gupta, B. *The Fulcrum of Asia: Relations amongst China, India, Pakistan and the USSR*. New Delhi, 1970.

Shah, S. 'Nepal's Economic Development Problems' *Asian Survey* 28, 1988, pp. 945–47.

Shaha, R. *Nepali Politics: Retrospect and Prospect*. New Delhi, 1978.

Shahi, A. *Pakistan's Security and Foreign Policy*. Lahore 1988.

Shaikh, F. *Community and Consensus in Islam: Muslim in Foreign Policy*, Cambridge, 1988.

Shakabpa, W. D. *Tibet: A Political History*. New York, 1984.

Shala, R. *Essays in the Practice of Government in Nepal*. New Delhi, 1982.

Shaw, I. *The Pakistan Handbook*. London, 1989.

Sheppardon, M. and Simmons. *The Indian National Congress 1885–1985*. Avebury, 1988.

Sherwani, L. A. *Pakistan, China and America*. Karachi, 1980.

Shome, P. *Social Security Institutions and Capital Creation: Singapore, the Philippines, Malaysia, India and Sri Lanka*. New York, 1981.

Sims, H. 'The State and Agricultural Productivity: A Comparative Study of Indian and Pakistan Punjab' *Asian Survey*, 26, 1986, pp. 483–500.

Singer, M. R. 'New Realities of Sri Lankan Power' *Asian Survey* 30, 1990, pp. 409–25.

Singh, J. 'Indian Security: A Framework for National Strategy' *Strategic Analysis* 11, 1987, pp. 898–917.

Singh, N. 'Can the US and India Really be Friends?' *Asian Survey* 23, 1983, pp. 1020–32.

Singh, O. P. *Strategic Sikkim*. New Delhi, 1985.

Singh, P. *India and the Future of Asia*. New Delhi, 1966.

Singh, S. N. 'Why India Goes to Moscow for Arms' *Asian Survey* 24, 1984, pp. 707–40.

Singh, U. S. *Burma and India, 1948–1962*. New Delhi, 1979.

Sisson, R. and Rose, L. *War and Secession: India, Pakistan and the Creation of Bangladesh*. Princeton, 1990.

Snodgrass, D. R. *Ceylon: An Export Led Economy in Transition*. Illinois, 1966.

Sreedhar and Subrahmanyam, K. *The Pakistan Bomb*. New Delhi, 1980.

Subrahmanyam, K. C. 'The Challenge of the Seventies to India's Security' *India Quarterly* 26, 1970.

Subrahmanyam, K. M. (ed.) *Nuclear Myths and Realities: The Indian Dilemma*. New Delhi, 1982.

Tambiah, S. J. *Sri Lanka: Ethnic Fratricide and the Dismantling of Democracy*. New Delhi, 1986.

Tansky, L. *The US and the USSR Aid to Developing Countries: A Comparative Study of India, Turkey and the UAE*. New York, 1967.

Terhal, P. 'Guns Vs. Grains: Macro-Economic Costs of India's Defence 1960–70' *Economic and Political Weekly* 16, 1981, pp. 1998–2014.

Thakur, R. et al. (eds.) *The Soviet Union as an Asian Pacific Power: Implications of Gorbachev's 1986 Vladivostok Initiative*. Boulder, 1987.

Thakur, R. 'Normalising Sino-Indian Relations' *Pacific Review* 4, 1991, pp. 5–18.

The Military Balance: 1989–1990. London, 1990.

Thomas, C. *In Search of Security: The Third World in International Relations*. Brighton, 1987.

Thomas, R. 'The Armed Services and Indian Defence Budget' *Asian Survey* 20, 1980, pp. 825–45.

Thomas, R. 'US Transfers and Dual-Use Technologies' *Asian Survey* 30, 1990, pp. 846–65.

Thomas, R. *India's Security Policy*. Princeton, 1986.

Thomas, R. *The Defence of India: A Budgetary Perspective on Strategy and Politics*. Lexington. 1978.

Thornton, T. P. 'Between The Stools: US Policy Towards Pakistan During the Carter Administration' *Asian Survey*. 22, 1982, pp. 959–70.

United Nations Year Book. Geneva, 1984.

Vajpayee, A. B. *New Dimensions of India's Foreign Policy*. 1979.

Van Hollen, C. 'The Tilt Policy Revisited' *Asian Survey* 20, 1980, pp. 352–73.

Varma, S. P. and Misra, K. P. *The Foreign Policy of South Asia*. New Delhi, 1969.

Venkataramani, A. L. *The American Role in Pakistan*. New Delhi, 1982.

Verma, R. *India's Role in the Emergence of Contemporary Bhutan*. New Delhi, 1985.

Vertzberger, *Sino-Pakistan Relations 1960–1980*. Washington Papers, 1981.

Vohra. *India's Aid Diplomacy*. New Delhi, 1980.

Waseem, M. *Pakistan Under Martial Law 1977–1985*. Lahore, 1987.

Waseem, M. *Politics and the State in Pakistan*. Lahore, 1989.

Wei, Wang Hong. 'Sino-Nepali Relations in the 1980s' *Asian Survey* 25, 1985, pp.

Weissman, S. and Krosney, H. *The Islamic Bomb: The Nuclear Threat to Israel and the Middle East*. New York, 1981.

Whitehead. *Far Frontiers People and Events in North-Eastern India*. London, 1989.

Wight, M. *Power Politics*. Leicester, 1978.

Williams, D. *The Specialized Agencies and the United Nations*. London, 1987.

Wilson, A. J. *Politics of Sri Lanka 1947–1979*. London, 1980.

Wilson, A. J. *The Break-Up of Sri Lanka*. London, 1988.

Wolf, M. *India's Exports*. World Bank Publication, 1982.

Wood, J. (ed.) *Contemporary State Politics in India*. Boulder, 1987.

World Bank Report. Washington, 1990 (and annually).

World Bank. *Economic Trends in Developing Economies*. Washington, 1989.

World Bank. *World Development Report on Poverty* Washington, 1990.

Younghusband, F. *India and Tibet: A History of Relations*. London, 1910.

Yu, T. George. *Intra-Asian International Relations*. Boulder, 1989.

Index

Afghanistan 21, 71–2, 75–6, 78, 82, 92, 94 *see also* Durand Line
Asian Development Bank (ADB), 6
Awami League, 31, 117, 127 *see also* Bangladesh, elections; Rehman, Mujib

balance of power, 32 *see also* military doctrines
Bandaranaike, Mrs R. D. B. (Prime Minister 1960–65, 1970–77), 54, 96, 106, 178 *see also* Sri Lanka, elections
Bangladesh
  aid, 34, 79, 175–6
  basic indicators, 5, 154, 174
  constitution and government, 35, 125–7, 130 *see also* Rehman, Mujib
  economic development, 127, 154, 176–7
  elections, 37, 124 *see also* Awami League; *individual names of leaders*
  environmental degradation, 39, 176
  Islamic Fundamentalism, 35, 128
  military coups, 128, 131
  military establishments, 39
  minorities, 124
  political parties, 129, 130-1
Bangladesh, foreign relations with
  China, 125, 127
  UN, 38, 83 *see also* Pakistan, foreign relations with Bangladesh; India, foreign relations with Bangladesh
  USA, 73–4
  USSR, 78
Begum Zia (Prime Minister 1991–), 131, 161 *see also* Bangladesh, elections

Bharitya Janata Party, 104, 137, 141, 186 *see also* India, Hindu revivalism
Bhutan
  basic data, 7, 173
  constitution and government, 7, 174
  economic development, 173
  political parties, 48
Bhutan, foreign relations with
  British India, 48
  China, 47–8
  UN, 83
  USA, 74
  USSR, 78
Bhutto, Benazir (Prime Minister 1988–90), 9, 30, 123, 164, 188, 212 *see also* Pakistan, elections; Pakistan's People's Party
Bhutto, Zulfika Ali (President 1971–73, Prime Minister 1973–77) 18, 33, 36, 70–1, 92, 115, 117–18, 187, 213 *see also* Pakistan, elections; Pakistan's People's Party
Buddhism, 7, 41, 53, 107, 146 *see also* Sri Lanka, constitution and government

Central Treaty Organisation (CENTO), 11, 68, 70
Chandra Senkhar (Prime Minister 1990–91), 10, 67, 104, 183 *see also* India, elections
collective security, 23, 76, 209, 214–16
Colombo Plan, 6, 54, 92, 161
Commonwealth, 52, 80, 90–2
Cuba, 75, 88

domestic energy requirements, 189, 211, 213 *see also* India, nuclear weapons programme
Durand Line, 25 *see also* Afghanistan

environmental degradation, 38, 40 *see also* Bangladesh, environmental degradation
Ershad, Mohammed (General 1982–85, President 1985–90), 10, 33, 97, 124, 129–30 *see also* Bangladesh, elections
European Economic Community (EC), 96, 163, 165, 167, 189

Gandhi, Indira (Prime Minister 1966–77, 1980–84), 35, 76, 105, 131, 136, 137, 157, 183 *see also* India, constitution and government
Gandhi, Rajiv (Prime Minister 1984–89), 10, 25, 44, 77, 104, 138, 160, 163, 184, 186 *see also* India, trade liberalisation, elections
General Agreement on Tariffs and Trade (GATT), 162, 165–6
Great Power, 15, 191, 195–7, 199, 201, 206, 217

Himalayan 'Zone of Peace' proposal, 50, 73–4, 79, 202
Hinduism, 47, 134 *see also* India, Hindu revivalism

India
   aid, 6, 74, 142, 155
   arms exports, 17, 120–1
   Assam, 34, 41
   basic indicators, 4–5, 15, 154, 181
   constitution and government, 104, 131–6 *see also* Gandhi, I.; Nehru, J.
   economic development, 181, 183–5
   elections, 10, 133–4 *see also* Indian National Congress Party; *names of individual leaders*
   Hindu revivalism, 134, 136, 141, 199, 219 *see also* Hinduism; Bharitya Janata Party; Vishwa Hindu Parishad
   Hindu-Muslim violence, 104, 137–9, 220

Indo-Soviet Friendship Treaty 69, 75
Indo-Sri Lankan Accord, 50–1, 55, 73, 148, 180, 198 *see also* Sri Lanka; Tamil parties
   Kashmir, 9, 25, 27–9, 30, 78, 81, 83, 92 *see also* Pakistan, Azad Kashmir
   military establishments, 17–20, 198
   minorities, 133, 138, 141 *see also* Sikkim
   nuclear weapons programme, 18, 64, 206, 208 *see also* energy requirements; Sarabhai Profile
   Sikh separatism, 139–41
   trade policy, 5, 65, 67, 76–7, 162, 164, 181, 190
   trade liberalisation, 157, 160, 184 *see also* Gandhi, R.
India, foreign relations with
   Bangladesh, 33–7 *see also* Bangladesh, foreign relations with India
   Bhutan, 34, 46
   China, 40–5, 77, 86
   Middle East, 95
   Nepal, 34, 46–9
   Pakistan, 24, 27, 30, 63, 90, 98, 203 *see also* Simla Accord
   Sri Lanka, 53–4
   UN, 66, 76, 81-2, 210 *see also* Non-Aligned Movement
   USA, 63–4, 66–7, 70–2, 162–3
   USSR, 12, 45–6, 75–7, 82, 207
Indian National Congress Party, 8, 24, 26, 31, 132 *see also* India, constitution and government; Nehru, J.
Indian Ocean 'Zone of Peace' initiative, 57, 58, 73, 94
Intermediate Nuclear Force Treaty (INF), 216
International Atomic Energy Association (IAEA), 204, 20–21, 212 *see also* international sanctions against nuclear threshold states
International Bank for Reconstruction and Development (IRBD) 39, 79, 162
International Monetary Fund (IMF), 6, 11, 46, 79, 83, 158–60, 162, 185, 188, 207
international sanctions against nuclear threshold states, 209–10, 214 *see also*

International Atomic Energy
   Association; Nuclear Non-
   Proliferation Treaty
Irredentism, 7–10, 78
Islamic Conference Organisation (ICO),
   38, 93–4, 97

Japan, 85, 98–9, 161, 163, 189, 190
Jayawardene, J. R. (Prime Minister
   1977–78, President 1978–88) 55, 73 *see
   also* Sri Lanka, constitution and
   government, elections
Jinnah, Mohammed (Governor-General
   1947–48), 21, 24, 26, 111, 218 *see also*
   Muslim League; partition; Pakistan,
   constitution and government

Kampuchea/Cambodia, 89
Khan, Ayub (President 1958–69), 69, 92,
   113–14, 156 *see also* Pakistan, military
   coups
Khan, Liquat Ali (Prime Minister 1947–
   51), 29, 92, 113
Khan, Yahya (General 1963–69,
   President 1969–72), 116–18 *see also*
   Pakistan, Civil War
Kotelawala, Sir John (Prime Minister
   1953–56), 52, 79, 146 *see also* Sri
   Lanka, foreign relations with China,
   foreign relations with USSR

Maldives, 3, 96, 163, 189, 198
   attempted coup, 56
military doctrines, 22, 57, 200 *see also*
   balance of power
Montreal Protocol, 87
Mountbatten, Louis (Viceroy March–
   August 1947), 25
Multi-Fibre Agreement, 166–7
Muslim League, 24, 110, 113, 127 *see
   also* Jinnah M.; Pakistan, constitution
   and government, elections

Nehru, Jawaharlal (Prime Minister
   1947–64), 12, 16, 29, 81, 83, 86, 132,
   218 *see also* India, elections; Indian
   National Congress
Nepal
   agricultural reforms, 171

aid, 47–9, 79
basic data, 4–5, 170
constitution and government, 7, 10,
   46, 49, 171–2
economic development, 170–2
political parties, 49
trade policy, 167, 170
Nepal, foreign relations with
   China, 47, 49
   UN, 50, 83
   US, 74
   USSR, 79
   see also India, foreign relations with
      Nepal; Pakistan, foreign relations
      with Nepal
New International Ecoonomic Order
   (NEIO), 82, 88, 90
New World Order (NWO), 11–12, 63,
   72, 202, 216, 220
Non-Aligned Movement (NAM), 16, 27,
   38, 64, 67, 63, 86–90, 204 *see also*
   India, foreign relations with UN; Sri
   Lanka, foreign relations with UN;
   Panscheel
Nuclear Non-Proliferation Treaty
   (NPT), 11, 76, 78, 202–6, 209–10 *see
   also* international sanctions against
   nuclear threshold states

Pakistan
   aid, 67, 75, 91, 116, 188
   Azad Kashmir, 28 *see also* India,
      Kashmir
   Baluchi separatism, 78, 120
   basic data, 4, 15, 154, 186
   Civil War, 9, 30–2, 117–18 *see also*
      Khan, Yahya; Pakistan, foreign
      relations with Bangladesh
   constitution and government, 103,
      110–11, 114–15, 119, 121, 124 *see
      also* Jinnah, M.; Muslim League;
      Pakistan People's Party
   economic development, 156, 186–7
   elections, 10, 103, 113, 116–17, 120–1,
      123 *see also* Muslim League;
      Pakistan's People's Party; *names of
      individual leaders*
   Islam, 24, 37, 94, 96, 107–9, 114, 119,
      121–2, 161 *see also* Zia-el-Haq

Islamic Fundamentalist parties, 109,
110, 120
military coups, 29, 71, 114, 121 see
also Khan, A.; Zia-el-Haq
military establishments, 20–3, 119, 200
minorities, 6, 109
nuclear weapons programme, 18, 208,
211–12
trade policy, 93, 96
Pakistan, foreign relations with
Bangladesh, 32, 36 see also
Bangladesh, foreign relations with
Pakistan, foreign relations with UN;
Pakistan, Civil War
China, 33, 36, 45, 53
Middle East, 68, 92–3, 96
Nepal, 50
Sri Lanka, 53–4
UN, 37, 82–3
USA, 22, 65, 67, 69, 70–1, 96, 200, 207,
212
USSR, 65 75, 77–8
Pakistan's People's Party, 103, 117–18
see also Bhutto, B.; Bhutto, Z.;
Pakistan, elections
Panscheel, 7, 41, 75, 218 see also Non-
Aligned Movement
partition, 10, 21, 24–6, 68, 133, 200 see
also Jinnah, M.
Peaceful Nuclear Explosion (PNE), 18,
199, 201, 210, 212, 217
Premadasa (President 1988-) 148, 180

realism, 1–2, 81, 104
Rehman, Mujib (Prime Minister 1971–
75, President 1975), 31, 35, 37, 117–18,
124, 127, 175 see also Awami League;
Bangladesh, constitution and
government

Sarabhai Profile, 213 see also India,
nuclear weapons programme
security complex, 15, 105, 187
Sharif, Naswar (Prime Minister 1990-),
30, 104, 188 see also Pakistan,
elections
Sheikh Mujib (Opposition Leader 1975-),
131
Sikkim, 7, 44, 47, 49–50 see also India,
minorities

Simla Accord, 32–3 see also India,
foreign relations with Pakistan
Singh, V. P. (Prime Minister 1989–90),
10, 99, 104, 138, 184, 198 see also
India, elections
South Asian Association of Regional
Cooperation (SAARC) 11, 40, 53, 128,
167–70
South East Asian Treaty Organisation
(SEATO), 11, 68
Sri Lanka
aid, 54, 79, 180
basic data, 4–5, 177
constitution and government, 145,
147–8 see also Buddhism; names of
individual leaders
economic development, 143, 156, 160,
178–9
elections, 144–5, 147 see also Sri
Lankan Freedom Party; United
National Party; names of individual
leaders
minorities, 52, 96, 142–3, 145
political violence, 144, 147, 179
Tamil parties, 9, 144, 148 see also
India, Indo-Sri Lankan Accord
Tamil separatism, 7, 52, 54
trade policy, 80, 96
Sri Lanka, foreign relations with
Bangladesh, 54, 56
China, 53–4 see also Kotelawala,
Sir J.
UN, 73, 79, 83
USA, 73
USSR, 53, 78–9
see also Koteawala, Sir J.; India,
foreign relations with Sri Lanka;
Pakistan, foreign relations with Sri
Lanka
Sri Lankan Freedom Party, 73, 79, 144,
146–7, 178 see also Sri Lanka,
elections
Strategic Arms Reduction Talks
(START), 216

Tashkent Agreement, 30

United National Party, 52, 54, 73, 146–7,
156, 161, 178 see also Sri Lanka,
elections

United Nations
  General Assembly, 75, 83–4, 89, 204
  Security Council, 29, 85, 202, 216
United Nations Conference on Trade
  and Development (UNCTAD), 81–2, 90

Vietnam, 65, 87, 182
Vishwa Hindu Parishad, 137 *see also*
  India, Hindu revivalism

World Bank, 46, 158–60, 165, 177–8, 188

Zia-el-Haq (General 1977–85, President
  1985–88) 28, 37, 72, 78, 164, 175, 187,
  212–13 *see also* Pakistan, Islam,
  military coups
Ziaul-Rehman (President 1978-81), 37,
  78, 97, 128, 167 *see also* Bangladesh,
  military coups